W9-AMC-690

CRACKING
the
CORPORATE
CLOSET

CRACKING
the
CORPORATE
CLOSET

The 200 Best (and Worst) Companies
to Work for, Buy from, and Invest in
If You're Gay or Lesbian—and Even
If You Aren't

DANIEL B. BAKER, SEAN O'BRIEN STRUB,
and BILL HENNING
in Association with the
National Gay and Lesbian Task Force Policy Institute

HarperBusiness
A Division of HarperCollins*Publishers*

HarperCollins books may be purchased for educational, business, or sales promotional use. For information, please write: Special Markets Department, HarperCollins Publishers, Inc., 10 East 53rd Street, New York, NY 10022.

FIRST EDITION

Designed by Irving Perkins Associates

Library of Congress Cataloging-in-Publication Data

Baker, Daniel B., 1946–
    Cracking the corporate closet : the 200 best (and worst) companies to work for, buy from, and invest in if you're gay or lesbian—and even if you aren't / Daniel B. Baker, Sean O'Brien Strub, and Bill Henning, in association with the National Gay & Lesbian Task Force Policy Institute.
        p.   cm.
    Includes index.
    ISBN 0-88730-691-8
    1. Vocational guidance for gays—United States.   2. Corporations—United States.   3. Job hunting—United States.   4. Gays—Employment—United States.   I. Strub, Sean O'Brien.   II. Henning, Bill.   III. Title.
HF5382.685.B35   1995   94-48463
338.7′025′73—dc20

95 96 97 98 99 PS/RRD 10 9 8 7 6 5 4 3 2 1

The authors would like to dedicate this book to our agent, Jed Mattes, for all his support and guidance.

Dan Baker dedicates his work to Bob Miller, with his love.

Sean Strub dedicates his work to Xavier Morales, with his love.

Bill Henning sends his dedication to Tom Ortiz, for all those lunches.

CONTENTS

PREFACE

The idea for this book came from the fertile brain of one of the co-authors, Sean Strub, who first suggested it to me during a long weekend on Fire Island. Sean has been involved with the gay community in a number of capacities over the years, and he was one of the first to see that workplace issues were going to be a major concern for gays and lesbians in the 1990s. The formation of influential employee groups, such as AT&T's LEAGUE, and the adoption of domestic partnership benefits by Lotus Development Corporation in 1991 signaled that discrimination against gay men and lesbians was at last becoming a "mainstream" issue and that some of "our" areas of concern were finally being addressed.

Not all companies, speaking just about the private sector, were addressing those issues at the same speed. In the 1980s Sean had co-authored a book, *Rating America's Corporate Conscience*, that dealt with the emerging issues of corporate responsibility. He saw that the way companies were dealing with gay issues was similar to how they had behaved on environmental and other issues in the past—there were a few cutting-edge corporations at the forefront, some that were very negative, and a large majority that had not even begun to cope with the new conditions. But who were these companies? Press and other media coverage had been scanty and often very anecdotal. Sean felt that the only way to get more reliable data was to systematically survey the companies and see how they stood on anti-discrimination protections, providing benefits for same-sex partners, and marketing to the gay community. So the idea for *Cracking the Corporate Closet* was born.

At about the same time, one of the two nationwide gay and lesbian lobbying groups, the National Gay and Lesbian Task Force (NGLTF), began to look at the same issues from a different perspective: How could influence be brought to bear on corporations so that they would see equal treatment for their gay employees as a matter of urgent concern? The Task Force felt that this was a pressing area where action was needed and that it would serve as the best medium for reaching out to companies. Under the direction of its then co-chairs, Elizabeth Birch and Christopher Collins, NGLTF set up the Workplace Project to work for these goals. It immediately became apparent that a first priority was to collect reliable information to serve as the basis for future action, and the Project formed a Data Committee to do this research.

Sean had been involved with NGLTF for many years and was a close friend of the Task Force's new executive director, Torie Osborn, and he quickly realized that we were all pursuing the same task. He proposed that we join forces, and this was agreed to by Torie and by the recently appointed head of the Workplace Project, George Kronenberger. The two different groups had developed slightly different questionnaires. We collaborated in sharing information we had gained in resurveying companies that had already completed one or the other of the two questionnaires. We worked very closely with the head of the Workplace Project's Data Committee, Howard ("Chip") Tharsing of Progressive Asset Management in Oakland, California, and his research assistant, Scott Isaacs, in making sure that both groups had access to all the information. Chip was a constant source of help and good advice. Without his involvement the book would have been much less complete. Without the support of Elizabeth, Chris, George, and Torie at the Task Force, the book would not have been possible. We acknowledge our deep gratitude to all of them.

Sean and I hired a mutual friend, Bill Henning, to assist us with sending out the questionnaires and tabulating the responses. It became clear that Bill was assuming a much larger role and, indeed, wrote a great deal of what went into the final book. We were, therefore, very pleased when he agreed to join us as one of the co-authors of *Cracking the Corporate Closet*.

We had a very pleasurable and productive working experience with our publisher, HarperCollins. I would particularly like to thank Rick Kot, Virginia Smith, Joshua Rutkoff, Adrian Zackheim, Mary Sue Rucci, and Mary Wieder for their assistance and encouragement.

In addition to these thanks, we want to acknowledge the many gay men and lesbians who contacted us to tell us about their job-related experiences, both negative and positive. It is their stories that you will find in this book. Their lives animate the otherwise dry data that we amassed and remind us that we are not dealing with abstruse ideas but with vital issues that have a daily impact on the lives of millions of people. We salute all of them.

Without the help of all of these people, *Cracking the Corporate Closet* would not have been possible. The authors, however, take full responsibility for any errors that inadvertently may have crept into its pages. In this fast-developing area of corporate concern, changes, usually for the better, happen every day. We look forward to the time when all the issues we discuss will no longer be a novelty, but will be seen as part of every corporation's duty to treat every employee decently and with equality, and when every employee can safely afford to be out on the job.

DANIEL B. BAKER
New York
February 1995

CRACKING
the
CORPORATE
CLOSET

1

HOW GAY-FRIENDLY ARE AMERICA'S COMPANIES?

In June 1993, members of the National Gay and Lesbian Task Force (NGLTF) Policy Institute's Workplace Project sent a short survey with questions about employment policies and benefits to the CEO's offices of 1,000 of America's largest publicly held companies. The 1,000 companies that were mailed the survey had appeared that April in *Fortune* magazine's annual "Fortune 500" and "Fortune Service 500" lists. They were asked to complete the survey and return it within a month.

In August 1993, the authors of *Cracking the Corporate Closet* developed their own questionnaire. When we saw the NGLTF questionnaire, we realized that we were asking for much the same information. We decided to combine our efforts and developed a follow-up survey to the companies that had either completed the NGLTF survey or responded with some information. The follow-up survey had a few further questions on employment policies and benefits, but focused on AIDS issues, charitable giving, marketing, and advertising. (These two surveys are Appendixes 2 and 3 of this book.) We also sent out an overall survey that was a composite of ours and NGLTF's, directing these to certain companies that were not included in NGLTF's original mailing because they were not in the Fortune 1,000: high-profile companies that are privately owned (Mars), large American companies that are divisions of foreign companies (MCA), and smaller companies that we knew had exceptionally good records (Ben & Jerry's) or bad records (H & H Music) on issues of importance to lesbians and gay men.

1

During the late summer and fall, companies that did not respond to the original survey received follow-up calls from either NGLTF Workplace Project volunteers or the authors. Some companies requested that the surveys be sent to them again, others declined to participate, still others gave us the runaround. All the companies listed in the Fortune 1,000, as well as the other companies approached by the authors, received follow-up calls.

In addition to information supplied by the companies, we also independently pursued information from several sources. Going back five or six years, we searched publications for stories involving companies and lesbians and gays or AIDS issues. We also sought firsthand information about companies from their current and former employees. Toward that end, notices asking for information appeared in lesbian and gay media. Co-author Sean Strub also placed a card requesting information from employees in his direct-mail company's *Sapphile* and *Community Cardpack*. Three times a year, *Sapphile* and the *Cardpack* are sent to 150,000 households across the country that have previously responded to a lesbian-, gay-, or AIDS-related mailing from either a merchant or a nonprofit organization. Employees who responded to either the notices in the gay media or to the *Sapphile* or *Cardpack* requests were interviewed about their experiences with their employers.

In January 1994 we rounded up all the surveys and other information we had received from companies, as well as press clippings and stories shared by employees, and began drafting chapters on each industry. As each chapter draft was completed, it was sent out to the companies listed on or below the charts at the end of each chapter so that they might review the chart and their profile for accuracy and fairness. At companies that had responded to our surveys—whether to cooperate or to decline—the draft was sent to the survey respondent. At companies that did not respond at all to our surveys—some of which only appeared listed under the charts as nonrespondents, while others had full write-ups based on outside information we had obtained—the draft was sent to the public relations department. Unsurprisingly, the sight of the drafts inspired a new deluge of information from the companies. Previously cooperative companies suggested factual corrections, supplied further information about programs they had not thoroughly described in their original response, and commented on the balance and fairness of our profiles. Many companies that had not previously responded suddenly became interested in completing our surveys. The chapters were then revised to include the new information.

THE QUESTIONS WE WANTED ANSWERED

After we had collected the results of our surveys, talked to a lot of people, and read various news reports and other studies, we were able to break down the measurable issues of corporate progress in dealing with the gay community into three large categories. These are: (1) whether or not the company includes sexual orientation in its anti-discrimination policy; (2) whether it offers domestic partnership benefits; and (3) whether it perceives the gay community as an important market and is sensitive about how to sell to that market. When we set out, we had hoped to find indicators of other areas of importance, notably the existence of a "glass ceiling" and more information on various corporations' funding of charitable and political organizations.

The glass ceiling is defined as the invisible barrier of unstated prejudice that keeps certain people from reaching the top ranks of a company. In today's corporate environment, women, people of color, and gays are the ones most usually mentioned; in the past, and to a lesser extent in the present, it included Jews and men from the "wrong" social background. By its very definition, a glass ceiling is difficult to measure. In the case of women and people of color, a rough determination can be made by taking all of the staff at or above a certain rank, such as vice president, and counting which ones belong to various categories. In the case of lesbians and gay men, this does not work because the question is not how many there are in total (which is not usually known), but how many of them are open about their homosexuality, or "out." That continues to be a very small number.

We had hoped to get a rough guide by asking how many directors and officers of the company were unmarried, fully realizing that being gay and single were far from being synonymous. At least we thought it would tell us whether being married was a prerequisite to high office. This did not work for a number of reasons: Most companies did not record this information, most of those that did refused to tell us, and in the few cases where they would tell us we could find no discernible patterns. Therefore our only information about the existence of the glass ceiling was through the anecdotal experiences of people we talked to. We know it exists, but how strong it is in different companies is almost impossible to judge.

In the case of charitable and political giving, most companies were happy to tell us how much, if any, their charitable foundations were giving to various AIDS causes, and we have included that information. Very few corporate foundations contribute to specifically gay causes. As for trying to judge how much corporations are giving to homophobic organizations and politicians, this is almost impossible to know without conducting a major study, such as has been done for significant funders like the Adolph Coors Company and Milliken & Company. Most companies give, at the national level, to politicians who sit on Congressional committees with jurisdiction over their businesses or who come from districts in which they have significant operations. While this necessarily includes the likes of Senator Jesse Helms and Congressmen William Dannemeyer and Bob Dornan, we would be surprised if any corporation contributed to their campaigns *because* they were anti-gay. What we would have liked to have learned is whether any corporations refused to fund them because of their homophobic politics.

ANTI-DISCRIMINATION GUARANTEES

What we found out is that the most basic measure of how an American corporation stands on treating its lesbian and gay employees as equals is whether or not it has an anti-discrimination policy or equal employment opportunity statement that includes the term "sexual orientation" or "sexual preference." We found that about half of the companies that responded to our survey did.

Every company we know of has some kind of anti-discrimination policy. This is a direct outgrowth of the civil rights movement of the 1960s, which insisted that African-Americans and women should receive the same treatment as their white male colleagues. This was rather quickly expanded to include other categories, such as ethnicity (as distinguished from race), religion, disability, and age. Most of these policies reiterate protections that are guaranteed by federal, state, and local laws. Following the Stonewall Revolution of 1969, the newly organized gay community began to insist on the same kinds of protections. The first large company we know of that did this was

IBM, in 1974. However, this category has not had the same kind of universal protection as the others have had. There is, of course, no federal anti-discrimination law that protects gays, and there are state laws only in Connecticut, Hawaii, Massachusetts, Minnesota, New Jersey, Vermont, and Wisconsin (as well as the District of Columbia), while several progressive large cities and college towns have them as well.

DOMESTIC PARTNERSHIP BENEFITS

The real cutting edge today for companies on lesbian and gay issues is whether they offer domestic partner benefits, or, as they are called in the human resources profession, DP benefits. One reason is that there are still only a small number of publicly traded companies that offer these benefits. These are the companies that have been willing to go out on a limb in a new area of employer/employee relations. Our research shows that a company that is prepared to offer benefits to the same-sex partners of its employees is going to offer a conducive environment for gay employees generally.

The second reason is that offering DP benefits is the one tangible thing that companies can do to show that their equal employment opportunity statements are not just so many fine-sounding sentiments. It's equality that can make a difference in our daily lives. As William Rubenstein of the American Civil Liberties Union (ACLU) pointed out, a company that does not offer DP benefits might as well place an ad in the local classifieds advertising a job that pays $40,000 a year for straights but only $30,000 a year if you are gay.

The first company to introduce DP benefits was the *Village Voice*, in 1982. This was followed mainly by municipalities (in such liberal areas as Berkeley, West Hollywood, Santa Cruz, San Francisco, and Seattle) and universities in subsequent years. In September 1991 Lotus Development Corporation of Cambridge, Massachusetts, became the first large, publicly traded company to do so.

The experience of most companies that offer DP benefits is that only a small percentage of employees sign up for them. This is mainly because many of the partners already have coverage through their own place of employment, and the IRS has ruled that, unlike benefits for married spouses, the cost of the insurance has to be counted as taxable income because the federal government does not consider unmarried partners to be dependents. There are also legal implications: By signing the affidavit that is usually required for enrollment, the couple may then become subject to community property laws and may face the potential for "palimony" suits if they break up. Because of these implications, the number of employees who sign up has been low: At groundbreaking Lotus it is less than 20.

The companies that have adopted DP benefits have been divided into two camps. Some of them, such as Lotus, offer them only to same-sex partners on the theory that opposite-sex partners could get married if they wanted to. Unlike municipalities, a smaller number of companies, such as Ben & Jerry's, offer them to any employee out of a sense of fairness. In those companies that offer DP benefits to both same-sex and opposite-sex partners, the number of opposite-sex partners who sign up is significantly higher. In 1993 there were 6 same-sex vs. 11 opposite-sex partners at the *Village Voice*, and 80 vs. 120 at Levi Strauss. In the city of Berkeley it was 20 same-sex vs. 105 opposite, and even in the supposedly gay mecca of West Hollywood it was 6 same-sex compared to 10 male/female. In the city of Austin, Texas, less than one-third of the 98 couples who signed up were gay.

There is some confusion about the difference between "soft" and "hard" benefits. Many companies offer benefits that directly affect an unmarried partner without explicitly allowing for that possibility. These are those that allow for anyone to be named as the beneficiary of a life insurance policy and joint and survivor pension benefits. Other benefits include family leave, employee assistance programs, adoption assistance, and relocation assistance. The "hard" benefits are those that are explicitly extended to an unmarried partner. In order to do this, the company has to define "unmarried partner" and extend to that person a benefit that was not previously available. In practical terms, this has largely meant health insurance. In response to our survey, companies often claimed to be offering DP benefits that turned out to be "soft" benefits, which would by their nature be available to any employee, married or unmarried, gay or straight. In the accompanying table, therefore, we have listed only those companies that have taken the significant step of offering "hard" benefits (health insurance).

One of the salient characteristics of "hard" benefits is that in order to receive them the employee has to make an explicit statement of living in a partnership relation with a member of the same sex. In some sense, therefore, it is a kind of coming-out statement in the work environment. Of course, the information is confidential, but it is one of the few times a person has to fill out a form that explicitly spells out that she or he self-identifies as being gay. In order to qualify for health insurance benefits the employee and partner normally have to sign an affidavit that they live together in a relationship that includes mutual financial responsibility.

One of the major factors that has impeded companies from instituting DP benefits is, of course, cost. The perception is that such coverage would significantly increase a company's health care insurance costs. This has, however, not proven to be true. Lotus was willing to go ahead only after Lotus's lesbian and gay employees group and the company's benefits consultant, Andrew Sherman of the Segal Company, showed management that the increased costs would not be significant. Costs have proven to be less than for heterosexual couples, mainly because the major cost in most health insurance schemes are those associated with pregnancy and birth. AIDS has not been a significant factor; the treatment costs for AIDS have turned out to be somewhat lower than for other major illnesses like cancer and heart disease. Studies have shown that gay couples are at no greater risks for these kinds of "catastrophic" illness than are straight couples. So far, because most of the enrollees have been young, the costs have been much less.

Now that the initial cost results are in, it is possible to sell DP health benefits as a low-cost way for a company to show its support for equal treatment. Richard Jennings, executive director of Hollywood Supports, a nonprofit group that lobbies the entertainment industry on gay and AIDS issues, summarized the situation well in a *Wall Street Journal* article of March 18, 1994: He said that health insurance is "a benefit that doesn't cost much of anything . . . [but that] sends an incredibly powerful message of a company's support of all of its employees, regardless of sexual orientation."

These results have put increasing pressure on other large corporations to adopt DP benefits. As a *New York Times* article of June 13, 1993, put it: it seems time for a really big domino—"an AT&T or Xerox"—to fall. Certain very large companies are actively considering such plans. AT&T would seem like a particularly likely target because their lesbian and gay employees group, LEAGUE, is very strong and is actively lobbying for a DP plan. As recently as March 1994, the company said that it had been unable to quantify the possible benefits employees would get. Two other large companies that we are aware of asked us not to reveal that discussions are going on, presumably because if the plans are rejected at the highest levels, lesbian and gay employees will feel enormously aggrieved. On the other hand, smaller companies are not able to offer DP benefits because they cannot find an insurance carrier who offers them, although this may be changing—Prudential Insurance announced that it would offer DP benefits to companies with 50 or more employees in California starting in January 1995. The larger companies are self-insured or have the clout to have the carrier tailor-make a policy for their needs.

In any case, those human resources professionals who predicted that Lotus had started a trend that would end up with only one company, Lotus, signing on have been proved wrong. The personnel manager at Ben & Jerry's says she receives phone calls practically every day from other companies asking about the ice-cream maker's plan. "It's the number-one question I get asked," she told the *Wall Street Journal.* It was also the number-one issue we used in singling out those American companies that seem to be especially gay-friendly.

MARKETING TO GAYS AND LESBIANS

Until recent years, lesbians and gay men were the unknown consumers. Never were two women pictured holding hands in an ad, even if it was by a mainstream advertiser in a gay publication. In fact, almost all of the ads in those publications were for sex-related items that were sold in a way that most large companies eschewed. In the last two or three years there has been a convergence of perceptions. Aspiring national gay publications have realized that they need large advertisers in order to survive and expand, and have therefore thought of ways to limit the sex advertising. Large corporations, on the other hand, have become aware of the size and potential of the gay market and have begun thinking of how to tap into it. One of the ways that we looked at companies in our research was to see just how willing they were to market to the lesbian and gay community through print and other media.

Numerous studies in recent years have tried to estimate just how big and rich the lesbian and gay market in the United States is. This is indeed a matter of dispute. The size of the market has been estimated at anywhere from 5 million people to 20 million. Many gay marketeers like to pull out studies (much disputed as they are) such as those done by Overlooked Opinions, a market research firm in Chicago, that shows that the gay male market, especially, is unusually affluent, with many disposable dollars to spend on leisure activities and other discretionary spending.

Obviously market research firms have a vested interest in having advertisers accept these propositions, and many gay people resent the notion that they are somehow more valuable to society because they have a lot of money to spend. However, common sense and anecdotal evidence seems to tell us that at least some of these perceptions are true. Most of the consciously gay market is an urban one made up of either single people or two working partners. There are a relatively small number of children. Therefore many gay people belong to those coveted groups of guppies (gay, urban professionals) and/or dinks (double income, no kids). These are people that marketers would like to get to know.

One of the most obvious consumer products that is marketed specifically to the gay community is alcoholic beverages. Because marketers of these products are limited in how they can advertise (most can't be on television, for example), they have had to look to nontraditional outlets to build brand image. The first mainstream product that spent big bucks advertising in the gay community was Absolut vodka, which, when the advertising started, was unknown in this country. Michel Roux, president of Carillon Importers, the company that brought the liquor over from Sweden, looked around for an untouched group of consumers and found us. The first Absolut ads began in the *Advocate* in 1979. The clever, full-color ads that Roux placed on the back covers of the *Advocate* and other gay publications kept many of those publications afloat. In later years Roux even sought out smaller gay publications such as *On Our Backs*, the lesbian erotic magazine, to advertise in. The result of all this was to create an astounding brand loyalty for the liquor.

Purveyors of alcoholic beverages are faced with a stagnant overall market in the United States. If they want to stay alive, they have to look for niche markets, and they see gays as being part of a bar culture. That is why major brands like Miller Beer (part of the Philip Morris empire) have been willing to be connected with gay events, including national ones like the Gay Games. Miller signed on as a sponsor for Gay Games IV, held in New York in June 1994, for a reported six-figure amount.

The other kinds of products most likely to be found conducting marketing or ad campaigns specifically directed to the gay community are tobacco companies and such clothing companies as Calvin Klein, Benetton, and The Gap and its affiliate Banana Republic, all of whom have done ads that are either openly gay-oriented or close enough that it doesn't make a difference. The fact that a company markets to gays does not, however, mean that it is gay-positive in its internal practices or even ready to be identified as marketing to the gay community. The Gap, for example, has refused to discuss its marketing strategies.

Of course, the thing that worries any company marketing to the gay community is the backlash that their product will receive from homophobic elements of society, especially the organized religious right. However, the strength of the right-wing backlash may well be overestimated. Probably the most concerted campaign to date was the one conducted by the Rev. Donald Wildmon's American Family Association to boycott Levi Strauss & Co. after the company withdrew funding for the Boy Scouts of America in response to its homophobic policies. The campaign included sending 100,000 preprinted postcards to Levi Strauss headquarters in San Francisco. A company spokesperson, however, said that the campaign had had no measurable effect and that in the year it was conducted, 1993, the company experienced record sales and profits. Miller Brewing reports that its sponsorship of the Gay Games elicited only a small and easily containable negative reaction.

On the other hand, as the experience of Absolut vodka shows, those companies that are willing to become identified with the gay community are often able to develop a devoted following. To take another example, Naya Water (not covered by our surveys), another sponsor of the Gay Games as well as many other gay events, has created a name for itself, and a practically guaranteed market, by becoming "our" water. We have overheard gay men in our neighborhood chiding their friends for buying some other brand.

This kind of success is being emulated by competing companies who have found that nontraditional means are often the best way to reach the gay community. A Naya competitor, Calistoga Water, handed out flyers at the most recent Gay Pride Parade in San Francisco reading, "We don't label people, just bottles." Perrier passed out a circular to all the houses at the gay resort of Fire Island Pines, reminding the residents of the dates for all of the summer's upcoming benefits and, incidentally, featuring a picture of their familiar green bottle.

Among the most recent appeals to the gay and lesbian markets have been the direct-mail campaigns of two major long-distance telephone companies, MCI and AT&T, to gay households, based on the large databases that have been developed by direct-mail marketers as a result of years of appeals for AIDS and civil rights causes. AT&T's recent campaign includes pictures of several same-sex couples and a letter from the co-chairs of LEAGUE, AT&T's lesbian and gay employees group, which is probably the largest and is certainly one of the most active in the country. AT&T was probably reacting to a similar campaign mounted by MCI a few months before.

The growing trend toward marketing to the gay community manifested itself increasingly in 1993 and 1994. In March 1994 the Swedish furniture and housewares chain Ikea (as a non-U.S. company, it was not part of our survey) began an advertising campaign in the United States that featured a gay male couple shopping for a dining room table together, discussing how they met and about possibly adding a leaf to the table if the relationship flourishes.

Ikea said that it was the first advertising featuring a gay couple to appear on "mainstream" television, as opposed to the much more extensive case of mainstream advertisers advertising in the gay press or other gay media outlets. The Ikea ad was run on local television in four major markets where Ikea has stores—New York, Los Angeles, Philadelphia, and Washington. The CEO of the ad agency that created the spot was quoted in the *New York Times* as saying that they had little concern about right-wing backlash because "the Donald Wildmon fans probably aren't Ikea shoppers in the first place."

While recognizing that a company's advertising to the gay community is motivated much more by the profit motive than by a concern for equal rights, we did think it significant if a company showed savvy in how it portrayed lesbians and gays in their advertising. Also, given the nature of the pop culture we live in, a lot of our perception of "reality" is governed by how we are portrayed in the media. It can only be a good thing if advertisers show us as the normal, consuming human beings that we are.

FACTORS INFLUENCING COMPANIES

The results of our surveys showed that it is not accidental when a company is at the forefront in addressing issues of concern to their lesbian and gay employees. One major determining factor is the nature of the company's business. The biggest strides have been made in the high-tech industries of Silicon Valley and elsewhere. There are some obvious reasons for this. One is that almost all of these are young, start-up companies. They do not have an entrenched, conservative corporate culture to overcome. The founders or current CEOs are often relatively young. They either grew up in or were influenced by the counterculture ideas of the 1960s. The very idea of discrimination is abhorrent to them, and they are not shocked by what two women or two men might be doing in bed.

Another major factor is that these companies are in a highly competitive environment where the major input is human brainpower. A highly skilled technician or programmer is extremely valuable, no matter what her or his sexual orientation is. If they can be attracted to a company because it offers a decent environment for homosexual employees (most especially if it offers something tangible like domestic partnership benefits), then the company will go out of its way to achieve such an environment.

What is true about the high-tech industries of Silicon Valley is also true to a somewhat lesser extent of the entertainment industry centered in Los Angeles. Again, the necessity of depending upon the creative ability of their employees has led these companies to create more open, liberal environments where creative talent can flourish. Led by such industry leaders as MCA/Universal, these companies are joining the high-tech industry as particularly welcoming places for lesbians and gay men to work. Even such relatively conservative entertainment companies as the Disney Corporation, while not exactly on the cutting edge, are noticeably more forthcoming than is the prevailing standard among American companies generally.

At the same time, there are other industries where lesbian and gay issues are only beginning to be addressed. The most blatant and unsurprising example is the defense industry, which hides behind the notoriously homophobic policies of the Pentagon in a way that actively discriminates against its homosexual employees. Likewise, most manufacturing industries are only now beginning to address the issues we discuss in this book. In fact, in our telephone conversations with many of these companies' spokespersons we were amused (at the same time that we were appalled) when they often expressed such sentiments as "You mean this is really something that people care about. Why, no one here has ever even mentioned it." Given the reaction their employees were likely to encounter, we daresay that's true.

We were more surprised about certain other sectors of the American economy that seem to be relatively untouched by the trend to provide complete equality to their lesbian and gay employees. For example, while they were highly reticent about their employment policies, what we did learn about the big advertising firms is not reassuring. We would have thought that this would be another industry that was highly sensitive to the competition for scarce human resources and a place where quirky creativity is nurtured. On the whole, however, the big advertising firms do not seem to encourage their employees to be out. We were somewhat less surprised to find that this seems to be true of accounting firms as well.

In other industries, the results seem to be mixed. The airline industry, for example, has companies, such as United and Continental, that are not bad and seem to be making efforts to deal with the homosexual reality; however, their competitor Delta has one of the worst records, based on information available to us. It is our hope, of course, that the good example shown by the high-tech and entertainment industries will create a domino effect not only for the companies who compete directly with each other but for American industry as a whole.

The other great determining factor that seems to make a difference in how a company treats its lesbian and gay employees is its location. It came as no big shock to learn that San Francisco, the Bay Area, and Silicon Valley to the south are hotbeds for lesbian and gay employee activism. Of course, many high-tech companies are headquartered in the area, and that is partially responsible for the good results. But beyond that, companies in other industries are noticeably skewed in our direction if they are headquartered in San Francisco.

Among utilities, Pacific Gas & Electric (headquartered at 201 Mission Street, San Francisco) is far ahead of its rivals in providing a good work environment for lesbians and gay men. Likewise, the San Francisco banks stand out among banking establishments, and Levi Strauss & Co. (1155 Battery Street) probably has the best record of any manufacturing company in the United States. Of the major oil companies in the country, only Chevron (at 575 Market Street) completed our survey, and what they had to tell us was very encouraging.

What is true for San Francisco is true to a lesser extent for New York and Los Angeles. Companies headquartered in those cities tend to be ahead of their rivals in the same industry in the extent to which they have committed themselves to providing true equality of treatment on the basis of sexual orientation. But it is a decidedly mixed picture. While some New York–based companies, such as many of the operating units of Time Warner, Inc., have been at the forefront of progress, others, such as those in the pharmaceutical industries and, as noted above, advertising firms, which are heavily concentrated in New York, have been laggards.

Elsewhere in the country, the picture is pretty much what one would expect. The South and Midwest are behind the two coasts when it comes to addressing lesbian and gay issues. An interesting case is that of Austin, Texas, which in recent years has become a notable center for high-tech industry and has the reputation of being the most socially liberal city in the state if not in the entire South. The municipality of Austin had instituted domestic partnership benefits for city workers in September 1993, but they were repealed in a popular referendum on May 7, 1994, by a margin of 62% to 38%.

In nearby Williamson County, a battle was fought over giving tax breaks to Apple Computer so that it could build a factory. The issue was the fact that Apple provides DP benefits, and the good people of Round Rock (the proposed site of the plant) were afraid that this would encourage homosexuality to flourish in their midst. One argument used in opposing the Apple plant was that the town would become just like Austin, 20 miles away.

It is also noteworthy that the two big computer companies headquartered in Texas, Dell in Austin and Compaq in Houston, are noticeably behind their Silicon Valley competitors in such indicators of lesbian and gay concerns as providing DP benefits. Texas, and Austin in particular, could well be the place to watch to see how the interplay of high-tech progressiveness and Sun Belt conservatism works out.

Another important factor in determining how a company stands on lesbian and gay issues is whether its previously homophobic actions have been challenged by a lawsuit or boycott. In many cases companies have been forced to incorporate antidiscrimination clauses or to take some other gay-positive action as the result of these kinds of outside pressures. In the telecommunications industry, for example, both Pacific Telesis and MCI were forced to pay damages to employees and/or job applicants who pressed suits claiming they had suffered discrimination because they were gay. In addition to monetary settlements, the two companies incorporated sexual orientation into their equal employment opportunity statements.

Likewise, several highly publicized boycotts by the gay community have had the effect of modifying behavior on the part of some of the largest corporations in the United States. The most notorious of these is the Adolph Coors Company, which has been the target of boycotts by various groups since the 1960s. As a result, Coors has developed notably gay-friendly policies at its plants, has actively marketed to the gay community, and has funded many gay events and organizations. However, the company continues to be controlled by the Coors family, which is a major funder of virulently right-wing organizations. A boycott of Philip Morris in the early 1990s because of its support for Senator Jesse Helms led the company to increase its charitable giving to AIDS organizations and to become more supportive of gay causes, including becoming a major sponsor of Gay Games IV through its Miller Brewing subsidiary.

More recently, American Airlines was the target of an incipient boycott because of the insensitivity of on-board personnel in dealing with lesbians and gays returning from the March on Washington in April 1993 and in dealing with a passenger with AIDS in November of that year. Outcry from the gay community forced American to increase its AIDS-sensitivity and diversity training and to augment its funding to AIDS charities. The weight of the evidence shows that it is definitely worthwhile to speak out in cases of injustice.

In a like vein, one of the major things we learned in doing this research is that an active, vocal lesbian and gay employees group is a key factor in effecting change within a corporation. Few indeed are the corporations that have instituted domestic partnership benefits without pressure from such a group. These groups do not function as labor unions by threatening work actions; rather they have been highly successful in changing attitudes by showing companies and their employees that many of their most valued co-workers are gay and are proud to let the world know it. Beyond that, they have quietly done research on the consequences of things like health insurance benefits for unmarried partners, showing that it is the right thing to do and, perhaps more to the point, will cost little. A list of these lesbian and gay employee groups can be found in Appendix I to this book.

Most of these lesbian and gay employee groups started out as informal social networks that then took the significant step of coming out of the closet by announcing their existence publicly and by soliciting people to come to their meetings. Once they started meeting formally, they began to look for ways in which they could work to improve the work environment for fellow lesbians and gay men. In almost all cases, they have been successful in accomplishing some of the things they set out to do. Many of the stories we tell in this book are about the people who took the brave step of organizing co-workers to work for positive change.

RATING THE COMPANIES

Our research showed that there are a couple of easily applied, objective criteria that can give a rough guide as to how gay-positive a company is. The first of these criteria is the most basic—whether or not the company includes the term "sexual orientation" or one like it in its personnel anti-discrimination policy. About half of the companies who responded to our surveys did not, and this automatically puts them in the bottom tier of our ranking. However, we should point out that the information is based on those companies who were willing to respond to our surveys. This alone indicates a certain sensitivity to the issues we discuss.

TABLE 1   *Companies That Do Not Include Sexual Orientation in Their Anti-discrimination Policies**

Air Products	Comerica
Allegheny Ludlum	Commonwealth Edison
American Home Products	Compaq
Bank of Hawaii	Coopers & Lybrand
Barnett Banks	Corning
Baxter	Dana Corporation
Boeing	Detroit Edison
Burger King	Diamond Shamrock
Caremark	Enserch
Cargill	Florida Power & Light
Carillon Importers	Fort Howard

General American Life
Genuine Parts
Hill and Knowlton
Hilton
Hoffman–La Roche
Home Depot
J.C. Penney
J.M. Smucker
Lands' End
Lockheed
Magma Copper
Marriott
Meridian Bancorp
Mobil
Monsanto
Motorola
Mylan Laboratories

Nordstrom
Owens–Corning Fiberglas
Panhandle Eastern
PBS
Pepsico
Phillips
PNC Bank
Reynolds Metals
Rite Aid
Southland
Sovereign
Sun Trust
Syntex
The Gap
Toys 'R' Us
Wachovia

* As of July 1994.

TABLE 2   *Companies That Include Sexual Orientation in Their Anti-discrimination Policies and Dates the Provision Was Added**

Advanced Micro Devices, 12/91
Aetna
Alamo, 9/20/93
Alberto-Culver, 11/93
Allstate, 1992
America West, 9/91
American, 6/93
American Cyanamid, 1/93
Apple Computer, 4/25/88
AT&T, 3/75
Bank of America, 1/78
Bank of Boston, 8/92
Bankers Trust, 1/85
Bay View Federal, 9/92
Bear Stearns
Ben & Jerry's
Boston Globe, 7/87

Burroughs Wellcome, 3/18/92
California Federal, 1/90
CBS, 1978
Chase Manhattan
Chevron, 5/93
Chubb, 10/93
CIGNA, 1/90
Citicorp
Colgate-Palmolive, 1/94
Comdisco
Continental, 7/92
Coors, 1/78
Corestates, 4/90
Cray Research, 1/81
Dayton Hudson
Del Monte
Delta

Digital, 7/86
Disney, 4/92
Dow, 12/15/92
Dow Jones
Dun & Bradstreet, approx. 1988
DuPont, 7/26/92
Eastman Kodak, 6/1/86
Equitable
Ernst & Young, 1/89
Fannie Mae, 5/7/92
First Bank System, 1/91
First Chicago, 1/92
Gannett, 7/92
GEICO
Genentech
General Electric, 5/92
General Motors, 9/29/90
H & R Block, 10/93
Harley-Davidson, 1/90
Harris Trust, 1/89
H. B. Fuller
Herman Miller, 1/90
Hewlett-Packard, 6/8/92
H. F. Ahmanson & Co.
Hibernia
Hoechst-Celanese, 1/94
Honeywell, 8/93
IBM, 11/74
International Data Group
Intel, 1/91
ITT Rayonier
J.P. Morgan & Co.
Kellogg
KPMG Peat Marwick
Levi Strauss & Co.
Lillian Vernon, 1/95
Lincoln National, 1991
Lotus
LSI Logic, 1/90
Mass Mutual, 9/5/91

Maxtor, 1/90
MBIA
MCA (Universal), 1/93
McCaw Cellular, 1980s
McGraw-Hill
MCI, 12/88
Mellon
Merck
Microsoft, 6/90
Midlantic, 1/92
MONY
Nestlé Beverage Co., 1/91
New York Life
New York Times, 8/93
Northern Trust
NYNEX, 10/87
Oracle, 9/15/86
Pacific Gas & Electric, 1/82
Pacific Telesis, 1980
Paramount, 1/92
Penn Mutual, 1/89
People's Bank, 1994
Pinnacle West Capital, 1/88
Piper Jaffray, 6/10/91
Polaroid, 1/90
Procter & Gamble, 9/15/92
Prudential, 10/17/91
Public Service Electric & Gas
Quark, 1/83
RJR Nabisco, 7/88
Ryder, 1993
San Francisco Federal, 1/80
Seagram, 1/88
Silicon Graphics, 1/90
Southern California Edison, 4/93
Southwestern Bell
Sprint, 3/90
St. Paul, 3/91
Sun Microsystems
Supermarket General, 6/84

Tambrands	US Bancorp
Tandem, late 1980s	US West, 1/88
3M, 1/92	Viacom
TIAA-CREF, 2/91	Village Voice, 1/77
UJB Financial, 1/92	Washington Mutual, 1/89
Union Carbide	Wells Fargo, 1/88
Unisys, 1/91	Xerox, 1/91
United, 7/93	Young & Rubicam
UNUM, 8/30/90	Ziff-Davis

*If no date is given, companies did not know or did not supply a date when the anti-discrimination clause was instituted.

Going beyond the basic anti-discrimination guarantees, the handful of companies that have extended domestic partnership benefits to their lesbian and gay employees are automatically in the forefront of American corporations on "our" issues:

TABLE 3   *Companies That Have Extended Health Insurance to Employees' Domestic Partners*

Apple	MCA (Universal)
Ben & Jerry's	Microsoft
Borland	Oracle
Boston Globe	Quark
Charles Schwab	Silicon Graphics
Fannie Mae	Sun Microsystems
Genentech	Time Warner*
International Data Group	Viacom
Levi Strauss & Co.	Village Voice
Lotus	Ziff-Davis

* Time Warner has extended benefits to its corporate employees and employees of some divisions (HBO, Time, Atlantic Records, Warner Brothers Pictures), but not all divisions.

In addition to the surveys that we mailed to companies, we also interviewed present and former employees of those companies and searched through press reports of corporate behavior on the issues that concerned us. This gave us a much more rounded, but necessarily subjective, view of just how gay-positive the companies were.

Based on this, we came up with the 12 American companies that provided the best environment for their lesbian and gay employees. These are the lesbian and gay corporate "winners":

TABLE 4

Apple Computer	Lotus
Ben & Jerry's	MCA (Universal)
Boston Globe	Pacific Gas & Electric
Charles Schwab	Quark
Fannie Mae	Viacom
Levis Strauss & Co.	Ziff-Davis

On the other hand, there are certain companies whose history of misbehavior condemns them to the bottom of the list. These are, in our opinion, America's corporate "losers":

TABLE 5

Abbott Laboratories	First Interstate Bank
American Home Products Corp.	General Electric
Circle K Corporation	Great Republic Insurance Co.
Coastal Corporation	Guardian Life Insurance Corp.
Cracker Barrel Old Country Store	H & H Music Company
Delta	HealthAmerica Corp.
	Milliken & Company

2
ACCOUNTING

As NOTED IN the introductory chapter, there is a definite pattern among companies in different sectors as to how they responded to our initial questionnaire and to our follow-up queries. Accounting firms, for example, are not notably progressive on gay and lesbian issues, but they do seem to be (no surprise here) anal retentive about replying to their mail. All except **Deloitte & Touche** wrote back to us. Unfortunately, most of them wrote to say, politely but firmly, that they could not answer our questions. **Coopers & Lybrand** stated that it hired only on the basis of job-related qualifications because "it is the right thing to do and makes good business sense." However, they did not include a copy of their equal employment opportunity policy and fudged on the question of whether it explicitly includes sexual orientation. Perhaps unique among all the companies surveyed, **KPMG Peat Marwick** has an equal employment opportunity policy that includes both sexual orientation and sexual preference.

The one company that did respond to the full survey, **Ernst & Young**, seems to be fairly good on "our" issues. This is, of course, a pattern. The companies with good policies are quite happy to return the questionnaire; the others are much more reticent. Ernst & Young has included sexual orientation in its written anti-discrimination policy since 1989. It has operations in most of the states and cities that include employment protections for gays and lesbians. It includes sexual orientation in its diversity training. However, so far the company has not gone beyond offering these basic anti-discrimination guarantees: it has no domestic partnership (DP) benefits and does not contribute to or match its employees' contributions to AIDS or gay organizations.

One senior manager, but nonpartner, at Ernst & Young told us that he thinks the accounting industry as a whole must be among the most conservative in the United States. He compares the large accounting firms to fraternities with their own rites, initiations, and cultures. If you want to "belong," you have to fit into that culture. This is reinforced by the hierarchical structure of these companies and by the fact that in order to make partner you have to be voted on by the other partners in your group. If a senior partner, almost all of whom are conservative white men, does not like you for any reason (such as, for example, the fact that you are gay), you will not make partner. He says this atmosphere stifles any desire to be open on the job.

This informant recounts the tale of the managing partner not knowing that the firm's anti-discrimination policy included "affectional preference" and being shocked that it did. The presumption is always of heterosexuality, and no one in the New York office is aware of any employee bringing a same-sex partner to a social event where significant others were invited.

CPA Rick Rodriguez, who talked to us about his on-the-job experiences, has worked at three of the "Big Six" accounting firms (Ernst & Young, Price Waterhouse, and Coopers & Lybrand). He reports that the attitudes at all three were very similar. He felt that he had been hired as the token Latino, and that it was only by far exceeding the company's expectations that he personally was given respect; meanwhile, he felt that he had made it easier for other non-white professionals to be hired. He says he saw instances where African-Americans, especially, were passed over for promotion. In this kind of atmosphere he felt his career would be in jeopardy if he were to be open about his sexuality.

In order to protect his career and stay on the promotion track, Rodriguez resorted to the stratagems that have been used since time immemorial. His best friend, a woman, became his "fiancée"; at one point he even introduced her at company functions as his wife. Rodriguez worked at offices in New York and Atlanta; he says that, although Atlanta might be a little less open, in his professional life he noticed no material differences in the two locations. In both cities, there was a large homosexual "underground" that knew each other socially but remained perfectly closeted on the job. In Atlanta, one "flaming queen" was known to be gay, and the conventional wisdom was that this had obliterated any chance he might have had to make partner. Rodriguez, who now works for a gay nonprofit organization as director of finance, says that he could never go back to the closeted atmosphere of the big accounting firms.

Rick Rodriguez's perceptions of the corporate culture in the accounting world are echoed by Jason Cohen, an accountant at the Chicago headquarters of **Arthur Andersen & Co./Andersen Consulting**, the largest accounting and consulting company in the United States. Arthur Andersen did not respond to our questionnaire, but we did hear from the Chicago office's informal gay and lesbian employees organization. Cohen, one of the founders of the group, shared his remembrances of how the group got started. His recollections mirror the reports of others involved in setting up employees groups—what motivated them and the obstacles they ran into.

Cohen says that he first felt the need for a gay and lesbian group when he was offended by homophobic comments and behavior at the office's annual picnic. He later found out that a group of like-minded employees had gotten together in a gay bar a couple of times, but that information was spread only by word of mouth. "That bothered me a lot," Cohen says. "If it remained limited to word of mouth, lots of people who'd be interested (like me) might never hear about it."

He proposed that the group become public and advertise its meetings on company bulletin boards. This scared a lot of people, according to Cohen: "Some of the people were very fearful that if, for instance, this cocktail hour were advertised on a poster at work, their manager or co-workers would show up outside the bar to see who would go in! The professional staff (partner-track consultants) absolutely believe there's a glass ceiling."

After a few months of procrastination, Cohen and a friend decided to advertise a meeting, even if some former attendees chose to limit their participation. They came up with a poster announcing a "Social Group of Lesbian and Gay Employees and Friends Within Arthur Andersen/Andersen Consulting" and tacked it up on bulletin boards on a total of 44 floors in two buildings. Within a couple of days all of the notices had been pulled down, but 22 people showed up for the first announced event in the summer of 1992. Within a couple of meetings, the group branched out from purely social events and started talking about networking with other Chicago gay and lesbian employees groups, such as those at AT&T and Commonwealth Edison, and about ways to effect change at Arthur Andersen.

As Cohen and his group continued to post notices, they were inevitably pulled down, mutilated, or defaced. Department heads complained to senior management. Satirical counter-posters were put up ("Straight employees and friends" were invited to get together for a tractor pull). In one case, the firm's equal employment opportunity officer (sic) tried to get the poster taken down, until he was told by the corporate head of human relations that it fit within company guidelines.

At about the same time as this incident, however, the Chicago office (not company headquarters) added sexual orientation to its equal employment opportunity statement. The gay and lesbian group began to notice some positive changes. Various co-workers came out to them or made positive comments about what they were doing. Colleagues took note of offensive words and began to censor themselves. Two upper-echelon managers came out to senior management and were asked their advice on how to expand diversity training to include gay and lesbian issues. Members of the group got an appointment with the senior human resources partner to discuss their concerns. The moral of this story: Being open about your sexual orientation is not easy, but it's the only way to make a difference.

ACCOUNTING

Company	Survey Response	Date Added	Policy	Soft Benefits	Hard Benefits	AIDS Education	Diversity Training	G/L Group	Authors' Choice
Coopers & Lybrand	♦								
Ernst & Young	♦♦♦	1/89	♦			♦	♦		
KPMG Peat Marwick	♦♦		♦						

Companies that declined to participate in our surveys: Arthur Andersen, Price Waterhouse
Company that did not respond at all: Deloitte & Touche

Key

Survey response	Sexual orientation included in anti-discrimination policy	Date sexual orientation added to anti-discrimination policy	Soft benefits (bereavement or family/personal/sick leave) extended to domestic partners	Hard benefits (health insurance) extended to domestic partners	AIDS education	Diversity training	Lesbian and gay employees group	Authors' choice
blank=None. ♦ = Provided some information, but didn't complete survey. ♦♦ = Completed one survey. ♦♦♦ = Completed both surveys.	blank=No, it is not, or unknown. ♦ = Yes, it is. UC= Under consideration.		blank=None known. ♦ = Has bereavement or family/personal/sick leave for partners. UC= Company is actively considering extending bereavement leave or family/personal/sick leave to domestic partners.	blank=No. ♦ = Yes, it is. UC= Company is considering extending health insurance to domestic partners.	blank=None known. ♦ = Yes, company conducts AIDS education.	blank=Unknown if company has any diversity training. none=Company has none. NI=Company has diversity training, but sexual orientation is not covered. ♦ = Sexual orientation is included in company's diversity training. UC= Company is actively considering including sexual orientation in its existing or proposed diversity training.	blank=None known at company. ♦ = Company has a gay and lesbian employees group. ♦♦ = Company has a gay and lesbian employees group that it officially recognizes.	♥ = The authors feel the company has distinguished itself on lesbian/gay and AIDS issues within its industry.

3
ADVERTISING AND PUBLIC RELATIONS

FOR ANYONE WHO LIVES in New York City it is old news that the large advertising and public relations agencies are filled with gay men and lesbians. The monthly meetings of the New York Advertising and Communications Network, a social and networking group for advertising professionals, fill the third floor of the Lesbian and Gay Community Services Center. The group now counts over 800 members.

That is why one of our greatest surprises in conducting this research was to discover that the big advertising and public relations agencies that employ these people are notably reticent on lesbian and gay issues. Of the several advertising companies that we sent our questionnaire to, only one (J. Walter Thompson) responded. We also heard from one public relations firms (Hill & Knowlton), but neither company was willing to complete the questionnaire. This did not strike us as being particularly good public relations.

Actually we suspect that these companies have a good reason for not responding to our inquiries: They have something to hide. In a major feature story in the *Adweek* issue of July 19, 1993, in which more than 100 lesbian and gay advertising professionals were interviewed, more than three-quarters "said that using their names might jeopardize their career prospects." In a number of cases, openly lesbian and gay executives were told by management—whom they believed accepted them completely—not to talk publicly. The most telling quotation was taken from a *New York Times* article in which the chairman of **Young & Rubicam, Inc.**, commented on the company's new creative director: "This guy is one of us. He's a gentleman. He has a lovely wife."

Of the two companies that did send us a letter, the one advertising agency, **J. Walter Thompson**, said that "information can be disclosed only as required by law." **Hill & Knowlton**, the large public relations firm, sent along a copy of its equal employment opportunity policy, which does not include sexual orientation. Outside of the categories that it does protect (race, sex, religion, etc.), other factors are included only insofar as they are prohibited by federal law or the state and local laws of the place of employment.

Hill & Knowlton has shown itself to be open in at least one important respect. Bruce Hayes, a swimmer who won a gold medal at the Los Angeles Olympics in 1984, is an account executive at Hill & Knowlton's New York office. Hayes is one of the few openly gay Olympic athletes and as such was a major publicist and spokesperson for the 1994 New York Gay Games. Hill & Knowlton was supportive of Hayes's activities, and he does not feel that his openness jeopardized his public relations career.

In spite of this one shining example, our impression is that the advertising and public relations professions are two of the most closeted in America today. We discussed this with Ron Antman, a partner in the small gay-oriented ad agency Ron Owen & Associates. Antman has worked at both J. Walter Thompson and **Grey Advertising**, where he was a creative director before striking out to found his own company. He says it is absolutely true that the major ad agencies are very loath to let their clients know that any of the employees they are dealing with are homosexual.

Inside the industry, it is well known that many of the creative people are gay, as is attested by the large number who attend the network meetings. But agency executives are so nervous about clients' fickle reactions that they actively discourage employees from being open on the job. Antman reports that he is convinced that one of his major clients would have dropped the firm or asked for another account executive if he had known that he was gay. "I loved my job too much to be confrontational," he says. Like many other gay professionals in similar situations, he did not concoct lies but rather "lied by omission." He never invented girlfriends or wives, but neither did he ever mention going home to his male lover.

Antman reports that he is much happier now that he can be open on the job. His own agency is taking advantage of the many companies that are trying to tap into the perceived potential of the gay market by coming up with ad campaigns specifically targeted to lesbians and gay men. As discussed elsewhere in this book, there is a boomlet of companies doing just that, and Antman's business is going well. Interestingly, he says that the industry that is most resistant to gay advertising is pet foods and pet care. One would think that, with all those lesbians with cats and all those gay men out walking their dogs, the manufacturers would see this as a highly lucrative market that should be tapped into immediately.

A more junior account executive, Andrew Beaver, who is now at Foote, Cone & Belding (which we did not survey), recounts that when he got his first job in advertising just a few years ago everyone in the agency soon became aware of the fact that he was gay. The agency's president asked a colleague, a senior executive at Ogilvy & Mather, to take Beaver to lunch. The purpose of the lunch was to ask him not to be open on the job for fear of frightening off clients.

The question for which there is no answer is whether the fears of these ad executives are justified. Our sources within the industry tell us that conditions have not really changed significantly in the last ten years. If questioned, they think that their bosses would argue that even though they are liberal themselves, the companies they have to deal with are not all from New York or San Francisco. Many are headquartered in the hinterlands where views are less progressive.

One of the things we learned in conducting research for this book is that things are changing everywhere, although admittedly more slowly in some places than others. We think that the ad companies are victims of that particular New York–centrism that thinks the rest of the world is made up of yokels. If they were more open about the large number of homosexuals in their midst (many of the heads of agencies themselves are known to be gay) and took such steps as including sexual orientation in their anti-discrimination policies, sponsoring diversity training, and instituting domestic partnership benefits, they would find that they were only just keeping up with their clients.

This may already be happening. **Saatchi & Saatchi Advertising Worldwide**, one of the biggest of the ad companies, had a potential client that was interested in marketing to the gay community. When Saatchi & Saatchi looked at its own written policies, it realized that they fell short. As a result, with the active involvement of the company's CEO, it is now in the process of adding sexual orientation to its anti-discrimination policy.

ADVERTISING AND PUBLIC RELATIONS

Company	Survey Response	Policy	Date Added	Soft Benefits	Hard Benefits	AIDS Education	Diversity Training	G/L Group	Authors' Choice
Hill & Knowlton	◆								
Saatchi & Saatchi	◆	UC						◆◆	
Young & Rubicam	◆	◆							

Companies that declined to participate in our surveys: Backer Spielvogel Bates, Grey Advertising, J. Walter Thompson
Companies that did not respond at all: McCann-Erickson, Ogilvy & Mather

Key

Survey response
blank=None.
◆ = Provided some information, but didn't complete survey.
◆◆ = Completed one survey.
◆◆◆ = Completed both surveys.

Sexual orientation included in anti-discrimination policy
blank=No, it is not, or unknown.
◆ = Yes, it is.
UC = Under consideration.

Date sexual orientation added to anti-discrimination policy

Soft benefits (bereavement or family/personal/sick leave) extended to domestic partners
blank=None known.
◆ = Has bereavement or family/personal/sick leave for partners.
UC=Company is actively considering extending bereavement leave or family/personal/sick leave to domestic partners.

Hard benefits (health insurance) extended to domestic partners
blank=No.
◆ = Yes, it is.
UC=Company is considering extending health insurance to domestic partners.

AIDS education
blank=None known.
◆ = Yes, company conducts AIDS education.

Diversity training
blank=Unknown if company has any diversity training.
none=Company has none.
NI = Company has diversity training, but sexual orientation is not covered.
◆ = Sexual orientation is included in company's diversity training.
UC=Company is actively considering including sexual orientation in its existing or proposed diversity training.

Lesbian and gay employees group
blank=None known at company.
◆ = Company has a gay and lesbian employees group.
◆◆ = Company has a gay and lesbian employees group that it officially recognizes.

Authors' choice
♥ = The authors feel the company has distinguished itself on lesbian/gay and AIDS issues within its industry.

4

AEROSPACE AND DEFENSE

As MIGHT BE EXPECTED within the tight-lipped aerospace and defense industry, response to our survey requests was dismal. Most companies did not even respond. However, General Dynamics, Litton, Lockheed, Martin Marietta, McDonnell Douglas, and Northrop did at least decline. Still, we were able to accumulate relevant information about several companies within the industry. Most of it suggests that these companies not only work for the Department of Defense but that their thinking on gays and lesbians may be beholden to the Pentagon as well.

For alleged anti-gay discrimination, we can look at a 1989 incident that spurred a lawsuit against **General Electric Corporation**. In the fall of 1988, James Wood was hired as an information systems engineer at GE's plant in King of Prussia, Pennsylvania; because his job included work for the Department of Defense, he applied for a government security clearance. Several months later, Wood received from a co-worker a memorandum that said, "Security processing indicates that you may be living a homosexual lifestyle," and proceeded with questions about Wood's sex life. Wood responded by giving the co-worker a letter asking that the unsigned memo be revised to identify the official sending it and that it be signed. There was no reply to Wood's letter. Wood was later told by GE officials that the company had agreed to a government demand that his request for a security clearance be withdrawn. Wood was fired in July 1989.

In mid-July of the same year, Wood filed suit against GE and the Department of Defense, charging that the company, at the government's request, had withdrawn his request for a security clearance solely because he was believed to be gay—violating Wood's right to equal protection under the law. On July 31, Wood was rehired by GE to a position with duties similar to his previous job but for which no security clearance was necessary. He also received back pay. Nevertheless Wood continued to pursue the lawsuit because the issue of his security clearance was unresolved. His lawyer alleged that the company had clearly violated Wood's rights in the matter by refusing to issue a decision on his security clearance application, or to detail the reasons for its withdrawal, or to give Wood a hearing on the matter and a chance to confront witnesses. Wood, GE, and the government reached a settlement of the suit (with undisclosed terms) in November 1989. GE amended its anti-discrimination policy to include sexual orientation in May 1992. The company's aerospace businesses were sold to Martin Marietta in 1993.

Similar incidents have cropped up at different GE divisions in other parts of the country. In July 1993, Jonathan Burrows, an employee of GE Capital Computer Leasing in Emeryville, California, filed a complaint against the company under the provisions of the state's fair employment and housing act, alleging discrimination on the basis of disability. Burrows has AIDS. He was hired by GE in 1991 after doing temp work at the company. In October 1992 he received a 9.1% raise—three times the average raise at GE in those tight economic times, according to Burrows. But then a hard-to-shake bout of viral bronchitis caused Burrows's health to deteriorate, and he took several sick days. Burrows says the company gradually became aware of his AIDS diagnosis; in fact, company officials stated they were aware of it in a meeting. On January 6, 1993, after two sick days, Burrows says he was told he was being suspended for "erratic behavior"—less than three months after receiving a pay increase that would suggest his performance was better than satisfactory and without being placed on probation or given any written warning about a performance problem. The next day, when Burrows tried to speak with his supervisor, he says he was told that his "personal problems" were of no interest and that termination was "the only route." Burrows filed his complaint and is on long-term disability, but his employment status is unclear. In a *San Francisco Bay Guardian* article on January, 12, 1994, GE attorney David Lidstone maintained that Burrows "has never been terminated; he is still an employee out on an approved absence." Burrows continues to receive disability benefits from the company. GE is self-insured for medical, life, and disability insurance; Burrows says statements were made in a meeting with GE human resources professionals that led him to believe that he was being terminated in order to cut the company's potential costs.

Burrows's complaint is still being processed by California's Department of Fair Employment and Housing. In the meantime, Burrows has been promoting a letter-writing campaign to boycott GE. In the course of this campaign, Burrows says he has met two people with AIDS who say they were also fired by GE and he is continuing to collect stories. The similarities of the experiences as recounted by Wood and Burrows—an assumedly biased dismissal, followed by a reversal of the firing or denial that it ever took place—at two very different company divisions on opposite sides of the country suggest that the GE corporate culture is not only homophobic and AIDS-phobic, but also does not attempt to veil those tendencies.

(For a discussion of GE's record at another of its non-defense divisions, see the discussion of NBC in chapter 9, "Entertainment.")

We did find a couple of small (and relatively dim) bright spots at **Lockheed**. Lockheed's corporate headquarters did not respond to our surveys, but Lockheed's Missiles & Space division in Sunnyvale, California (in the heart of Silicon Valley, a veritable hotbed of gay and lesbian activity), has adopted an anti-discrimination policy that includes sexual orientation and a gay/lesbian/bisexual employees group called GLOBAL (Gays, Lesbians or Bisexuals at Lockheed).

GLOBAL started in September 1990 with an informal gathering of about 25 people for a potluck dinner. In April 1991, they sent a letter to the president of the company, announcing the formation of their group. They received an unpleasant letter back from the vice president of human resources, requesting that they not use Lockheed's name because the group was not a company-recognized organization. The group then applied for membership in LERA, the Lockheed Employees Recreational Association. They were turned down because GLOBAL was not considered to be "recreational" in nature (this in spite of the fact that LERA included other employee groups, including those for Christians, women, and people of various races and ethnicities). GLOBAL then filed a discrimination complaint with the Human Resources Department. The department at first refused to consider the complaint, claiming it was outside their jurisdiction. When pressed, it did review the dispute and then passed down a judgment that no discrimination had taken place.

This attitude changed somewhat when a new vice president of human resources took over and worked to bring about a "compromise" at a meeting of the concerned parties in April 1993. GLOBAL was not admitted to LERA but was made a member of the Missile and Space Division's chapter of the National Management Association's "Diversity Roundtable." As part of its Diversity Roundtable activities, GLOBAL plans to sponsor gay pride events in June 1994; it will bring in outside speakers to address Lockheed employees on diversity issues concerning sexual orientation. Since it is a member of the Diversity Roundtable, GLOBAL says that it expects, but cannot guarantee, that it will receive company backing.

It should be emphasized that GLOBAL is not a company-wide organization and has had no contacts with gay and lesbian employees at other Lockheed facilities. The fact that the Missile and Space Division is located in Sunnyvale meant that many of its professionals were members of High-Tech Gays, a group of Silicon Valley gay professionals, and other organizations and carried over their commitment to equality to the Lockheed workplace.

One of the founders and a former co-chair of GLOBAL is Frederick Parsons, who works as a budget analyst in Lockheed's Sunnyvale plant and has been with the company for 13 years. Parsons became an activist following a year of on-the-job harassment. He had come out to two of his co-workers. In the course of a security clearance investigation, one of these colleagues revealed Parsons's sexual orientation to government investigators, who grilled him for six hours about his sex life and threatened to tell his parents about his homosexuality. He was forced to come out to his parents in order to forestall having it revealed by the investigators.

Parsons was turned down for the security clearance, thereby blocking his career advancement. His sexuality became generally known in the office, and he was subject to verbal "jokes" and outright harassment. When he advertised for a roommate on the staff bulletin board, the word "FAG" was scrawled across the announcement. One co-worker said, "Why don't you go to work at Apple, where you belong?" When Parsons complained to the Human Resources Department, they said there was nothing they could do. For Parsons, this was "the most miserable year of my life."

Parsons decided to fight back and helped found GLOBAL. Even though GLOBAL is still not a company-recognized group, its efforts have made possible several advances: An AIDS Awareness Program was incorporated into the company's "Wellness" program, and on World AIDS Day, December 1, 1992, the Sunnyvale facility displayed an AIDS Quilt panel dedicated to Lockheed employees who had died. In the summer of 1993, sexual orientation was added to the Missile and Space Division's anti-discrimination clause.

Parsons says that in helping to found GLOBAL and in getting the group to press for positive change at Lockheed, he was motivated by his own experiences: "I didn't think that anyone should have to go through what I had gone through. Basically, at some point you have to say you don't care if you get fired if it means standing up for your rights."

Surprisingly, we were able to locate another gay and lesbian employees group at an aerospace company. Seattle-based **Boeing Company** has a group called BEAGLES (Boeing Employee Association of Gays and Lesbians). BEAGLES is not officially recognized by the company because it is not open to all Boeing employees (like the chess club is). Sexual orientation is not included in the company's equal employment opportunity policy, and because Boeing declined to respond to our survey, we do not have further information about gays and lesbians and Boeing. Public records, however, may lend some indirect insight into the company's thinking. Whether one is comfortable with the term "gay and lesbian" or prefers the more expansive term "queer," which is often accepted by younger gay men and lesbians to refer to themselves as well as to bisexuals, transvestites, transgendered people, and other sexual minorities, the records of a lawsuit filed against Boeing by a transgendered employee show the company to be reasonably open-minded.

After years of struggling with his sexual identity, a male engineer hired by Boeing in 1978 had concluded by 1984 that he was a transsexual and wished to undergo gender-reassignment surgery and treatment to become a woman. He informed his supervisors of his diagnosis and intentions in 1985 and asked Boeing management to accommodate him in his need to live for one full year prior to the surgery in the social role of a female (as recommended by gender-reassignment specialists). Boeing refused to allow the engineer to use the women's rest rooms or to dress in "feminine" attire until the completion of his surgery, but it did agree to significant accommodations. The engineer was allowed to wear unisex clothing to work, including blouses, flat shoes, nylon stockings, earrings, lipstick, and foundation makeup, but obviously feminine clothing such as dresses, skirts, or frilly blouses was forbidden. The engineer's psychologist and treating physician agreed that the accommodations were sufficient to enable him to prepare for his surgery. Nevertheless the engineer felt the accommodations were inadequate and did not observe them. Between June and September 1985 Boeing received about a dozen employee complaints regarding his attire and use of the women's rest rooms. He was issued a written warning to comply with Boeing's directives; his supervisor was instructed to review his appearance each day during a probation period to determine whether his attire was acceptable.

When his attire was judged to be acceptable on the first day of the probationary period, the engineer expressed disappointment and said he would "push it" the next day. A strand of pink pearls that he wore the following day was deemed to make him appear excessively feminine, and when he refused to remove them he was fired. The engineer filed a lawsuit against Boeing, alleging discrimination based on handicap (his gender dysphoria). Washington law requires employers to make reasonable accommodations to an employee's needs. The case went all the way to the Washington State Supreme Court, which found that Boeing had not discriminated on the basis of the handicap.

The wisdom of the individual accommodations agreed to by Boeing (and approved by the engineer's doctors) can be debated, but it cannot be denied that the company made a concerted effort to help the engineer continue to work while pursuing gender reassignment. We were not surprised to learn from Boeing, then, that by the time of the engineer's gender-reassignment surgery, eight other Boeing employees (out of a total of 121,000) approached the company seeking accommodations for gender reassignment. About ten more have sought similar accommodations since then. In a difficult industry, Boeing's sensitivity and professionalism in accommodating employees undergoing gender reassignment bodes well for gay and lesbian employees.

AEROSPACE AND DEFENSE

Company	Survey Response	Policy	Date Added	Soft Benefits	Hard Benefits	AIDS Education	Diversity Training	G/L Group	Authors' Choice
Boeing	◆								
General Electric	declined	◆	5/92					◆	◆
Lockheed	declined						◆	◆	

Companies that declined to participate in our surveys: General Dynamics, General Electric, Litton, Lockheed, Martin Marietta, McDonnell Douglas, Northrop

Companies that did not respond at all: EG&G, Grumman, Raytheon, Rockwell International, Teledyne, Textron, Thiokol, TRW, United Technologies, Westinghouse

Key

Survey response
blank = None.
◆ = Provided some information, but didn't complete survey.
◆ = Completed one survey.
◆ = Completed both surveys.

Sexual orientation included in anti-discrimination policy
blank = No, it is not, or unknown.
◆ = Yes, it is.
UC = Under consideration.

Date sexual orientation added to anti-discrimination policy

Soft benefits (bereavement or family/personal/sick leave) extended to domestic partners
blank = None known.
◆ = Has bereavement or family/personal/sick leave for partners.
UC = Company is actively considering extending bereavement leave or family/personal/sick leave to domestic partners.

Hard benefits (health insurance) extended to domestic partners
blank = No.
◆ = Yes, it is.
UC = Company is considering extending health insurance to domestic partners.

AIDS education
blank = None known.
◆ = Yes, company conducts AIDS education.

Diversity training
blank = Unknown if company has any diversity training.
none = Company has none.
NI = Company has diversity training, but sexual orientation is not covered.
◆ = Sexual orientation is included in company's diversity training.
UC = Company is actively considering including sexual orientation in its existing or proposed diversity training.

Lesbian and gay employees group
blank = None known at company.
◆ = Company has a gay and lesbian employees group.
◆ = Company has a gay and lesbian employees group that it officially recognizes.

Authors' choice
♥ = The authors feel the company has distinguished itself on lesbian/gay and AIDS issues within its industry.

5
AUTOMOBILES, AUTO PARTS, AND MACHINERY

No INDUSTRIAL OR FARM equipment companies were willing to complete our surveys. We fared slightly better with automakers and auto parts companies.

Toledo-based **Dana Corporation**, one of the world's leading manufacturers of a wide variety of vehicle parts, declined to complete our surveys but did provide some information on their policies and benefits. They told us flatly that their benefits programs do not provide benefits for same-sex partners and that they place no limitations on employees with HIV or HIV-related illness. On policy matters, Dana was not as revealing—although just as clear—claiming that decentralization made it impossible to answer our questions: "Each facility may adopt policies that are appropriate for its people. Consequently, a particular facility may be subject to state or local regulations which could prompt a policy which differs from one adopted by a facility in another location." Dana obviously is not willing to go beyond the requirements of local ordinances in protecting its employees from discrimination.

Genuine Parts, the auto parts wholesaler behind the yellow NAPA sign, also declined to participate in our survey. However, attached to their polite letter were several blank copies of our survey *and* one that had been completed—apparently sent by mistake. While we must consider the information conveyed to be unofficial at best, we are happy to share it. Genuine Parts does not include sexual orientation in its anti-discrimination policy, nor is it considering doing so. The company's diversity training does not include sexual orientation, and management has "no knowledge of any" lesbian and gay employees group at the company. Genuine Parts has not run or considered running any ads in the lesbian and gay media or done any marketing toward lesbians and gays. The self-insured company extends no benefits to domestic partners, and it places no job or insurance restrictions on employees with HIV. AIDS awareness or education programs are provided "when requested or needed." The wholesaler is headquartered in Atlanta, a city that protects lesbians and gay men from employment discrimination.

Milwaukee's **Harley-Davidson** makes motor homes, travel trailers, and commercial vehicles but derives the lion's share of its income and its image from its motorcycles. Harley has included sexual orientation in its anti-discrimination policy since 1990 and has apparently been developing greater sensitivity to its lesbian and gay employees since then. Currently there is no diversity training in place, but it is being developed and most likely will contain sexual orientation when it is instituted. Similarly, there is no known lesbian and gay employee group at the company, but in its survey response Harley indicated that, if one formed, "we would support the group." The only benefit the company listed as being available to same-sex domestic partners was relocation assistance, which we assume is based on who lives at the employee's place of residence rather than on any codified extension of the benefit to domestic partners.

Of the "big three" automakers, only **General Motors**, the world's largest company, participated in our survey. GM has been in the vanguard of U.S. companies providing AIDS education ever since panic swept its Clinton, Mississippi, plant in the mid-1980s when it became known that an employee had been dignosed with AIDS. Workers refused to touch equipment or use bathrooms that the infected employee had used, and many threatened not to report for work if the diagnosed worker returned to the job. In response, GM launched a $2 million AIDS education program and quickly took steps to guarantee the confidentiality and rights of employees with the disease. Every GM plant has developed an extensive AIDS library from which employees can borrow materials, and the company has held teleconferences linking all plants to presentations by AIDS experts. Together with the United Auto Workers, GM developed an AIDS education booklet that was sent to the homes of 500,000 of its U.S. employees. GM has also expanded its education efforts to the general public. Another educational booklet was produced and

500,000 copies were distributed in schools; in September 1993, an informational AIDS television special underwritten by GM was broadcast in Michigan during prime time. GM has also been steadfast in its provision of benefits to AIDS-affected employees and their dependents. Ryan White, the Kokomo, Indiana, youth who became a media symbol of AIDS and AIDS discrimination in 1986 and whose mother worked for a GM subsidiary, was fully covered by the company's benefits during his illness.

Looking beyond its exemplary work on AIDS, General Motors looks good on policy. The company has included sexual orientation in its anti-discrimination policy since September 29, 1990, and orientation is also included in the company's diversity training. Management is not aware of the existence of any lesbian and gay employees group at GM but assured us that, should one form, it would be welcomed. Unfortunately GM's actual record on issues of concern to lesbians and gay men (besides AIDS) has been spotty. In October 1991, Carolyn Mauch, a former manager at GM's Electronic Data Systems (EDS) subsidiary in Dallas, filed suit in federal court alleging that the company had an unwritten policy of not hiring gays, lesbians, diabetics, or people with drinking or weight problems, and that she had been fired when she refused to carry out the policy. The suit was settled out of court; both sides agreed not to disclose details of the settlement. It should be noted that GM had bought EDS (founded by H. Ross Perot) in 1984; the abhorrent policies described in Mauch's suit, if they existed, may have predated GM's control.

We are not aware of any other incidents of alleged discrimination at GM, but the Mauch suit at EDS and several glaringly homophobic actions in GM's marketing and advertising sugggest that the company's thinking about lesbians and gays as detailed in its official employment policies is not being communicated to all of its divisions and departments as effectively as AIDS education has been. In 1992 the Gay and Lesbian Alliance Against Defamation (GLAAD) urged consumers to boycott the automaker because it had pulled its ads from two episodes of *L.A. Law* in the previous season, citing either "gay theme" or "lesbians" as its reasons for withdrawing the ads, when questioned. Skittishness about advertising on programs with gay themes is common among major American companies (and GM insists it pulled its ads from the episodes because the material involved was about *gay-bashing*, not lesbians and gays in general), but these incidents followed a much more serious problem with the automaker's marketing in 1990.

A video sent by a marketing arm of GM to its dealers and sales-people in August 1990 for use at a trade show promoted the company's Geo pickup truck by attacking Japanese-made trucks. The tape denigrated the Japanese models by calling one of their pickups a "little faggot truck." Responding to the immediate outcry against the use of the epithet in the video, GM quickly discontinued use of the promotional tape, which never made it to the trade show. Amazingly, a company spokesman told the *Detroit Free Press* that GM officials did not realize the comment was offensive, likening it to the phrase "little yuppie truck." Some of the methods and commitment GM displayed in pursuing AIDS education so effectively over the past decade are clearly needed to bring the company's environment for lesbian and gay employees and customers up to speed with its policies.

We have no information on employment policies, benefits, or marketing at **Chrysler**, but a February 1993 *Business Week* cover story included the company in a list of major American corporations that have "paltry" AIDS education efforts.

Ford Motor Company, the last of the "Big Three," did not respond to our surveys. Like GM, it also has had problems where lesbians and gays intersect its advertising. Prestige Ford, a dealership in Garland, Texas, had been running small ads in the *Dallas Voice*, the local lesbian and gay paper, for some time. The ads listed openly gay salesman Jeff Hanson, as well as the name of the Ford dealership, and Prestige found that its ads drew customers. Then, in March 1992, a flurry of articles about the lesbian and gay market and its supposed affluence appeared in papers across the country, including *USA Today*. One such article appeared in the *Dallas Morning News*, and it used the success of the Prestige ad in the *Dallas Voice* as its lead. Suddenly Prestige was flooded with angry calls and letters from people in the conservative suburb of Garland who demanded that the dealership stop advertising in the lesbian and gay paper. Angry citizens also complained to Ford, and, according to salesman Hanson, Ford pressured dealership owner Randall Reed to pull the ads from the *Voice*. Cowardly Ford officials insisted that they did not want to take a stand on whether or not the company's products should be advertised in the lesbian and gay press; they simply wanted the controversy to end. Reed acceded to Ford management's request and pulled the ads.

There is an interesting postscript to the story. Reed has since bought another Ford dealership—this time in Dallas's gay-friendly Oaklawn section—and he and salesman Hanson (who now works out of the Oaklawn location) have once again begun advertising in the *Voice.* The small ads list a phone number and ask interested car buyers to contact Hanson, but, in order to avoid the scrutiny and wrath of Ford management, they list neither Ford nor the name of the dealership, Park City Ford. Reed and Hanson are apparently businessmen who learned from their original experience that advertising to the lesbian and gay community is good business.

For perspective on Ford and GM's paranoia concerning lesbians and gays and advertising, we can consider an ad featuring Toyota's Ultima Seca placed by two Australian dealerships, one in Sydney and one in Melbourne. Instead of just placing generic advertisements in the lesbian and gay press, the dealers have apparently designed an ad specifically for lesbians and gays. The ad features a Seca, parked in front of a home, being loaded for what looks to be a weekend trip or vacation. Two handsome twentysomething men, dressed in khakis and button-down shirts with sweaters draped over their shoulders, are loading the car with leather luggage, tennis rackets, a picnic basket, and a pair of contented dalmatians. The ad's slogan? "The Family Car."

At the risk of nudging stereotypes, the savvy dealers have meticulously crafted an ad that demonstrates their awareness of the tastes of the gay market. Furthermore, they've gone a step further by adding the ironic slogan, which demonstrates their political awareness by apparently taking a stand for the acceptance of nontraditional families. Going beyond the politics of placing ads in the lesbian and gay press, the ad capitalizes on the gay community's hunger to see itself portrayed in advertising for general consumer products. That makes good business sense, and Toyota has not interfered. American automakers have just recently begun to reverse two decades of decline in the face of competition from foreign automakers (particularly the Japanese) by building better cars and relearning how to market them. Unfortunately the contrast between the Australian Toyota ad and Ford and GM's clumsiness around lesbian and gay consumers suggest that American automakers still have a lot of catching up to do.

AUTOMOBILES, AUTO PARTS, AND MACHINERY

Company	Survey Response	Policy	Date Added	Soft Benefits	Hard Benefits	AIDS Education	Diversity Training	G/L Group	Authors' Choice
General Motors	◆◆	◆	9/29/90			◆	◆		
Harley-Davidson	◆◆	◆	1/90	◆			UC		
Dana Corporation	◆								
Genuine Parts	*								

* Genuine Parts sent a letter declining to participate, but enclosed with that letter and several blank photocopies of the survey was one that was completed. Information given is unofficial.

Companies that declined to participate in our surveys: Cooper Tire, Cummins Engine, Deere, Goodyear Tire

Companies that did not respond at all: Caterpillar, Chrysler, Eaton, Ford, B.F. Goodrich, Ingersoll-Rand, Navistar International, Toro

Key

Survey response	Sexual orientation included in anti-discrimination policy	Date sexual orientation added to anti-discrimination policy	Soft benefits (bereavement or family/personal/sick leave) extended to domestic partners	Hard benefits (health insurance) extended to domestic partners	AIDS education	Diversity training	Lesbian and gay employees group	Authors' choice
blank = None. ◆ = Provided some information, but didn't complete survey. ◆◆ = Completed one survey. ◆◆◆ = Completed both surveys.	blank = No, it is not, or unknown. ◆ = Yes, it is. UC = Under consideration.		blank = None known. ◆ = Has bereavement or family/personal/sick leave for partners. UC = Company is actively considering extending bereavement leave or family/personal/sick leave to domestic partners.	blank = No. ◆ = Yes, it is. UC = Company is considering extending health insurance to domestic partners.	blank = None known. ◆ = Yes, company conducts AIDS education.	blank = Unknown if company has any diversity training. none = Company has none. NI = Company has diversity training, but sexual orientation is not covered. ◆ = Sexual orientation is included in company's diversity training. UC = Company is actively considering including sexual orientation in its existing or proposed diversity training.	blank = None known at company. ◆ = Company has a gay and lesbian employees group. ◆◆ = Company has a gay and lesbian employees group that it officially recognizes.	♥ = The authors feel the company has distinguished itself on lesbian/gay and AIDS issues within its industry.

6
BANKS AND SAVINGS INSTITUTIONS

ONLY TWO NEW ENGLAND banks answered our surveys, both fully completing it. In Bridgeport, Connecticut, **People's Bank** is currently revising its anti-discrimination policy to conform to Connecticut state law and include sexual orientation. Its diversity training already includes sexual orientation. The company has not extended any benefits to include domestic partners and has no gay and lesbian employee group. People's has recently started marketing two different "affinity" credit cards to gay men and lesbians—Uncommon Clout (in an arrangement with one of the coauthors, Sean Strub, and his partner) and Point One. In conjunction with the card's launch, the bank expects to spend in excess of $500,000 in gay and lesbian media in the first year as well as in event sponsorship and marketing partnerships with gay businesses. People's marketing campaign includes materials featuring same-sex couples.

Bank of Boston told us that sexual orientation is already included in both the company's anti-discrimination statement and its diversity training. The company recognizes an employee Gay and Lesbian Resource Group, which it also provides with facilities and in-house publicity. The bank conducts AIDS education and places no insurance or employment restrictions on employees with HIV/AIDS. No benefits have been extended to include domestic partners, and the bank has not marketed toward gay men and lesbians. It has sponsored the local AIDSWalk and has made donations to the AIDS Action Committee and the Urban Health Project. A special emphasis seems to have been placed on AIDS education for youth, with donations to a Teen AIDS Expo and Risky Times, which teaches kids about the disease. Bank of Boston only matches its employees' gifts to educational institutions.

Midlantic Corporation, of Edison, New Jersey, responded to the first of our surveys. The bank includes sexual orientation in its diversity training and its anti-discrimination policy, to which the provision was added in January 1992.

New York's **J.P. Morgan & Company**, the nation's fifth-largest banking institution, focuses on loans and services to governments, large corporations, and wealthy individuals. Morgan declined to complete our survey but did supply some information. Sexual orientation is included in the bank's anti-discrimination policy. Diversity training is limited to the company's managers but does include sexual orientation. The eighth-largest U.S. bank, **Bankers Trust** is a universal banking company that operates in the world's financial markets. Bankers Trust fully completed our surveys. Sexual orientation was added to the bank's anti-discrimination policy in January 1985; the company reports that no claims have been filed under the provision. Bankers Trust includes sexual orientation in its diversity training, and its medical department provides ongoing AIDS education. No job or insurance restrictions are placed on employees with HIV/AIDS. Bankers Trust is self-insured and has extended no benefits to include domestic partners. No marketing has been done toward gays and lesbians. Bankers Trust has contributed to the New York City AIDS Fund and to the Gay Men's Health Crisis (GMHC), the New York–based AIDS service organization.

We had no response from New York's largest and best-known consumer banking institutions: Chase Manhattan, Chemical, and Citicorp. We do have published reports, however, that **Citicorp**—the nation's largest bank—includes sexual orientation in its anti-discrimination policy. Sexual orientation is also included in the anti-discrimination policy at **Chase Manhattan**—the second largest issuer of bank credit cards in the country, behind Citicorp. We also know that in 1989, as part of its "executive loan" program, Chase loaned one of its top executives—a vice president and senior credit specialist—to the Washington-based National AIDS Network for one year. The executive contributed financial management skills to the AIDS organization while remaining on the Chase payroll.

Philadelphia's **Corestates Financial** has been making good progress. Corestates responded to our first survey, telling us that it added sexual orientation to its anti-discrimination policy in April 1990 and includes sexual orientation in its diversity training. The bank recognizes Mosaic/Corestates' Gay and Lesbian Employee Association and provides the group with facilities and access to in-house media. Corestates did not indicate that it conducts formal AIDS education, but it does sponsor an Employee AIDS Network and has carried AIDS information in the company magazine. Similarly, while bereavement leave and family/personal/sick leave have not been officially extended to include domestic partners, the company told us that its broad policies are designed to allow for the discretion of managers within their business units and that they "encourage managers to permit leaves of absence for partner care when requested."

Meridian Bancorp, of Reading, Pennsylvania, also completed our first survey but had considerably less to report. Although sexual orientation is reported to be included in the bank's diversity training, it is not included in its anti-discrimination policy, and Meridian wrote that its inclusion is not currently being considered. Meridian's Reading neighbor, **Sovereign Bank**, completed our full survey. Sexual orientation is not included in the bank's anti-discrimination policy, nor is it included in their diversity training, which was just instituted in 1994. Sovereign's respondent to our survey was particularly frank, saying, "We're barely into racial/national heritages, let alone sexual sensitivity." She repeatedly referred to the "conservative," "suburban" location of the bank and asked for any help we might give as the bank "gently" raises awareness in the future. Not surprisingly, benefits have not been extended to include domestic partners, and Sovereign has not marketed toward gay men and lesbians. Still, AIDS education has been conducted, and no insurance or job restrictions are placed on employees with HIV/AIDS. Sovereign has made contributions to AIDS service groups, such as the Berks AIDS Network, Lancaster AIDS Project, and Rainbow Home. They also actively search out AIDS groups to support in the bank's service area.

Farther west, Pittsburgh's **PNC Financial** operates 17 banking subsidiaries, including Pittsburgh National Bank, Marine Bank, and Bank of Delaware, and it is America's leading mutual funds bank manager. PNC did not complete our survey but sent a letter that indicates that sexual orientation is not included in the company's anti-discrimination policy. PNC's neighbor **Mellon Bank** also declined to complete our survey, but wrote that it does include sexual orientation in its equal employment opportunity policy.

North Carolina is home to the fourth-largest U.S. bank, **Nations-Bank**, which did not respond to our survey. Winston-Salem's **Wachovia** declined to participate in our survey but did send a letter that stated that the company "does not discriminate on the basis of sexual orientation." Unfortunately Wachovia did not indicate whether or not that prohibition exists in its written policies. Atlanta's **SunTrust Banks**, which combines Florida's SunBanks, the Trust Co. of Georgia, and Tennessee's Third National Corp., also declined to be surveyed but sent a letter and a copy of its anti-discrimination policy, which does not include sexual orientation. (As an interesting side note, SunTrust's Trust Co. subsidiary helped with Coca-Cola's original underwriting in 1919 and has held 12 million shares of Coke stock since then. The only written copy of the formula for Coca-Cola is kept in a Trust Co. vault.) Jacksonville's **Barnett Banks** is the number-one bank in Florida and also has a significant position in the Georgia banking industry. Barnett completed our first survey, indicating that it includes sexual orientation in its diversity training but has not yet added it to the bank's anti-discrimination policy. The clause's addition to the policy is currently being considered.

New Orleans's **First Commerce** also said in its response to our first survey that it is considering adding sexual orientation to its anti-discrimination policy. At the same time, the bank indicated that it is "currently evaluating options for developing a corporate diversity training program." First Commerce told us that it sometimes makes "special work adjustments" for employees with HIV/AIDS. First Commerce's New Orleans neighbor **Hibernia National Bank** declined to complete our survey but wrote that its "general policy" is that "discrimination in the workplace based on race, sex, sexual orientation, creed or national origin is unacceptable." Still, sexual orientation is not included in the bank's written anti-discrimination policy. Hibernia seems to have a problem with commitment. Sexual orientation is included in diversity training for managers, but no diversity training is offered to other employees. Similarly AIDS education is not conducted for the whole company; rather it is "conducted by the bank's Employee Assistance Program in departments where an employee has HIV/AIDS" or—and this is very worrisome—where an employee "is suspected of being infected."

Detroit's **Comerica** told us in its full survey response that, although sexual orientation is included in the bank's diversity training, it is not included in its anti-discrimination policy. Their respondent was unaware of any gay or lesbian employees group at the company or of any marketing directed at gays and lesbians. The bank places no job restrictions on employees with HIV/AIDS, but it does not conduct formal AIDS education, leaving interested employees to seek information through Comerica's Employee Assistance Program. Chicago's **Northern Trust Company** also does not regularly conduct AIDS education but has actively done so periodically. It has regularly contributed to the AIDS Foundation of Chicago. Northern Trust includes sexual orientation in both its anti-discrimination policy and its diversity training. No benefits are currently available that include employees' domestic partners, but the company's corporate diversity council is reportedly exploring sexual orientation issues in the workplace and has hired consultants as part of that process. The largest bank in Chicago and America's third-largest credit-card issuer is **First Chicago**, which answered our first survey. First Chicago added sexual orientation to its anti-discrimination policy in January 1992 and includes it in the bank's diversity training. The company has extended family/personal/sick leave to include domestic partners, but not bereavement leave or more significant benefits. First Chicago did not inform us of any formal AIDS education conducted by the bank.

Chicago's **Harris Trust & Savings Bank** completed our full survey. Harris added sexual orientation to its anti-discrimination policy in January 1989 and, while it wouldn't disclose specific information about claims filed, did state that "issues regarding sexual orientation have been raised, addressed and resolved." The company's diversity training covers sexual orientation "generally, not specifically." Harris does not currently have a gay and lesbian employees group but did say it would consider placing employment ads in the gay and lesbian press. The company is self-insured and has extended bereavement leave and family/personal/sick leave to include domestic partners. AIDS education is conducted at Harris, and no job or insurance restrictions are placed on employees with HIV/AIDS. The company has contributed to Horizon Hospice and San Miguel Apartments, which are residences for people with HIV. Harris noted that many of its employees have participated in Chicago's annual AIDS Walk, but the company itself has not sponsored any events for gay and lesbian or AIDS organizations, nor has it done any marketing toward gays and lesbians. Harris matches its employees' gifts to a list of designated organizations at a ratio of 1:1, but also matches their gifts to other organizations (including gay and lesbian ones) if the employee meets certain requirements as a volunteer for the group.

Our last stop in the Midwest is Minneapolis, the headquarters of the multistate **First Bank System**, which fully completed our surveys. Since it added sexual orientation to its anti-discrimination policy in January 1991, no claims have been filed. Sexual orientation is included in First Bank's diversity training, and the bank reported that gay and lesbian employees groups have been formed in both the Twin Cities and Denver. First Bank also added that it would consider placing job ads in the gay and lesbian press. The self-insured company extends bereavement leave and family/personal/sick leave to include domestic partners. Employees with HIV/AIDS do not face any job or insurance restrictions at the bank, but First Bank does not conduct any AIDS education. It has not done any marketing toward gays and lesbians. First Bank indicated that it has contributed to AIDS groups, including the San Francisco AIDS Foundation and the Minnesota AIDS Project.

In the Pacific Northwest, we had responses from only one bank and one savings bank. Portland's **US Bancorp** answered our first survey, indicating that it includes sexual orientation in both its anti-discrimination policy and its diversity training. The response to our surveys from savings and loan institutions was not nearly as broad as the response from banks, which is probably understandable, given the turmoil in the savings field over the past several years. The few responses that we did receive from S&Ls, however, were fairly detailed and encouraging. Seattle's **Washington Mutual Savings Bank**, one of America's ten largest, fully responded to our surveys. Washington Mutual added sexual orientation to its anti-discrimination policy in January 1989, and no claims have been filed under the provision since then. Sexual orientation is also included in the company's diversity training. Washington Mutual has no employee groups. The company is self-insured and has not yet extended any benefits to domestic partners. It places no job or insurance restrictions on employees with HIV/AIDS and conducts AIDS education in conjunction with the Northwest AIDS Foundation, which it funds and whose annual AIDS Walk it sponsors. Washington Mutual also told us it has sponsored choral concerts in the gay and lesbian community and has even advertised its financial services in gay and lesbian publications.

As expected, we had a good level of response from the gay-friendly San Francisco Bay area. San Mateo's **Bay View Federal Bank** completed our full survey. The bank added sexual orientation to its anti-discrimination policy in September 1992 and has had no claims filed under the provision since then. Bay View has diversity training that includes sexual orientation; it conducts separate training for lending personnel that teaches that sexual orientation cannot be considered as a factor in the lending process. The bank recognizes no employee groups and has done no marketing toward gay men and lesbians. No employee benefits have been extended to include domestic partners. We were surprised to learn that Bay View conducts no AIDS education for its employees. The bank has contributed to the San Francisco AIDS Foundation, Project Open Hand, and the AIDS Legal Referral Panel. No job or insurance restrictions are placed on the bank's employees with HIV/AIDS.

San Francisco Federal also fully completed our survey. The savings institution added sexual orientation to its anti-discrimination policy in 1980 and was frank with us about the record of complaints under the provision: "We have had complaints, investigated them and took disciplinary action where necessary. One employee was terminated for sexual harassment." The company recognizes no employee groups, but it does have diversity training that includes sexual orientation. San Francisco Federal indicated that, although it has a limited recruitment budget, it would consider placing employment ads in the gay and lesbian press. Like many San Francisco businesses, the company has extended bereavement leave and family/personal/sick leave to include same-sex and opposite-sex domestic partners. SF Fed conducts AIDS education and places no job or insurance restrictions on employees with HIV/AIDS. In fact, they told us a viatical endorsement option has been added to their life insurance plan, allowing terminally ill employees to sell their insurance in order to get a portion of the proceeds. The respondent was unaware of any marketing initiatives by SF Fed toward gay men and lesbians. The company has been a regular sponsor of AIDS Walk San Francisco.

The ninth-largest bank in America is **Wells Fargo & Company**. The company has more than 600 branches—all of them in California. Wells Fargo fully completed our survey. The company includes sexual orientation in its diversity training and added the provision to its anti-discrimination policy in January 1988. Wells Fargo recognizes no employee groups. The self-insured bank has extended no benefits to include domestic partners. No insurance or job restrictions are placed on employees with HIV/AIDS. In fact, Wells Fargo has been a model for corporate responses to AIDS since the beginning of the health crisis. Wells Fargo was the first major American company to formulate a comprehensive response to AIDS. In 1983 a Wells Fargo employee who had come down with the disease took his doctor's advice and prepared to return to work. Wells Fargo was immensely supportive and moved quickly to educate the workers in the man's division about the disease. His co-workers threw him a "welcome back" party upon his return. Wells Fargo has continued aggressively conducting AIDS education ever since. A company spokesperson, quoted in the *Wall Street Journal* about companies' responses to the disease, outlined policies that are almost identical to what we have used as criteria for rating corporate AIDS response: He said that AIDS must be treated as any other serious illness, that employees must be supported if they choose to continue working, that screening prospective employees or curtailing health benefits for people with AIDS would be "immoral if not illegal," and that companies must instead educate their employees about the disease because that is the only way to limit costs. Wells Fargo had this well-thought-out policy in place by the time of the article's appearance—in 1985.

Wells Fargo has not advertised in the gay and lesbian press or produced any advertising specifically designed to appeal to gay men and lesbians. However, the bank has distinguished itself from most American companies by sponsoring many events in the gay and lesbian community, including the Los Angeles Pride Parade, San Francisco's LAVA (Lesbians of Achievement, Vision and Action) Dinner, and the Cable Car Awards. It has also done extensive charitable work in the community. Recipients of grants include GLAAD Los Angeles, San Diego's Gay/Lesbian Center, San Francisco's Community United Against Violence, and Los Angeles's Gay and Lesbian Latinos Unidos.

When it merged with Security Pacific in 1992, **Bank of America** became America's second-largest bank. The San Francisco–based bank has operations throughout the West and dominates the California and Washington markets. Bank of America, which completed the first of our surveys, added sexual orientation to its anti-discrimination policy in 1978 and also includes sexual orientation in its diversity training. The bank extends "soft" benefits, including bereavement leave and family/personal/sick leave to include both opposite-sex and same-sex domestic partners. Further benefits have not been extended and, according to a 1990 *Advocate* story, an assistant vice president at Bank of America subsidiary Seafirst Bank has filed suit in Seattle District Court, seeking full coverage for his domestic partner. Bank of America has been very proactive in AIDS education. AIDS information regularly circulates in management and employee publications, and the bank's life-threatening illness policy, formulated in 1985, focuses on enabling ill employees to keep working for as long as they like. Without a response to our follow-up survey, we do not have detailed information on Bank of America's charitable work; however, we did see published reports that at one point the bank provided free office space to the San Francisco AIDS Project.

We also are aware of an unpleasant incident that has caught Bank of America between gay-rights organizations and the Boy Scouts of America. In highly publicized events in recent years, the Boy Scouts have repeatedly expelled gay scouts and scoutmasters from their organization. When a lawsuit filed by one expelled member resulted in a 1992 court ruling that, as a private organization, the Scouts can legally exclude gays from their ranks, gay rights groups sought other ways to put pressure on the group to change its homophobic policies. This effort was particularly vocal in San Francisco, where the local affiliate of the United Way discontinued its funding for the Scouts. Major corporations were also urged to halt contributions, and many, including Bank of America and Levi Strauss, did just that. The success of the effort to de-fund the Scouts resulted in a strong countermovement, and Bank of America came under increasing fire for its move, with Scout supporters reportedly removing millions of dollars from the bank by closing their checking, savings, and credit-card accounts. In response to these losses, Bank of America (unlike Levi Strauss) backed down and resumed its Scout funding. Queer Nation and other gay rights groups have called for a boycott of the bank after its cowardly reversal.

A recent reversal by a major Los Angeles–based bank can be better categorized as disingenuous rather than cowardly. **First Interstate Bank** operates in 11 Western states and formerly included sexual orientation in its anti-discrimination policy. Yes, First Interstate stands alone among American companies as having instituted and then removed protections against sexual orientation–based discrimination. The bank quietly dumped "sexual orientation" from its policy in late 1993, instead substituting the phrase "or any other basis protected by federal, state or local law." First Interstate spokesperson Ken Preston said the change was necessary "to establish common policies throughout all our banks. . . . Our banks were basically operating autonomously . . . and there's a major cost associated with that. So in moving to common policies, we were establishing one set of policies and procedures for all of our banks and in essence were able to reduce a lot of costs." The company has downplayed the impact of the change: "Our corporate policy basically states the company's position against any type of employment discrimination, but it allows for a maximum of flexibility in meeting federal, state and local laws." But California is the only state in which First Interstate operates that includes sexual orientation in its anti-discrimination laws. With the exception of those who live in a few cities that also have ordinances, employees in the ten other states have been made vulnerable by the policy change. Since it was probably considering making the change when our surveys went out, we are not surprised that First Interstate did not respond to our inquiries.

Two Los Angeles–based savings institutions, **California Federal Bank** and **H.F. Ahmanson & Company**, whose Home Savings of America is the nation's largest, responded to our survey; both include sexual orientation in their anti-discrimination policies. **Bank of Hawaii** declined to complete our questionnaires, noting that it is against their policy "to release any [company] policy to outside organizations." They did pique our curiosity by stating, "Our company has had written non-discrimination policies in place for over 25 years, and our policies include all forms of discrimination." All forms of discrimination? It sounds to us as if sexual orientation is not specifically listed in their policy.

BANKS AND SAVINGS INSTITUTIONS

Company	Survey Response	Policy	Date Added	Soft Benefits	Hard Benefits	AIDS Education	Diversity Training	G/L Group	Authors' Choice
Bank of America	◆◆	◆	1/78	◆		◆	◆		◆
Bank of Boston	◆◆◆	◆	8/92			◆	◆	◆◆	
Bank of Hawaii	◆					◆			
Bankers Trust	◆◆◆	◆	1/85			◆	◆		
Barnett Banks	◆◆	UC					◆		
Bay View Federal	◆◆◆	◆	9/92				◆		
Chase Manhattan		◆							
Citicorp		◆							
Comerica	◆◆◆						◆		
Corestates	◆◆	◆	4/90				◆	◆	
First Bank System	◆◆◆	◆	1/91	◆			◆	◆◆	◆
First Chicago	◆◆	◆	1/92	◆			◆	◆◆	◆
First Commerce	◆◆	UC		◆			UC		
Harris Trust	◆◆◆	◆	1/89	◆		◆	◆		◆
Hibernia	◆	◆							
Mellon	◆	◆							
Meridian Bancorp	◆◆	◆					◆		
Midlantic	◆◆	◆	1/92				◆		
J.P. Morgan & Co.	◆	◆							
Northern Trust	◆◆	◆					◆		
People's Bank	◆	◆	1994				◆		
PNC Bank	◆								
Sovereign	◆◆					◆	NI		
SunTrust	◆								
US Bancorp	◆◆	◆		◆			◆		◆
Wachovia	◆					◆			

	Survey response	Sexual orientation included in anti-discrimination policy	Date sexual orientation added to anti-discrimination policy	Soft benefits (bereavement or family/personal/sick leave) extended to domestic partners	Hard benefits (health insurance) extended to domestic partners	AIDS education	Diversity training	Lesbian and gay employees group	Authors' choice
Wells Fargo	◆◆◆	◆	1/88	◆		◆	◆	◆	◆
H.F. Ahmanson & Co.	◆	◆							
California Federal	◆◆	◆	1/90						
San Francisco Federal	◆◆◆	◆	1/80	◆	◆	◆	◆	◆	◆
Washington Mutual	◆◆◆	◆	1/89	◆		◆	◆	◆	◆

Companies that declined to participate in our surveys: Coast Savings, Commercial Federal, Downey, Farm & Home, First Fidelity, First Union, Norwest, Golden West

Companies that did not respond at all: Anchor, Banc One, Bank of New York, Charter One, Chase Manhattan, Chemical, Citadel Holding, Citicorp, CSF Holdings, Dime, Firstfed Financial, Firstfd Michigan, First Interstate, Fleet Financial, Glenfed, Great Western, KeyCorp, MBNA, Metropolitan Financial, National Westminster, National City, NationsBank, NBD Bancorp, Republic NY, Rochester Community, St. Paul, Standard Federal, TCF Financial

Key

Survey response
blank=None.
◆ =Provided some information, but didn't complete survey.
◆◆ = Completed one survey.
◆◆◆ = Completed both surveys.

Sexual orientation included in anti-discrimination policy
blank=No, it is not, or unknown.
◆ =Yes, it is.
UC=Under consideration.

Soft benefits (bereavement or family/personal/sick leave) extended to domestic partners
blank=None known.
◆ =Has bereavement or family/personal/sick leave for partners.
UC=Company is actively considering extending bereavement leave or family/personal/sick leave to domestic partners.

Hard benefits (health insurance) extended to domestic partners
blank=No.
◆ =Yes, it is.
UC=Company is considering extending health insurance to domestic partners.

AIDS education
blank=None known.
◆ =Yes, company conducts AIDS education.

Diversity training
blank=Unknown if company has any diversity training.
none=Company has none.
NI=Company has diversity training, but sexual orientation is not covered.
◆ =Sexual orientation is included in company's diversity training.
UC=Company is actively considering including sexual orientation in its existing or proposed diversity training.

Lesbian and gay employees group
blank=None known at company.
◆ =Company has a gay and lesbian employees group.
◆◆ =Company has a gay and lesbian employees group that it officially recognizes.

Authors' choice
◆ =The authors feel the company has distinguished itself on lesbian/gay and AIDS issues within its industry.

7

CHEMICALS, METALS, BUILDING MATERIALS, AND FOREST PRODUCTS

Tucson's **MAGMA COPPER COMPANY** responded to our full survey and is apparently just beginning to deal with sexuality issues. The addition of sexual orientation to their anti-discrimination policy is currently under consideration. It is not included in their diversity training, and the company recognizes no employee-organized groups. Magma is self-insured and imposes no job or insurance restrictions on employees with HIV/AIDS. The company did indicate that it conducts AIDS education for its employees. It listed no charitable giving, either to lesbian and gay or AIDS groups or to any other civil rights organizations. Because the company sells a commodity, copper cathode, rather than a consumer product, our questions on marketing and advertising initiatives were not applicable.

Located in Richmond, Virginia, **Reynolds Metals Company** declined to complete our survey but did write to tell us that it has no corporate policy specifically addressing sexual orientation. Reynolds stated, "The laws concerning sexual orientation vary from jurisdiction to jurisdiction. Reynolds' general policy is to comply with federal, state and local laws in jurisdictions in which it does business."

The only steel company to respond to our surveys was **Allegheny Ludlum Corporation**. Although the survey was thoroughly completed, Allegheny Ludlum had little progress to report. Sexual orientation is not included in the company's anti-discrimination policy; although the company is headquartered in Pittsburgh, which bans orientation-based discrimination, the addition of such a provision is not currently being considered. The company has no diversity training and recognizes no employee groups. It is self-insured and places no job or insurance restrictions on employees with HIV/AIDS. The company does conduct AIDS education, but it reported no donations to AIDS organizations or to lesbian and gay ones.

Moving from metals to renewable resources, the response rate from forest-product companies was similarly poor, but the companies were much less forthcoming. Connecticut-based **ITT Rayonier** declined to complete our survey but did send a copy of its anti-discrimination policy, which was revised on September 28, 1993, to include sexual orientation. **Fort Howard Corporation**, headquartered in Green Bay, Wisconsin (a state that prohibits discrimination based on sexual orientation), seemed to suggest that its anti-discrimination policy includes sexual orientation: "Fort Howard supports Equal Employment Opportunity for all applicants and employees, regardless of race, color, creed, gender, or sexual orientation. Our employment practices and our Affirmative Action plans document this commitment." However, they did not send a copy of their policy, leaving us in doubt as to whether sexual orientation is actually listed in their written policy. When Fort Howard's letter continued with "as a matter of corporate policy we do not adopt employment policies that would benefit one particular special interest group over all other special interest groups," our doubts were exacerbated and, in a subsequent telephone call, confirmed.

In the diverse field of building-material manufacturers, only one company answered our survey. Toledo's **Owens-Corning Fiberglas Corporation** completed the first of our surveys, reporting gradual progress. The company is currently considering adding sexual orientation to its anti-discrimination policy. It did not indicate whether or not it conducts diversity training, and it does not have a lesbian and gay employees group. The company does, however, extend family/personal/sick leave and bereavement leave to cover employees with domestic partners.

The chemicals industry was the most responsive sub-group of companies in this category, in both number and quality of responses. **Union Carbide**, the nation's fourth-largest chemical company, based in Danbury, Connecticut, includes sexual orientation in both its anti-discrimination policy and its diversity training. The company did not indicate when the provision was added to its policy, but its inclusion was noted in a *Business Week* article in 1984; that pre-dates the inclusion of sexual orientation by any of our other respondent chemical companies by almost a decade. Union Carbide tells us no claims have been filed under the policy. The company has no lesbian and gay employees group. Since it has no consumer products, it is not surprising that the company has not advertised to lesbians and gay men. No benefits have been extended to include domestic partners by the self-insured chemical maker. No insurance or job restrictions are placed on employees with HIV/AIDS, and Union Carbide does conduct AIDS education as part of its Employee Wellness Program. The company indicated that it has contributed to AIDS groups but did not provide any details of that giving.

Half as large as Union Carbide is **Air Products and Chemicals**, of Allentown, Pennsylvania, which declined to complete our survey. When the company declined, members of Air Products' Gay and Lesbian Empowered Employees (GLEE) volunteered to provide what information they could, so the following information is unofficial. GLEE was formed in January 1992; in May of that year the term "sexual orientation" was added to Air Products' anti-discrimination policy. Unfortunately, rather than prohibiting discrimination based on sexual orientation at the company, the wording of the clause says that the company will comply with all federal, state, and local laws regarding non-discrimination on the basis of the characteristics listed. No such laws regarding sexual orientation apply at the company's headquarters in Allentown. Still, while not extending its protections beyond those required by law, Air Products seems to have made some advances consistent with the addition of the term to its policy. While GLEE's members knew of no claims filed under the provisions of the new policy, they were aware of management reprimanding several "non-complying managers whose actions were not supportive" of the inclusion of sexual orientation. GLEE is recognized by Air Products, which also includes the group in its regular diversity activities and the diversity newsletter. No benefits have been extended to include domestic partners by the self-insured company, which conducts AIDS education and places no insurance or job restrictions on employees with HIV/AIDS. Like Union Carbide, Air Products has not marketed toward lesbians and gays since it has no consumer products. The company does match its employees' gifts to any 501(c)3 nonprofit organization at a ratio of 1:1. Air Products itself has contributed to Allentown's FACT (Fighting AIDS Continuously Together).

Dow Chemical Company, America's second-largest manufacturer of chemicals, has operations all over the world, but its headquarters are in Midland, Michigan. In addition to chemicals and plastics, the company has a significant presence in the household products and pharmaceutical industries, with products such as Fantastik, Cepacol, Saran Wrap, and Nicorette nicotine gum. Dow added sexual orientation to its anti-discrimination policy on December 15, 1992, and reports that no claims have been filed under the provision since its addition to the policy. Dow does include sexual diversity in its diversity training but has had no requests to form a lesbian and gay employees group. The company is self-insured and places no job or insurance restrictions on employees with HIV/AIDS. It does conduct AIDS education for its employees. Dow extends bereavement leave and family/personal/sick leave to cover its employees with domestic partners. The company reported no marketing initiatives directed at lesbians and gays, and no charitable contributions to gay or AIDS organizations, adding that most of its contributions are directed toward general education.

Hoechst-Celanese Corporation, of Bridgewater, New Jersey, did not respond to our surveys. However, we were able to locate an informal, underground lesbian and gay employees group called Gay Community @ HCC; when management also ignored the employee group's request that they complete our survey, members of the group agreed to provide unofficial information about the company's record. At the time of our survey, Hoechst's anti-discrimination policy did not include sexual orientation, but the term was added in January 1994. Members of Gay Community @ HCC say that before sexual orientation was added to the company policy, several cases of harassment had been reported to management (possibly bolstered by the fact that New Jersey state law prohibits employment discrimination based on sexual orientation) and that at least one such case had been dismissed by the company as unfounded. Sexual orientation is not included in Hoechst's diversity training, although the company's Equality Forum (a group of about 15 employees that meets with management to discuss diversity issues) includes lesbian and gay employees and has covered orientation issues.

Hoechst is self-insured and has no job or insurance restrictions for employees with HIV/AIDS. It has no ongoing AIDS education program; employees report that a brochure on AIDS was mailed to workers' homes "about seven years ago" but that there has been no follow-up since then. Although Hoechst does contribute to local and national civil rights groups as well as to the United Way, Gay Community members were unaware of any unilateral company contributions to lesbian and gay or AIDS charities, but Hoechst will match employee contributions to those groups. Hoechst has not done any marketing toward lesbians and gays.

St. Louis–based **Monsanto** is America's third-largest chemical company. For the most part, the company eschews the consumer products market, but does have the high-profile product NutraSweet. Monsanto does not have a company-wide policy prohibiting discrimination based on sexual orientation, claiming that, due to its decentralized operations, written policy "varies by operating unit." Sexual orientation is included in the company's diversity training. While Monsanto does recognize employee-organized groups, it does not yet have a lesbian and gay group. Nor does it extend any benefits to include employees' domestic partners. In its survey response, Monsanto noted that company benefits are available to employees' "spouses" and that "where a state recognizes same-sex or opposite-sex, unmarried partners as 'spousal' relationships, we also recognize and provide benefits under those circumstances." Clearly Monsanto is not planning to lead on domestic partner benefits, nor is it ready to lead on AIDS issues. The company supports the St. Louis Effort for AIDS, but AIDS awareness at the company itself seems to be lacking. Asked what support it gives to employees with HIV/AIDS, Monsanto responded, "We have yet to realize a first case. However, we will treat those individuals with the same care, respect, and attention given other employees living with catastrophic illnesses." Their sentiment is laudable, but it is hard to believe that in 1994 there exists an American company with 21,000 employees that has not had a single AIDS case. In fact, during communications after the original survey, Monsanto officials said that they had recently learned that they do have employees with HIV or AIDS. If the company was unaware of any cases among its employees or their covered dependents prior to just recently, it would suggest that the atmosphere at the company inhibits disclosure.

Indeed, we have had reports about the atmosphere at Monsanto. Interestingly, like Monsanto's anti-discrimination policy, the reports vary widely from facility to facility. Jim Kempland, who was a Monsanto employee for 12 years, wrote to us with homophobic tales from his time at NutraSweet. He transferred to NutraSweet in late 1989 and at first found the company to be neither exceptionally homo-phobic nor homo-friendly. In 1991 he got his first whiff of homo-phobia at NutraSweet, when employees there were given diversity training that included an educational video. The training had no discussion of sexual orientation as a diversity matter, focusing exclu-sively on gender and race (specifically, just women and African-Americans). The training was built around an educational video, and the video's only reference to sexual orientation was when a dramati-zation featured an African-American man being sexually harassed by a male co-worker. Kempland was shocked that a diversity training video that didn't even bother to cover sexual orientation as an area of diversity did introduce stereotypical images of the gay man as sexual predator. Kempland did not make a formal complaint but did make his feelings known to a woman he was friendly with in Human Resources; he had no response from the friend or the department and was not with the company long enough to experience further diversity training. NutraSweet officials tell us that the diversity train-ing program that offended Kempland was discontinued in 1991 and that the new training covers sexual orientation.

Soon after his diversity training, Kempland began to pick up on what he believes was a company pattern of lesbians and gay men being terminated, being asked to leave, or being given gradually reduced responsibilities until they left. Kempland himself was fired in July 1992, within hours of being told he was being investigated by the company's "ethics committee" (which he had never heard of before) for an irregularity on one of his expense reports in 1991. There was no warning issued, and Kempland was given no oppor-tunity to defend himself against the allegations. He admits that there was an incorrect entry on his expense account involving tickets to a baseball game that he planned to attend with a client but that the client was unable to attend (a situation that he claims is not uncom-mon at the company and that is rarely made a point of investigation). When appeals to the company for reinstatement—complicated by NutraSweet's refusal to allow Kempland on company property—proved fruitless, Kempland hired a lawyer and filed complaints of anti-gay discrimination. Chicago bans employment discrimination based on sexual orientation, but because NutraSweet is located in Cook County, the Chicago Human Rights Commission ruled that it did not have jurisdiction in the case. Cook County did not approve an anti-discrimination ordinance for sexual orientation until March

1993. Kempland's legal attempts to be reinstated were quickly exhausted. NutraSweet is one of Monsanto's divisions that does not include sexual orientation in its anti-discrimination policy. Since our survey, Monsanto has reported that it has begun the process of adding sexual orientation to the anti-discrimination policies of all of its operating units.

Another Monsanto company, G. D. Searle, already has an anti-discrimination policy that includes sexual orientation. One of their employees sent us a copy of the policy. When we became aware of Jim Kempland's complaints about NutraSweet, we asked our contact at Searle if he knew of any similar incidents of homophobia at Searle. Although not widely out to his co-workers, our contact told us that he had made a request of Monsanto corporate that it unify the policies at its subsidiaries and ban discrimination based on sexual orientation at all of them. He said he knew of no events such as Kempland had described at NutraSweet occurring at Searle and did not see any evidence of homophobia at the company.

America's largest chemical company is **E. I. du Pont de Nemours and Company**, of Wilmington, Delaware. With a stable of ubiquitous consumer-product materials that includes Corian, Dacron, Lucite, Mylar, Teflon, Tyvek, and Lycra, DuPont is almost as important a wordsmith as it is a chemical maker. With its 1981 acquisition of Conoco, it is also a power in the oil business. DuPont added sexual orientation to its anti-discrimination clause on July 26, 1992, and management knows of no formal claims being filed under the provision since then. Sexual orientation is included in the company's diversity training, and the company has an employee group called Bisexuals, Gays, Lesbians and Allies at DuPont (BGLAD), which it recognizes and provides with facilities and in-house publicity. The group seems to have a good rapport with company management; in fact, a member of the employee group was included on the team that completed DuPont's response to our surveys. Recently, when some DuPont employees challenged corporate support for BGLAD, management issued a strong reaffirmation of the rights of lesbian, gay, and bisexual employees to enjoy a respectful work environment and reminded employees that discrimination against or harassment of lesbian, gay, or bisexual employees, customers, or vendors would not be tolerated. Nevertheless, beyond the policy stage, the company seems to be lagging on issues of importance to lesbians and gay men. No company benefits have been extended to include domestic partners. And while informational materials about AIDS are available to employees, there has not been any formal, systematic AIDS education. The self-insured company does not place any job or insurance restrictions on employees with HIV/AIDS.

Because DuPont is such a large, diversified corporation, with operations spanning the globe, the team completing our surveys could not rule out the possibility of the company having marketed toward lesbians and gays or in lesbian and gay media, but they report that as a company they have not consciously done so. With a similar disclaimer, they said that the company has not changed its advertising plans at any point in response to boycott threats by conservative groups. As for charitable giving, the company has not contributed to lesbian and gay groups but has supported several AIDS projects and events over the years. This has not been a major focus of their corporate contributions program, which focuses primarily on educational and environmental initiatives.

CHEMICALS, METALS, BUILDING MATERIALS, AND FOREST PRODUCTS

Company	Survey Response	Policy	Date Added	Soft Benefits	Hard Benefits	AIDS Education	Diversity Training	G/L Group	Authors' Choice
Air Products	*					◆	◆	◆◆	
Dow	◆◆◆	◆	12/15/92	◆		◆	◆	◆◆	▶
DuPont	◆◆◆	◆	7/26/92				◆	◆◆	
Hoechst-Celanese	*	◆	12/93			◆	NI	◆	
Monsanto	◆◆						◆		
Union Carbide	◆◆◆	◆				◆	◆		
Allegheny Ludlum	◆◆◆					◆	none		
Fort Howard	◆								
ITT Rayonier	◆	◆							
Magma Copper	◆◆◆	UC				◆	NI		
Owens-Corning Fiberglas	◆◆	UC		◆					
Reynolds Metals	◆								

* Air Products declined and Hoechst-Celanese did not respond to our surveys. Information was provided by members of their lesbian and gay employees group and is unofficial.

Companies that declined to participate in our surveys: Air Products & Chemicals, Alcoa, Armstrong World Industries, Consolidated Papers, FMC, Georgia-Pacific, Hercules, Homestake Mining, International Paper, James River, Kimberley-Clark, LaFarge, Manville, Mead, Westvaco

Companies that did not respond at all: AMAX, American Standard, Bethlehem Steel, Boise Cascade, Champion International, W.R. Grace, Great Lakes Chemical, Hoechst-Celanese, Inland Steel, LTV, Lukens, National Steel, Nucor, PPG Industries, Scott Paper, Sherwin-Williams, St. Joe Paper, Union Camp, Union Carbide, USX, Weyerhauser

Key

Survey response	Sexual orientation included in anti-discrimination policy	Date sexual orientation added to anti-discrimination policy	Soft benefits (bereavement or family/personal/sick leave) extended to domestic partners	Hard benefits (health insurance) extended to domestic partners	AIDS education	Diversity training	Lesbian and gay employees group	Authors' choice
blank=None.	blank=No, it is not, or unknown.		blank=None known.	blank=No.	blank=None known.	blank=Unknown if company has any diversity training.	blank=None known at company.	♥ =The authors feel the company has distinguished itself on lesbian/gay and AIDS issues within its industry.
♦ =Provided some information, but didn't complete survey.	♦ =Yes, it is.		♦ =Has bereavement or family/personal/sick leave for partners.	♦ =Yes, it is.	♦ =Yes, company conducts AIDS education.	none=Company has none.	♦ =Company has a gay and lesbian employees group.	
♦♦ = Completed one survey.	UC=Under consideration.		UC=Company is actively considering extending bereavement leave or family/personal/sick leave to domestic partners.	UC=Company is considering extending health insurance to domestic partners.		NI=Company has diversity training, but sexual orientation is not covered.	♦♦ =Company has a gay and lesbian employees group that it officially recognizes.	
♦♦♦ = Completed both surveys.						♦ =Sexual orientation is included in company's diversity training.		
						UC=Company is actively considering including sexual orientation in its existing or proposed diversity training.		

8
COMPUTERS AND BUSINESS MACHINES

Of THE COMPANIES that manufacture computer hardware, there is one standout as far as gay and lesbian issues are concerned: **Apple Computer** of Cupertino, California, in the heart of Silicon Valley. In fact, one could say that Apple has been the archetypal Silicon Valley high-tech company ever since Steven Jobs and Stephen Wozniak started the company in a garage in Santa Clara in 1976. Apple's success in selling microcomputers by making them user-friendly is mirrored in the way the company has strived to make its personnel policies employee-friendly.

Apple responded to both the NGLTF survey and to our follow-up. The company has included sexual orientation in its anti-discrimination policy since 1988. Apple was one of the very few companies participating in the survey that was willing to discuss any claims filed under this clause: Five claims have been filed under that provision since then, and "appropriate steps were taken."

John Sculley, CEO of Apple until June 1993, was particularly supportive of gay and lesbian rights within the company. In June 1992 Apple began to offer limited domestic partner (DP) benefits, including child care, family leave, and relocation benefits. In January 1993 the gay and lesbian employees group requested a meeting with Sculley to discuss the possibility of extending these benefits. Sculley opened the meeting on January 28, 1993, by announcing that it was going to offer full benefits, including health insurance, to the unmarried same-sex partners of its employees. With Sculley's announcement, the whole tenor of the meeting changed. In the words of many of the employees who were there, it was one of the most emotional and uplifting experiences of their lives.

The chief of litigation at Apple, Elizabeth Birch, is the co-chair of the National Gay and Lesbian Task Force (NGLTF). Birch introduced Sculley to many of the national leaders of the gay and lesbian civil rights movement. When Torie Osborn, then executive director of NGLTF, met with President Clinton in his historic meeting with gay and lesbian leaders a few days before the April 1993 March on Washington, the president told her, "John Sculley is a big fan of yours." At the rally following the march, Sculley was introduced on the speaker's platform to the one million demonstrators assembled on the Mall.

Apple has shown that its commitment to gay human rights and to its own DP benefits policy was not shallow by standing up to homophobic bigotry in Williamson County, Texas. The government of Texas had lured Apple to the state by offering various financial incentives. As a result, Apple commited to build a new customer service center in Round Rock, a fast-growing suburban area 20 miles north of Austin, which is becoming a center for high-tech companies. However, unlike liberal Austin, which extended DP benefits to municipal employees in September 1993, the folks of Williamson County, where Round Rock is located, were influenced by the religious right to reject Apple because its DP benefits policy "encouraged" homosexuality.

Therefore, in spite of the fact that Apple proposed to spend $80 million to build the new facility that would employ 700 people, the County Commission voted on November 30, 1993, to deny the company the $750,000 tax abatement that would make construction possible. The vote made the front page of the *New York Times*, as well as other papers across the country. County Commissioner David Hays was quoted as saying, "If I had voted yes on the abatement, I would have had to walk into my church with people saying, 'There is the man who brought homosexuality to Williamson County.' " (Dream on, David.)

Apple stuck to its guns and made it clear that it would rather keep its DP benefits policy than build in Round Rock. With that, the Commission voted (with much less publicity) one week later to approve the tax abatement, but it also approved a resolution deploring Apple's DP policy, thereby having their cake and eating it too. The brouhaha over Apple's policy had a delayed and disappointing aftereffect: it energized conservative groups in the area and probably played a role in the outcome of a referendum in May 1994 in which Austin's new DP benefits were repealed.

Apple has a plant that employs 1,300 people in Colorado Springs, Colorado, the epicenter of the movement to enact Colorado's Amendment 2, denying gays and lesbians equal treatment under the law. The company was very active in the movement to defeat the referendum. It bought full-page ads in Colorado newspapers, urging voters to vote against the initiative pushed by the religious right; the ad was signed by David J. Barram, vice president of worldwide corporate affairs. The ad stated: "Employment discrimination based on (an) individual's sexual orientation is unjust. . . . Initiatives such as Amendment 2 are not in the best interest of sound business." Once the referendum passed, Apple sent a letter to its employees, reiterating the company policy not to discriminate. Signed by Kevin Sullivan, a senior vice president, it read in part, "We believe that initiatives of this sort are not in accord with our corporate values."

Apple has marketed its products specifically to the gay community, including an ad for its laptop PowerBook computer that first appeared in the October/November 1993 issue of *Out* magazine. The ad was the first time a large, high-tech company had advertised in a gay and lesbian publication. The ad shows a young, male pre-law student and an older established lawyer. On the student's list of files on his PowerBook is a sexually ambiguous phrase: "love letter to Kelly." Gay staffers at Apple campaigned successfully with the advertising department to use the name "Kelly" rather than "Kimberly" (of course, it could have said "Keith," but by such small steps is progress made).

Apple sponsored a giant fund-raiser for the National Gay and Lesbian Task Force at its Cupertino headquarters in October 1993— Silicon Valley Celebrates NGLTF. In the central courtyard of Apple's modernistic headquarters building, hundreds of high-tech queers (as many of them like to be called) from all over the peninsula south of San Francisco munched on elegant hors d'oeuvres, sipped Napa Valley wines, and listened to the likes of former presidential candidate Paul Tsongas and Philippe Kahn, president of Borland Computers, talk intelligently and articulately about the stupidity of discrimination in the workplace.

While Apple has received the lion's share of press and public recognition for its dedication to gays and lesbians, it must be noted that one smaller Fortune 500 computer manufacturer with a much lower profile quietly extended DP benefits to its employees *before* Apple did. Located in Mountain View, California, **Silicon Graphics** pioneered visual computing and produces highly specialized computers that are used, among other things, to create special visual effects, such as the ones used to animate the morphing, liquid-metal cyborg villain of the film *Terminator 2*. The company extended full DP benefits on October 1, 1992. Its policy prohibiting discrimination based on sexual orientation had been written down in 1990. Silicon Graphics includes sexual orientation in its diversity training and has a gay and lesbian employees group called Lavender Vision. AIDS education is conducted by the company, which places no job or insurance restrictions on employees with HIV/AIDS. Without a consumer product, Silicon Graphics has not marketed toward gays and lesbians, but it is one of only a few American companies that has advertised employment opportunities in the lesbian and gay press— and it has done so on several occasions. Silicon Graphics has contributed to several AIDS groups and was a sponsor of the Silicon Valley Celebrates NGLTF fund-raiser that was held at Apple headquarters in October 1993.

Moving back to the big boys, Apple's main competitor, **IBM** (Armonk, New York), was one of the first companies in the United States to include sexual orientation in its anti-discrimination policy—way back in 1974. In its response to our questionnaire, IBM says that since that time only two complaints have been filed under its provisions and that they were dealt with "appropriately based on findings." The current chairman, Lou Gerstner, has expanded upon the company's equal employment opportunity policy by writing this to all employees: "Implicit in our policy is a working environment free of harassment based on sex or sexual orientation, race or ethnic origin, religion, age, disability, or veteran status. In respecting and valuing the diversity among our employees and all those with whom we do business, managers are to ensure a work environment free of all forms of discrimination and harassment."

IBM has not yet provided health insurance for the domestic partners of its employees. We feel certain that the computer giant is well aware of the move toward partner benefits in the industry and is feeling some pressure to extend those benefits. Still any extension of benefits that could be perceived as increasing costs has to be weighed thoroughly by IBM management in light of the fact that its employees just began picking up a part of the cost of their benefits for the first time ever in April 1994. Like many companies, however, IBM does allow for certain "soft" benefits: Employees can designate whomever they wish for any survivor benefits and anyone can be joint owners of the stock purchased in the company stock option program.

If IBM has not been on the cutting edge in providing DP benefits, it has made a notable effort in providing diversity training for its employees. In its most recent video on the subject, which is part of a two-day diversity training required for all the company's managers, there is a panel that includes an openly gay man, as well as representatives of other groups. There is footage from the April 1993 March on Washington and a discussion as to whether there is a glass ceiling for women, people of color, and homosexuals.

IBM seems to be making real efforts to be open to its gay employees. Ted Childs, who is in charge of the company's diversity programs, hosted a dinner in Washington for IBM employees and their partners who were attending the 1993 march. In 1994, for the first time, the company's annual workplace diversity brochure pictures and talks to people who openly identify as being gay. Also, for the first time in 1994, the company invited employees to bring "someone important to you" rather than a spouse to the gala events put on for top corporate achievers. IBM does not, however, have any recognized employee groups, so there is no formal mechanism for gay and lesbian employees to network.

IBM has been active in donating to the AIDS field, matching its employees' contribution to AIDS education organizations at a ratio of 5:1. It has made several significant contributions to AmFAR (the American Foundation for AIDS Research).

Xerox of Rochester, New York, responded to our full survey. The company added sexual orientation to its anti-discrimination policy only in January 1991. It offers no DP benefits and does not market to the gay community. It does conduct diversity training and has an AIDS awareness campaign. It provides recognition and meeting facilities for its gay and lesbian employees group—GALAXE. The previously reticent company may, however, be getting its toes wet in becoming more involved with the gay community. Xerox thought long and hard before deciding not to become a major sponsor for Gay Games IV in New York City in June 1994. Under the instigation of its special events director, Linda Evans, it did, however, end up supplying a great deal of photocopying equipment and services at bargain prices.

Hewlett-Packard of Palo Alto, California, responded to our full survey. It has included sexual orientation in its anti-discrimination policy only since June 1992. Hewlett-Packard does not have a recognized gay and lesbian employees group, although one is in formation, following new company guidelines instituted in 1992 that allow formation of such groups. As late as April 1991, Mary Lou Simmermacher, a company spokesperson, was quoted in the *New York Times* as saying, "We don't see a business need to sponsor organizations based on sexual preference." A company spokesperson now recognizes that "there's a business purpose for HP to support employee network groups . . . [that] help members assimilate into the HP culture and provide an opportunity to air common problems and help one another." Simmermacher was further quoted in the 1991 *New York Times* article as saying, "We base our health policy on marriages legally recognized by the state. Extending health insurance to others is not under consideration at this time." The policy has not changed, but the company now admits that it continually reviews the competitiveness of its benefits package and would not rule out extending benefits to include domestic partners before the state legally recognizes the status of such relationships; it is watching its competitors. HP does not market to the gay community.

Hewlett-Packard has a large plant that employs 7,500 people making oscilloscopes in Colorado Springs. Unlike Apple, HP did not participate actively in the campaign to defeat Amendment 2, but following passage of the referendum, it did send a letter to its Colorado employees saying that the company's policies explicitly prohibited discrimination on the basis of sexual orientation.

Cupertino's **Tandem Computers** was started by a former HP marketing manager; it specializes in fault-tolerant computer systems that are essential in applications such as ATM networks and airline reservation systems, which must process thousands of transactions a second without interruption. Tandem completed our survey, telling us that it added sexual orientation to its anti-discrimination policy in the "mid to late 1980s." The company currently has no diversity training but does recognize a Gay and Lesbian Association (GALA) of its employees and provides the group with E-mail facilities. The self-insured company has not extended any benefits to include domestic partners and conducts no regular AIDS education. No job or insurance restrictions are placed on employees with HIV/AIDS. Without consumer products, Tandem has not marketed toward gays and lesbians. It has regularly contributed to AIDS walks.

Sun Microsystems, a Silicon Valley manufacturer of computer work stations, also completed our survey. Sexual orientation is included in both its anti-discrimination policy and its diversity training. Sun has a gay and lesbian employees group called Gays, Lesbians and Friends (GLAF) that it recognizes and provides with facilities and funding. Sun extended full company benefits to include employees' domestic partners in 1993. Unlike most other companies that have extended DP benefits, Sun allows employees to sign up opposite-sex domestic partners but charges more for the privilege. The company conducts AIDS education for its employees.

Unisys, based in Blue Bell, Pennsylvania, declined to complete our survey but did respond with some information. Sexual orientation was added to the company's anti-discrimination policy in January 1991. The company conducts diversity training but did not indicate that sexual orientation is specifically covered, and Unisys does not conduct AIDS education. No benefits have been extended to include domestic partners, and the company does not have a gay and lesbian employees group. It does not market to gay men and lesbians.

The Texas-based computer companies do not rate very well on gay and lesbian issues. Although **Compaq Computer Corp.** of Houston did respond to our full survey, the information it had to impart was dismal: its anti-discrimination clause does not include sexual orientation, it does not have DP benefits, market to the gay community, or have a recognized gay and lesbian employees group.

Although we suspect that **Dell Computer Corp.** of Austin would have the same dreary responses, the company refused even to respond to the survey. When told that they would be the only large computer manufacturer in the United States that refused to answer questions about its gay and lesbian employees, the company spokeswoman said that they "didn't care." Tom Rielly, founder and co-chair of Digital Queers, the new, highly respected, national organization of computer technology professionals that has mobilized on a wide variety of gay and lesbian causes, says that he would like to have five minutes of company founder and president Michael Dell's time to tell him "to get with the program."

Digital Equipment Corporation of Maynard, Massachusetts, responded to the NGLTF survey. It has had a sexual orientation clause since 1986. Digital has been at the forefront of providing diversity training. Kim Cromwell, the company's U.S. diversity manager, says that "our approach focuses explicitly on trying to create an environment where every employee feels free to contribute to the success of the company." One of the courses offered is "Understanding the Dynamics of the Gay, Lesbian, and Bisexual Difference," informally known as "Gay 101." Included in the course are role-playing exercises, such as explaining to co-workers the fun weekend you just had in Provincetown and the "special" person you met there. Ron Glover, corporate employee relations manager at Digital, says that "diversity is an engine for creativity."

Of course, things are not perfect. One of the instructors for "Gay 101" says that some of his co-workers do not welcome his openness, often couching their disapproval in religious terms. Cromwell has remarked, "Some people will say that when you talk about sexual orientation at work you're talking about sex, which is not the case. People don't realize that when they're talking about their husband or their wife they're talking about their sexual orientation."

Digital's supportiveness extends to AIDS awareness as well. It began its AIDS awareness policy in 1987. It was one of the pioneer companies in organizing dialogues between employees who were openly HIV-positive and their co-workers. It has used trauma intervention teams to counsel employees when one of their co-workers died of AIDS. Paul Ross, the manager of the HIV/AIDS program, says that he feels that the company's enlightened policy has helped to contain AIDS costs by encouraging HIV-positive employees to seek early treatment for the disease without fear of retaliation.

Digital does not provide DP benefits, largely, says Cromwell, because of the company's difficult financial situation (it has had to lay off several thousand employees in the last few years), which makes it very problematical to institute any new employee benefits, but it does have a gay and lesbian employees group, Digital Equipment Corporation People Like Us (DECPLUS).

COMPUTERS AND BUSINESS MACHINES

Company	Survey Response	Policy	Date Added	Soft Benefits	Hard Benefits	AIDS Education	Diversity Training	G/L Group	Authors' Choice
Advanced Micro Devices	◆◆	◆	12/91				◆		
Apple	◆◆◆	◆	4/25/88	◆	◆	◆	◆	◆◆	✔
Comdisco	◆◆	◆				◆	◆		
Compaq	◆◆◆						none		
Cray Research	◆◆◆	◆	1/81	◆		◆	NI		
Digital	◆◆	◆	7/86			◆	◆	◆◆	
Hewlett-Packard	◆◆◆	◆	6/8/92			◆	◆	◆◆	
Honeywell	◆◆◆	◆	8/93			◆	◆	◆◆	
IBM	◆◆◆	◆	11/74			◆	◆		
Intel	◆◆	◆	1/91	◆		◆	◆	◆◆	
LSI Logic	◆◆◆	◆	1/90			◆	NI		
Maxtor	◆◆◆	◆	1/90				◆		
Motorola	◆◆	UC							
Silicon Graphics	◆◆◆	◆	1/90	◆	◆	◆	◆	◆◆	✔
Sun Microsystems	◆◆◆	◆		◆	◆	◆	◆	◆◆	✔
Tandem	◆◆◆	◆	late 1980s				NI		
Unisys	◆	◆	1/91						
Xerox	◆◆◆	◆	1/91			◆	◆	◆◆	

Companies that declined to participate in our surveys: Data General, Gateway 2000, Seagate Technology
Companies that did not respond at all: Conner Peripherals, Dell, National Semiconductor, Pitney Bowes, Texas Instruments, Wang

Key	*Survey response*	*Sexual orientation included in anti-discrimination policy*	*Date sexual orientation added to anti-discrimination policy*	*Soft benefits (bereavement or family/personal/sick leave) extended to domestic partners*	*Hard benefits (health insurance) extended to domestic partners*	*AIDS education*	*Diversity training*	*Lesbian and gay employees group*	*Authors' choice*
	blank=None. ♦=Provided some information, but didn't complete survey. ♦♦=Completed one survey. ♦♦♦=Completed both surveys.	blank=No, it is not, or unknown. ♦=Yes, it is. UC=Under consideration.		blank=None known. ♦=Has bereavement or family/personal/sick leave for partners. UC=Company is actively considering extending bereavement leave or family/personal/sick leave to domestic partners.	blank=No. ♦=Yes, it is. UC=Company is considering extending health insurance to domestic partners.	blank=None known. ♦=Yes, company conducts AIDS education.	blank=Unknown if company has any diversity training. none=Company has none. NI=Company has diversity training, but sexual orientation is not covered. ♦=Sexual orientation is included in company's diversity training. UC=Company is actively considering including sexual orientation in its existing or proposed diversity training.	blank=None known at company. ♦=Company has a gay and lesbian employees group. ♦♦=Company has a gay and lesbian employees group that it officially recognizes.	♥=The authors feel the company has distinguished itself on lesbian/gay and AIDS issues within its industry.

9
ENTERTAINMENT

THE ENTERTAINMENT INDUSTRY is one of those, along with high-tech companies in Silicon Valley and elsewhere, that have made the greatest strides toward providing equal treatment to their lesbian and gay employees. As expected, however, there are wide variations between different companies.

In 1991 **MCA (Universal)** (a division of the Japanese electronics giant Matsushita) became one of the first companies in the country to offer benefits to employees' domestic partners, calling them "spousal equivalents." Former employee Tony Middleton says that "the company needs to be recognized for that accomplishment." Employees we spoke with almost unanimously agree that the company is "gay positive." MCA and its head, media mogul Sid Sheinberg, were singled out by the L.A. Gay & Lesbian Community Services Center for their contributions to the lesbian and gay community. Sheinberg founded Hollywood Supports, an organization that uses some of the biggest names in show business to raise money for AIDS causes. Hollywood Supports is also very outspoken in fighting homophobia and AIDS-phobia in the movie industry.

Under Sheinberg's sponsorship, Hollywood Supports hosted a luncheon at MCA headquarters in March 1994 for the human resources directors of other large entertainment companies, to inform them about MCA's domestic partner (DP) benefits and to encourage them to work for them in their own companies. Sheinberg instituted DP benefits in his company without pressure from the company's lesbian and gay employees group, EAGLE, which formed only in January 1994. When asked where he thinks the impetus came from, Tony Middleton says that he and a fellow employee stuffed a note to that effect in the company suggestion box just six months before the benefits were adopted. We suspect, however, that he may not have been alone in making the suggestion.

Given MCA's early introduction of DP benefits and its rave reviews from lesbian and gay employees, we were surprised to learn from the company's completed survey that sexual orientation was not added to the company's anti-discrimination policy until January 1993. MCA told us that claims have since been filed under the provision but would not elaborate on the claims or their resolution. Sexual orientation is included in the company's diversity training. AIDS education is conducted by the company, which places no job or insurance restriction on employees with HIV/AIDS. In response to our survey, MCA management indicated that it had not done any marketing toward lesbians and gays, pointing out, however, that it does not have a central marketing department. With other entertainment companies advertising first-run films, videos, book clubs, and CDs in lesbian and gay media, we speculate that that situation will soon change. MCA has made contributions to numerous AIDS groups, including AIDS Project Los Angeles, Project Angel Food, the Elton John AIDS Foundation, and Chris Brownlie Hospice. The company has also made significant contributions to lesbian and gay organizations, such as the Los Angeles Gay and Lesbian Community Services Center, GLAAD, and the National Gay and Lesbian Task Force.

Another Japanese-owned studio, **Sony Pictures Entertainment,** (not included in our survey), announced that it would extend DP benefits to its employees effective January 1, 1995.

A former employee of MCA described the situation at his new employer by delicately saying **The Walt Disney Company** is "a little further behind." It did include sexual orientation in its anti-discrimination clause before MCA, in April 1992. The company does not, however, have any DP benefits, not even the soft ones, and is only now working on putting a diversity training program together. Disney does include sexual orientation and "AIDS in the workplace" training for its human resources professionals. It has two lesbian and gay employees groups: LEAGUE in California, and Alliance in Florida. The two groups are listed in the Disney employee newsletter, giving lesbian and gay employees in far-flung outposts of the Disney empire a chance to associate with like-minded colleagues elsewhere.

The California group was formed in September 1992. Like most such groups, it was initially formed as a way for lesbian and gay employees to meet each other and socialize. The company's offices in Los Angeles are spread out in buildings "all over the place." As Garrett Hicks, a Disney employee and the contact for the lesbian and gay group, says, "There was also a desire to see who else showed up." Since then, the group's agenda has broadened, and it has worked very actively to get DP benefits for company employees. Concentrating its efforts, LEAGUE has recently formed a Workplace Issues Committee to put together a presentation on the costs and benefits of DP benefits to present to the senior vice president for Law and Human Resources.

Disney was under fire for a long time for not allowing same-sex dancing at its theme parks. Following an earlier suit that ruled that Disneyland had arbitrarily discriminated by not allowing such behavior in the late 1970s, in April 1987 three gay men, Eric Hubart, Jeff Stabile, and Christopher Drake, filed suit in Orange County Superior Court alleging that they had been discriminated against at the Videopolis Ballroom. Lambda Legal Defense and Education Fund took the case. Following the bad publicity, and not wishing a repeat of the earlier decision, Disney settled quietly out of court. Since then, girl-girl and boy-boy dancing at Disneyland and Disney World have been tolerated, if not exactly encouraged.

Billy Kolber of *Out and About* (a gay travel newsletter) reports that fall 1993's advertised Gay Night (which was actually about 60% lesbian) at Disneyland in Anaheim, California, was actually the result of gay tour company Odyssey Adventures renting out the park; it was not an event sponsored by Disney, a fact that Disney makes abundantly clear. The evening went smoothly, although Kolber reports that Mickey and Goofy shied away from party-goers intent on posing with the cartoon characters in "suggestive" ways. For the last four years, various gay groups have gotten together for a Gay and Lesbian Day at Orlando's Walt Disney World in early June. For the first couple of years, it was largely unpublicized beyond central Florida. The most recent two events received some notoriety when a few school and church groups complained about the large number of lesbians and gays in the park. Disney responded that it "does not discriminate against anyone's right to visit the Magic Kingdom." Kolber also mentioned that it is widely known, but totally unofficial, that Thursday night is gay night at the disco at Disney World.

Paramount Communications added sexual orientation to its antidiscrimination policy a few months before Disney—on January 1,

1992. It has no employees groups but does provide diversity training and has invited guest speakers to talk to employees about HIV and AIDS.

Viacom, which beat out non-respondent QVC in a bidding war to purchase Paramount, includes sexual orientation in its anti-discrimination policy and says that "we treat people as people." The company also includes health benefits for gay domestic partners. The company is starting an HIV/AIDS awareness and education program. Viacom owns the Nickelodeon cable channel, which is the home of the animated *Ren & Stimpy Show*. The openly gay producer of the show, Jim Ballantine, discussed in an *Advocate* article whether the two characters might be gay; after all, they share the same bed.

The biggest media conglomerate, **Time Warner, Inc.**, also declined to respond to our survey. This may well be because, with 40 operating divisions, there was no way to give one answer for any question that would apply to the whole. Each of the divisions sets its own human resources policies. Some of them, starting with HBO in July 1993, have instituted DP benefits. In addition to HBO, the list includes Time Warner Corporate; Time, Inc.; Atlantic Records; and Warner Brothers Pictures. Other divisions, like the Book-of-the-Month Club (which was one of America's first mainstream marketers to approach lesbians and gay men), Warner Books, Time-Life Books, and D.C. Comics, have been laggards. As Richard Mayora, co-chair of Lesbians and Gay Men at Time Warner and an HBO employee, says, "If people are not out there forcing the issue, nothing will happen."

When HBO put in DP benefits, it came after a good deal of groundwork was done by the employees group. The Human Resources Department had approached chairman Michael Fuchs twice before he said yes. His final decision probably owed a lot to the internal lobbying carried out by the employees group and to the discreet outside support that it got from Hollywood Supports, the organization founded by Sid Sheinberg of MCA. Since then, the employees group has worked toward helping the various divisions set up better diversity training programs. Tellingly, when a Diversity Council was set up at HBO, the co-chair of the lesbian and gay employees group was asked to join, but Time, Inc., forgot to include any lesbian or gay representatives on its council. Oops!

Lesbians and Gay Men at Time Warner was founded by Steve Petoniak, then an employee of pre-merger Time, Inc. He posted a notice calling for a meeting of interested parties for June 1, 1990, at

New York's Lesbian and Gay Community Services Center. He got some negative reaction: a few anonymous phone calls yelling "fag" and a few torn-down posters. On the whole, however, management was supportive. He expected 15 people; 120 showed up.

Petoniak says that he had four reasons for wanting to form the group: (a) social, (b) advocacy, (c) networking, and (d) education. The group wanted to serve as a conduit from organizations like the Gay and Lesbian Alliance Against Defamation (GLAAD) to one of the largest media forces in the country. He says that the networking aspect was also very important. Time, Inc., was notorious for its "old boy" network in which male employees from Ivy League schools give each other a helping hand up the corporate ladder. Petoniak wanted to set up a network in which lesbians and gays could help each other out as well.

Lesbians and Gay Men at Time Warner achieved its greatest social success in November 1993, when it sponsored an executive forum for top management from all the divisions at the company. They (and the lesbian and gay members who attended) listened to a panel discussion that was made up of k.d. lang, Urvashi Vaid (former executive director of the National Gay and Lesbian Task Force), Congressman Barney Frank, and author Paul Monette.

So far, the television networks have not followed MCA and HBO in establishing DP benefits. Not surprisingly for institutions that do so much to shape America's popular culture, they have all been involved at some time in controversies concerning their programming and how it portrays lesbians and gay men.

PBS did not complete our questionnaire but did return a copy of their anti-discrimination policy, which includes sexual orientation. For years, PBS has been involved in controversies with lesbian and gay rights groups, especially GLAAD, over the issue of increasing the quantity and quality of its gay and lesbian programming and projecting more positive images of homosexuals. PBS provoked a national controversy in June 1991, when about half of its affiliates refused to show Marlon Riggs's documentary *Tongues Untied* about gay African-American men. The network was hit by anger from gay rights groups that objected to the censorship as well as by equal outrage by such conservatives as Senator Jesse Helms, who demanded that public funding of PBS be cut off. The network tried to sidestep a similar controversy a few months later, in September 1991, when it canceled a scheduled airing of a documentary called *Stop the Church*, which dealt with ACT UP/New York's demonstration at St. Patrick's Cathedral in December 1989. There was a strong feeling among activists that PBS got scared at the possible reaction of the Catholic Church and Congressional funding sources and cravenly backed down.

Without a doubt, PBS regularly broadcasts significantly more programs involving AIDS and lesbian and gay issues than either its broadcast or cable counterparts. In the 1993/94 season it aired *Before Stonewall; Portrait of a Marriage; Silverlake Life: The View from Here;* interviews with Larry Kramer and Armistead Maupin; and documentaries on the making of *Angels in America,* on AIDS, and on the escalating conflict between lesbians and gays and religious fundamentalists. And not all of those programs were aired in Gay Pride Month (June) or around World AIDS Day (December 1), when the cable and broadcast networks express an increased interest in lesbian and gay or AIDS programming.

Still, PBS has proven to be unreliable in its support. The year 1994 brought the most dramatic and appalling example of the company's cowardice. In January it aired a six-hour miniseries version of Armistead Maupin's *Tales of the City,* the classic serial epic of San Francisco life in the 1970s. Watching the show, lesbians and gay men around the country remarked that they could not believe what was coming out of their TV sets: a natural and honest vision of parts of their lives that they had never seen on the little screen before. The audience for the show was even larger than that, however, and PBS enjoyed its highest ratings in over a decade with the program. Imagine the shock, then, in April when PBS announced that it was pulling out of plans for a sequel. In Georgia and Oklahoma, conservatives outraged at the show's content had succeeded in threatening local funding for PBS, while the PBS affiliate in Chattanooga had received a bomb threat in response to the scheduled airing of *Tales.* The pressure from the right was on, and it no doubt found a sympathetic ear in Ervin Duggan, a former Bush appointee to the Federal Communications Commission, who the *Advocate* reported had campaigned for "decent family values." Duggan became president of PBS in February 1994, between the airing of *Tales* and the canceling of the sequel. In his *New York Times* column, Frank Rich said of Duggan, "PBS can hardly afford a president who recklessly tells both the gifted creators and discerning audience of the most successful prime-time drama in years to get lost." But that is apparently what PBS is doing, and it comes as no surprise to lesbians and gay men; when the heat is on, PBS always seems to back down and slink off with its tail (or *Tales*) between its legs. We were not surprised when the company declined to complete our survey.

CBS includes sexual orientation in its anti-discrimination policy and has done so for the last 16 years. Its diversity training program for managers does include sexual orientation. Diversity training for all employees is conducted in the network's Los Angeles offices, but not in the entire company. There is no lesbian and gay employees group. Personal leave is the only company benefit currently extended beyond employees' spouses to include domestic partners. CBS began AIDS education with a company-wide newsletter on the subject in 1986. The company's AIDS policy states, "AIDS (Acquired Immune Deficiency Syndrome) is to be treated the same as any other illness. CBS policy prohibits discrimination based on AIDS in the terms and conditions of employment, including hiring, promotion and termination." In addition, CBS policy prohibits "the refusal to work with an AIDS victim or the refusal to cover assignments relating to AIDS." (Obviously, CBS has not heard that it is offensive to refer to people with AIDS as "AIDS victims," a term that is disempowering.)

In 1990 CBS was involved in a very public controversy after *60 Minutes* commentator Andy Rooney made homophobic remarks in a television interview on December 20, 1989. Rooney compounded his problems by granting an interview to the *Advocate*, in which he said, "I generally feel sorry for you guys. I've been around long enough to know about homosexuality, but I still don't think it's normal. . . . I think that homosexuality is inherently dangerous." He also made insulting remarks about African-Americans. The network suspended Rooney for three months without pay as a result of the ensuing controversy.

CBS's record of programming has generally been better than the Rooney incident would suggest. CBS was the first network to produce its own AIDS awareness campaign, *AIDS: Facts for Life*, in 1988 and since then it has regularly given exposure to AIDS awareness and educational messages from numerous groups. Public affairs and entertainment programs focusing on the disease include the 1983 special *Our Times with Bill Moyers*, the 1989 movie *The Littlest Victims* (that word, again!), and the religious documentary *Confronting AIDS: Compassion and Conflict*. CBS has also reliably made efforts to integrate lesbian and gay characters into its regular entertainment programming. The network introduced daytime TV's first gay character in

1988 on *As the World Turns,* and the following year had a positively portrayed gay male recurring role on prime-time's *Doctor, Doctor.* The Gay and Lesbian Alliance Against Defamation presented CBS with awards for the inclusion and portrayal of both characters, as it did more recently for 1993's *CBS Schoolbreak Special* entitled "Other Mothers," which depicted a youth being raised by a lesbian couple. That landmark program was also lauded by the American Women in Radio and Television, which gave another award to CBS for the *Designing Women* episode entitled "Killing All the Right People," which attacked AIDS-phobia and homophobia. And, lest we forget, CBS's *Northern Exposure* has traced the television community's origins to its lesbian founders, and in May 1994 showed the marriage of its two recurring gay characters.

General Electric–owned (see the Aerospace and Defense chapter for a thorough review of the parent company) **NBC** was the first network to present a TV movie that dealt with AIDS when it screened *An Early Frost* in 1985. In that movie, the grandmother of the character played by Aidan Quinn was not allowed to say that she liked his lover because that might appear to be an endorsement of homosexuality. In spite of good ratings and favorable reviews, there was a gap of six years before ABC aired another TV movie about AIDS.

TV journalist Stephen Gendel, chief medical correspondent for NBC's cable channel, CNBC, is co-chair of the Association of NBC Gay and Lesbian Employees. Gendel says that the former head of NBC News, Michael Gartner, was very supportive of lesbian and gay employees. After a meeting with representatives of the National Lesbian and Gay Journalists Association in December 1992, Gartner reaffirmed the company's policy of non-discrimination: "There is no room for bias of any kind at NBC News." Gendel says that current management (perhaps reflecting the corporate outlook of parent company GE?) has been less forthright in their support. When asked if they would put an openly gay reporter or anchorperson on television, they said, "Of course, but how would anyone know whether they were gay or not?" We think they are missing the point. After all, isn't Katie Couric being open about her sexuality when she talks about her husband and kids?

Gendel himself made news on July 15, 1993, when he came out on the CNBC program *Real Personal.* The topic of the discussion was an article in *Science* magazine discussing the "gay gene." When asked whether he would take part in the on-screen discussion, Gendel said

ENTERTAINMENT

Company	Survey Response	Policy	Date Added	Soft Benefits	Hard Benefits	AIDS Education	Diversity Training	G/L Group	Authors' Choice
CBS	◆◆	◆	1978	◆					
Walt Disney	◆◆	◆	4/92			◆		◆◆	
MCA (Universal)	◆◆◆	◆	1/93	◆	◆	◆	◆		◆
Paramount	◆◆	◆	1/92			◆	◆		
PBS	◆								
Time Warner		◆		◆*	◆*		◆		◆
Viacom	◆	◆		◆	◆	◆			◆

* Domestic partner benefits have been extended at several major Time Warner divisions, but not all. See the company profile for details.
Company that declined to participate in our surveys: Polygram
Companies that did not respond at all: 20th Century Fox, Capital Cities/ABC, Multimedia, Time Warner, Turner Broadcasting

Key

Survey response	Sexual orientation included in anti-discrimination policy	Date sexual orientation added to anti-discrimination policy	Soft benefits (bereavement or family/personal/sick leave) extended to domestic partners	Hard benefits (health insurance) extended to domestic partners	AIDS education	Diversity training	Lesbian and gay employees group	Authors' choice
blank=None. ♦ = Provided some information, but didn't complete survey. ♦♦ = Completed one survey. ♦♦♦ = Completed both surveys.	blank=No, it is not, or unknown. ♦ = Yes, it is. UC = Under consideration.		blank=None known. ♦ = Has bereavement or family/personal/sick leave for partners. UC=Company is actively considering extending bereavement leave or family/personal/sick leave to domestic partners.	blank=No. ♦ = Yes, it is. UC = Company is considering extending health insurance to domestic partners.	blank=None known. ♦ = Yes, company conducts AIDS education.	blank=Unknown if company has any diversity training. **none** = Company has none. **NI** = Company has diversity training, but sexual orientation is not covered. ♦ = Sexual orientation is included in company's diversity training. UC=Company is actively considering including sexual orientation in its existing or proposed diversity training.	blank=None known at company. ♦ = Company has a gay and lesbian employees group. ♦♦ = Company has a gay and lesbian employees group that it officially recognizes.	♥ = The authors feel the company has distinguished itself on lesbian/gay and AIDS issues within its industry.

"yes." When asked in what capacity, he said that he would do so as a reporter and as a homosexual. Management approved, and during the broadcast he told the show's host, Bob Berkowitz, "As you know, and as our audience is about to find out, I am a gay man." Gendel is thought to be the first "mainstream" television personality to come out on the air. He says that his superiors and fellow workers at CNBC were nothing but supportive.

ABC has aired a gay storyline on its popular daytime soap opera *One Life to Live.* In 1990, ABC ran an episode of *thirtysomething* in which two gay men were shown in bed together. The infamous American Family Association then called for an advertisers' boycott campaign that cost ABC an estimated $1.5 million in revenue. In response, ABC declined to include that episode when it reran the season's shows during the summer. A spokesman for ABC said, "I guess our position is that we've already run it once." In May 1991 ABC showed a sensitively produced AIDS movie called *Our Sons,* which starred Julie Andrews and Ann-Margret. And then, of course, it was on ABC that Roseanne Arnold had her infamous kiss with Mariel Hemingway in March 1994.

On October 1, 1994 Capital Cities/ABC became the first television network to institute domestic partners' benefits for its employees.

Turner Broadcasting System, parent organization of CNN, declined to return our survey. We had received allegations, by persons who asked to remain anonymous, claiming that the Atlanta-based company had had instances in which openly gay people had been rejected for employment by a homophobic on-screen personality. Given the network's uncommunicativeness, we were unable to substantiate these charges.

10
FINANCIAL SERVICES

U<small>JB</small> F<small>INANCIAL</small> C<small>ORPORATION,</small> based in Princeton, New Jersey, has included sexual orientation in its anti-discrimination policy since 1992 and includes sexual orientation in its diversity training. UJB also indicated in its response to our survey that child-care benefits are available to same-sex domestic partners and that it does not recognize any employee groups. It does conduct AIDS education programs for its employees.

MBIA, the Municipal Bond Investors Assurance Corporation of Armonk, New York, responded to our survey with copies of its policies. Sexual orientation is included in its equal employment opportunity statement but it is not specifically addressed in its anti-harassment policy. Although several anti-harassment workshops have been conducted at MBIA, diversity training has not yet been instituted. AIDS education is slated to begin sometime in 1994.

Teachers Insurance and Annuity Association–College Retirement Equities Fund (**TIAA–CREF**) is the world's largest private pension system. Headquartered in New York, its anti-discrimination policy has included sexual orientation since February 1991. Sexual orientation is also included in TIAA–CREF's diversity training. The company does not recognize any employee groups.

The **St. Paul Companies** have included sexual orientation in their anti-discrimination policy since March 1991. Company diversity training also includes sexual orientation. In response to our survey, St. Paul indicated that an "informal" gay and lesbian employee group has recently started at the company and that the company has provided facilities for the fledgling group's use.

Located across the river from Saint Paul, in Minneapolis, **Piper**

Jaffray Companies completed our surveys. They have included "affectional preference" in their anti-discrimination policy since June 1991 and informed us that no complaints have been filed under the policy since then. Their diversity training also includes sexual orientation issues. Piper Jaffray is self-insured and places no job or insurance restrictions on employees with HIV/AIDS. Unfortunately they do not offer any AIDS awareness or education programs. The company has not marketed its services directly to gay men and lesbians. Nor have they advertised job listings in the gay or lesbian media, because they do such advertising only in the largest mass market publications. Piper Jaffray has made company contributions to the Minnesota AIDS Project. It matches employee gifts to organizations with 501(c)3 nonprofit status from the IRS, except religious, political, fraternal, professional, or veterans organizations, making gifts to most lesbian and gay organizations possible. Piper Jaffray does require that the employee be not only a donor but also a volunteer with the group.

American Express, America's second-largest financial services company, did not respond to our survey. However, we are aware of plans for an upcoming marketing program targeted at gay men and lesbians. As part of its promotional campaign for Cheques for Two—traveler's checks that can be used by one or both members of a couple—in the fall of 1994 Amex plans to run ads in gay and lesbian magazines, specifically *Out* and *10 Percent*. Rather than running its standard ad for the special traveler's checks, which usually features the signatures of husbands and wives, the company will alter the ads so that the checks pictured carry the signatures of same-sex couples. The program will make Amex one of the largest and most prominent American companies to begin marketing toward gay men and lesbians. We wish we knew if the American Express employment policies and benefits bear any resemblance to the spirit of this progressive marketing campaign.

H & R Block, America's largest tax preparer and the owner of CompuServe, the leading on-line service for personal computer users, fully completed our surveys. Block's main office is in Kansas City, but its operations are spread throughout the United States. At the time of our survey, the company was considering the addition of sexual orientation to its anti-discrimination policy; it was added in October 1993. Similarly, the company does not currently conduct diversity training, but training is being developed now, and Block indicated that the program would include sexual orientation issues when completed. Block has not previously advertised employment opportunities in the gay and lesbian press but indicated that it would consider doing so in the future. The company is self-insured and has no job or insurance restrictions for employees with HIV/AIDS. Bereavement leave is available to employees with same-sex domestic partners, and same-sex partners may be included in the company pension program. Block has not done any marketing toward lesbians or gays. The company limits its matching-gifts program beneficiaries to United Way members, but the company itself has given to various AIDS organizations, including Heartstrings, the Good Samaritan Project, the Kansas City Free Health Clinic, and the Heart of America Community AIDS Partnership, to which Block gives annually.

Bear Stearns and Company, the New York–based investment banking firm and brokerage house, did not respond to our surveys but is reported to have an anti-discrimination policy that includes sexual orientation.

Another brokerage house that did not respond to our surveys, but about which we have good news to report, is **Charles Schwab**. With 45% of the market, Schwab is the nation's largest discount brokerage. It is also the only brokerage to have domestic partner (DP) benefits. In July 1993 the health, dental, and vision plans available to spouses of Schwab employees were made available to employees' domestic partners and the dependent children of domestic partners. The extension of benefits stemmed from the formation of an employee task force to study "diverse-family issues" as part of a recent focus on company diversity. As reported in Schwab's employee journal, the task force—formed just six months prior to the announcement granting DP benefits—also developed "a set of guidelines to make sure that when policies and procedures regarding employees and family benefits are being developed, the company is as inclusive as possible." It is changes like this, signifying that a company's philosophy is evolving to include an ongoing consciousness of its gay and lesbian employees, that are most heartening in studies of gay and lesbian workplace issues. Schwab is the only major brokerage house headquartered in San Francisco. As we see in our profiles of other industries, companies located in gay-friendly areas and companies that have active groups of "out" employees are most likely to lead their industries on issues of importance to gay men and lesbians.

The Federal National Mortgage Association, located in the District

FINANCIAL SERVICES

Company	Survey Response	Policy	Date Added	Soft Benefits	Hard Benefits	AIDS Education	Diversity Training	G/L Group	Authors' Choice
Bear Stearns		◆							
H & R Block	◆◆	◆	10/93	◆		◆	UC		
Fannie Mae	◆◆◆	◆	5/7/92	◆	◆	◆	◆	◆◆	◆
MBIA	◆	◆							
Piper Jaffray	◆◆◆	◆	6/10/91						
Charles Schwab				◆	◆		◆		◆
St. Paul	◆◆	◆	3/91				◆		
TIAA–CREF	◆◆	◆	2/91				◆		
UJB Financial	◆◆	◆	1/92			◆			

Companies that declined to participate in our surveys: American General, American International, Christopher Street Financial, Freddie Mac, General Re, ITT, Kemper, Loews, Marsh & McLennan, Paine Webber

Companies that did not respond at all: American Express, Bear Stearns, Beneficial, Capital Holding, Dean Witter Reynolds, Household International, Merrill Lynch, Morgan Stanley, Primerica, Sallie Mae, Salomon, Transamerica

Key

Survey response	Sexual orientation included in anti-discrimination policy	Date sexual orientation added to anti-discrimination policy	Soft benefits (bereavement or family/personal/sick leave) extended to domestic partners	Hard benefits (health insurance) extended to domestic partners	AIDS education	Diversity training	Lesbian and gay employees group	Authors' choice
blank=None.	blank=No, it is not, or unknown.		blank=None known.	blank=No.	blank=None known.	blank=Unknown if company has any diversity training.	blank=None known at company.	♥ =The authors feel the company has distinguished itself on lesbian/gay and AIDS issues within its industry.
♦ = Provided some information, but didn't complete survey.	♦ = Yes, it is.		♦ = Has bereavement or family/personal/sick leave for partners.	♦ = Yes, it is.	♦ = Yes, company conducts AIDS education.	none = Company has none.	♦ = Company has a gay and lesbian employees group.	
♦♦ = Completed one survey.	UC=Under consideration.		UC=Company is actively considering extending bereavement leave or family/personal/sick leave to domestic partners.	UC=Company is considering extending health insurance to domestic partners.		NI=Company has diversity training, but sexual orientation is not covered.	♦♦ = Company has a gay and lesbian employees group that it officially recognizes.	
♦♦♦ = Completed both surveys.						♦ = Sexual orientation is included in company's diversity training.		
						UC=Company is actively considering including sexual orientation in its existing or proposed diversity training.		

of Columbia and better known as **Fannie Mae**, was created by President Franklin Roosevelt in 1938 as a source of credit for low- and moderate-income home buyers. Today, as a private corporation, it dominates the secondary real estate market, buying mortgages from banks and savings and loans. With no fanfare and little or no notice by the media, in September 1993 the company quietly decided that, effective January 1, 1994, all company policies and benefits covering spouses would be extended to opposite- and same-sex domestic partners. Fannie Mae fully completed our surveys and has included sexual orientation in its anti-discrimination policy since May 7, 1992. The company considers information on claims filed under its anti-discrimination policy to be confidential and would not say if any had been based on sexual orientation. Fannie Mae is self-insured and places no job or insurance restrictions on employees with HIV/AIDS. It does conduct AIDS education for its employees.

Fannie Mae has a gay and lesbian employees group that it recognizes and provides with facilities and publicity. Comically, the group goes by the name Fannie FLAG. Fannie Mae does no marketing targeted at gays and lesbians. Nor has it advertised job opportunities in the gay and lesbian press, although it indicated that it would consider doing so in the future. Fannie Mae matches its employees' charitable giving to any IRS-recognized 501(c)3 nonprofit group at a ratio of 2:1 for the first $500 and 1:1 up to $10,000. With its survey response, Fannie Mae included a lengthy list of its contributions to AIDS groups. Recipients include Whitman Walker, the district's primary AIDS services provider; Food and Friends; and AIDS Housing of Washington. The company also contributed to Planned Parenthood of Washington for the production of an HIV prevention video for children in grades 4 to 6!

11

FOOD, TOBACCO, BEVERAGES, AND FAST FOOD

Mɪɴɴᴇᴛᴏɴᴋᴀ, Mɪɴɴᴇsᴏᴛᴀ, is home to **Cargill**, the largest privately owned company in the nation and the second-largest service company (behind AT&T). Not a household name, Cargill buys, produces, transports, processes, and packages commodities, including grain, seed, juice, coffee, sugar, and cotton. Cargill also produces and trades steel. While Cargill completed our full survey, they had little progress to report. Their diversity training does not include sexual orientation, nor does the company have a lesbian and gay employee group. Sexual orientation is not included in their anti-discrimination policy, and Cargill was frank enough to tell us that one claim of discrimination based on sexual orientation had been filed with the company but that it found no evidence of discrimination. Still, Cargill is not considering adding sexual orientation to their policy. The company is self-insured and offers no benefits that include domestic partners. It conducts AIDS education and places no job or insurance restrictions on people with HIV/AIDS. Cargill does not match its employees' charitable giving, and the company itself made no donations specifically to AIDS groups or to lesbian and gay organizations, but noted that it does contribute to the United Way, which in Minnesota funds the Gay and Lesbian Community Action Council.

Moving on to food companies whose names are better known to consumers, jam-maker **J. M. Smucker Company** is located in Orrville, Ohio. Smucker's anti-discrimination policy does not include sexual orientation, and its addition is not currently under consideration. The company noted that its corporate equal employment opportunity policy is in accordance with Title VII of the 1964 Civil Rights Act, so it appears that Smucker does not plan to extend protections in advance of the federal government. Smucker did say that in its benefit plans AIDS is treated as any other sickness or terminal illness.

San Francisco's **Del Monte Foods** did not complete our survey, but sent copies of its policies. We were surprised to see that sexual orientation is included in their equal employment opportunity statement but is not specifically listed in their anti-discrimination policy. Upon further investigation, we discovered that the discrepancy stems from differences in protections across the United States: Del Monte's equal employment opportunity statement is based on California state law, while its anti-discrimination policy is modeled on federal law.

Located in Waterbury, Vermont, **Ben & Jerry's Homemade** is not a Fortune 1,000 company and, despite the ice-cream maker's status as a household name, with 600 employees it is dwarfed by even the smallest companies in this chapter. Nevertheless this book would be incomplete without a mention of Ben & Jerry's because the company extended full benefits to employees' same-sex and opposite-sex domestic partners back in November 1989. While groundbreaking, the company's move was not surprising because Ben & Jerry's was launched not just with a commitment to quality and economic growth but also with a strong commitment to social issues. From top to bottom, Ben & Jerry's is run on a new model of socially responsible and individually empowering management: From the production line to management, employee dress is casual; an outstanding 7.5% of the company's pre-tax profits are dedicated to charitable giving; full staff meetings are held every two months, with input from all employees welcomed (and Ben and Jerry frequently attend); and employees are encouraged to design community service projects that may be pursued during a portion of company time.

Ben & Jerry's includes sexual orientation in its anti-discrimination policy, but indicated in its survey response that it has no diversity training and no employee-organized groups—probably because they are unneeded. There have been no requests to form employee groups and, in addition to employing an equal-opportunity vocabulary in company writings ranging from memos to handbooks, all company communications are neutral in terms of gender and sexual orientation. For lesbians and gay men, the atmosphere at the company is reported to be ideal. In her survey response, human resources manager Liz Lonergan wrote ". . . it's o.k. to be gay and be out (really out!) here, and that makes it a better place for all our employees." Her comments echo the remarks of a gay employee, as quoted in a 1992 article in *Personnel Journal,* "No one here is in the closet. . . . This is a company that's very open and accepting; there aren't any lines drawn. I can't imagine any typical company making me feel this comfortable." Neither can we.

McCormick & Company, the Sparks, Maryland–based diversified food specialty company best known for its spices and flavorings, fully completed our surveys. The company does not include sexual orientation in either its anti-discrimination policy or its diversity training. McCormick did note, however, that a formal proposal for adding such a provision to its anti-discrimination policy has been made and is currently under review. There are no employee groups of any kind sponsored by McCormick. The company is self-insured and has extended no benefits to include domestic partners. No job or insurance restrictions are placed on employees with HIV/AIDS. McCormick apparently does not formally conduct AIDS education, but did mention that it supplies AIDS information to its employees. The company indicated that it has done no marketing or advertising targeted at lesbians and gay men since "our products appeal to all individuals, regardless of sexual orientation." McCormick matches the charitable donations of its employees to any organizations recognized by the IRS as 501(c)3 nonprofits. This would make many AIDS and lesbian and gay organizations eligible. McCormick itself has contributed to AIDS Action Baltimore.

Cereal giant **Kellogg Company**, of Battle Creek, Michigan, declined to participate in our survey, but an *Advocate* story in 1990 reported that the company does include sexual orientation in its anti-discrimination policy. Otherwise Kellogg is notable (and notorious) only for one of its ads, which broke new ground in advertising by using homophobia's comic punch to sell a product. A 1990 ad campaign for Kellogg's Nut & Honey Crunch was built on the comedic potential of having one person ask another one what he or she was eating and having that person respond "Nut & Honey," only to be misinterpreted as having answered "Nothin', honey." When one such commercial featured a group of burly men seemingly about to beat up a man they thought had addressed one of them as "honey," lesbian and gay organizations attacked the cereal maker for the ad's blatant homophobia and its encouragement of anti-gay violence.

Nestlé Beverage Company of San Francisco is a division of Nestlé USA, which is in turn an arm of the Swiss food maker. Nestlé Beverage added sexual orientation to its anti-discrimination clause in January 1991 and has been moving steadily on AIDS issues and issues of concern to lesbians and gays since then. It also includes sexual orientation in its diversity training. The employee group Gay and Lesbian Associates of Nestlé Beverage Company was formed in February 1993 and is recognized by management, which provides facilities and internal publicity to the group. Nestlé Beverage is self-insured and currently extends bereavement leave and family/personal/sick leave to employees with domestic partners. No job or insurance restrictions are placed on employees with HIV/AIDS. Currently all manufacturing sites are involved in an HIV/AIDS awareness program, which is slotted for expansion in 1994.

Nestlé Beverage has not directly advertised toward lesbians and gay men but has sponsored events for lesbian and gay or AIDS groups, including the Golden Gate Business Association, Project Inform, Out and Equal in the '90s, and the National Gay and Lesbian Task Force. Nestlé Beverage has actively contributed to both AIDS and lesbian and gay organizations, including Project Open Hand, the San Francisco Names Project, Community United Against Violence, as well as the groups for which it has sponsored events, listed above. The company generally matches its employees' charitable giving only to United Way charities, but it does make one exception by matching contributions to AIDS Walk San Francisco. On the whole, Nestlé Beverage Company has been progressive on issues of importance to lesbians and gay men; however, we did find one negative incident. According to a report in the *Oakland Tribune*, a lawsuit alleging anti-gay discrimination was filed against the company by a former temporary employee in August 1992. The suit was one of seven $1 million lawsuits filed simultaneously in California to highlight the need for the addition of sexual orientation to the list of protected categories in the state's anti-discrimination law. The amendment to the law had been vetoed by Governor Pete Wilson in 1991 but has since been enacted. Unfortunately we were unable to locate further information on the discrimination suit against Nestlé Beverage. In an unrelated incident at another division of the Swiss company, Purchase, New York's Nestlé Chocolate and Confection Company dropped basketball star Magic Johnson as a spokesperson for its products after he announced he was HIV-positive. When Johnson originally announced his infection, Nestlé Chocolate denied that it would drop him but subsequently declined to renew his contract.

In 1985 when R. J. Reynolds, the tobacco company behind popular brands like Winston, Salem, and Camel, bought cookie-king Nabisco Brands, the result was one of the world's largest tobacco and food companies, **RJR Nabisco**. The company has operations around the world, but the majority of its employees are located in New Jersey and North Carolina. RJR Nabisco thoroughly completed our surveys. The company includes sexual orientation in its diversity training and has listed the term in its anti-discrimination policy since July 1, 1988. No claims have been filed for discrimination based upon sexual orientation since the policy was amended. At the time of our original survey, the company had no lesbian or gay employees group, but one has since formed at Nabisco Foods Group in East Hanover, New Jersey. RJR Nabisco is self-insured and has yet to officially extend any benefits to include domestic partners. In responding to our survey, the company noted, however, that bereavement leave and family/ personal/sick leave are available at "manager discretion."

The person completing our survey was not aware of any formal research by RJR Nabisco's marketers on the lesbian and gay market. At a time when most tobacco companies are keenly focused on developing niche markets, RJR Nabisco has in fact lagged behind its competitors by not placing ads in lesbian and gay media. They made a point of telling us, though, that the company has repeatedly defied boycott threats by advertising on the few television programs with lesbian and gay characters, including *L.A. Law, Roseanne,* and *Melrose Place.* RJR Nabisco has often sponsored events for AIDS organizations, including AIDS Walk Washington and numerous events for the Gay Men's Health Crisis. Recipients of the company's charitable donations include those and other AIDS groups—Whitman Walker Clinic, Food and Friends, and the Community Health Project—as well as several lesbian and gay organizations, including the Victory Fund, the 1993 March on Washington, and the Gay and Lesbian Alliance Against Defamation. The company's matching gifts program is limited to educational institutions and arts and cultural organizations.

Three times larger than RJR Nabisco in both sales ($50 billion) and number of employees (170,000), **Philip Morris Companies** is also a tobacco company that moved mightily into foods in the 1980s. Already the top cigarette company in the world, its purchases of

General Foods in 1985 and Kraft in 1988 made Philip Morris the largest food company in the United States. The New York company's brands include Marlboro, Cheese Whiz, Miller, Entenmann's, Jell-O, Maxwell House, and Oscar Mayer. Unfortunately Philip Morris did not respond to our survey. However, because the food and tobacco leader has had interactions with the lesbian and gay community and with AIDS activists on many fronts, we have no shortage of material on the company.

Within the context of our book, Philip Morris is perhaps best known for its charitable giving and marketing. The most notable incident sprang from the former and impacted the latter. In the summer of 1990, gay and AIDS activists were alerted that Philip Morris was the largest corporate donor to North Carolina's outspokenly homophobic and AIDS-phobic senator Jesse Helms. The company had been a long-time contributor to the Republican senator because he had always been a strong supporter of the tobacco industry, an important economic engine in North Carolina. Nevertheless the activists were outraged by the company's support of one of their most vocal and effective enemies and at the same time saw a rare opportunity to bring national attention (and hopefully national opposition) to Helms's unusually vulnerable re-election campaign that year. A boycott of Philip Morris was suggested, and AIDS and lesbian and gay groups around the country quickly signed on to what became a high-profile media effort. The boycott targeted all Philip Morris products but focused on its Marlboro cigarette and Miller beer brands. ACT UP chapters around the country plastered their cities with parodies of the granddaddy of advertising icons: Posters featuring jowly Senator Helms in a ten-gallon hat and identifying him as the "real Marlboro Man" described his offensive positions and then focused on Philip Morris's contributions. More dramatically, activists in many cities dumped case after case of Miller beer into the streets outside gay bars, which had canceled their Miller orders and removed Marlboro cigarettes from their vending machines. Seeing such spectacle, the mainstream media quickly picked up the story. Even the *Wall Street Journal* devoted ink to speculation about the boycott's effects on the company's bottom line.

Philip Morris said it would not comply with the boycotters' demand that it stop giving money to Helms. The company did meet with bar owners and activists in many cities to discuss its stance and point out its previous commitment to lesbians and gays through its sponsorship of events as well as its donations to AIDS charities. Nevertheless the boycott continued for almost a year—long after Helms had won re-election. It was further exacerbated when activists learned that, aside from its donations to Helms's political campaign, Miller had been a major funder of the Jesse Helms Museum project in North Carolina. Media coverage, which had lagged after the boycott's photogenic launch, resumed when activists loudly dogged the Philip Morris–sponsored national tour of a copy of the Bill of Rights. Finally, on May 30, 1991, ACT UP announced the end of the boycott, not because Philip Morris had agreed to stop funding Helms but because the company had agreed to increase its contributions to AIDS charities over a period of four years from $1.3 million to $2.6 million. The boycott's effects on the company's earnings had been negligible, but concerns about its public image had kept Philip Morris seeking some settlement with the activists throughout the year.

With the boycott ended, Philip Morris slowly but steadily resumed its courtship of the lesbian and gay market. More ads appeared in local gay publications, and in 1992 Philip Morris became the first tobacco company to advertise in a national gay magazine when it included ads in *Genre* as part of its new ad campaign for Benson & Hedges Special Kings. Philip Morris also took the unusual and laudable step of moving into the political arena for lesbians and gays when Miller joined several other large businesses, including Levi Strauss, in supporting California's proposed gay rights law in 1992. Corporate opposition had been cited by Governor Pete Wilson as a factor when he vetoed a similar bill in 1991. In late 1993 Philip Morris made its highest-profile lesbian and gay marketing commitment to date when Miller Brewing Company signed on (with Continental Airlines) as one of the first major, mainstream companies to sponsor June 1994's Gay Games IV and Cultural Festival in New York City, the year's premier lesbian and gay event.

Still the company is so large and its interests so diverse that its relations with the lesbian and gay community continue to be as awkward as the compromise that ended the boycott. Although its vice-peddling corporate siblings Philip Morris USA and Miller Brewing Company have certainly been at the fore of mainstream corporations marketing toward lesbians and gays, food maker Kraft General Foods asked that none of its products be advertised on a March 1994 episode of *Roseanne* that would feature a lesbian kiss. In a memo inadvertently leaked by the company's ad agency, Grey, the company's reason for prohibiting the showing of its ads was because the episode "deal[t] with homosexuality." Kraft has previously advertised on programs with gay content, however, including *Northern Exposure, Melrose Place,* and the first TV movie about AIDS, *An Early Frost.* Without a survey response from Philip Morris Companies, we do not know if the corporation's employment and benefit policies are similarly conflicted when it comes to homosexuality. We do know that as recently as September 1990 the company was reported not to include sexual orientation in its anti-discrimination policies, when an *Advocate* article remarked that the company, which has advocated the inclusion of smokers' rights in civil rights legislation, did not see the necessity of written protection for its lesbian and gay employees. We would hope that the company's attitude toward its lesbian and gay employees has since shown progress to mirror the blossoming of the company's marketing push. We would also hope that any progress made in protecting and recognizing lesbian and gay employees would be uniform at all the company's divisions, not just at those impervious to boycott by the religious right.

Speaking of boycotts, from the late 1970s into the 1980s, **Adolph Coors Company**, located in Golden, Colorado, was the constant target of strikes and boycotts resulting from alleged discriminatory and unfair labor practices. Among the most-repeated charges against Coors was the claim that it had done polygraph testing on prospective employees and that among the questions asked during the tests were inquiries about sexual practices and sexual orientation. Coors denied the charges and, as a direct result of the controversy, in 1978 became one of the first companies in the country to add sexual orientation to its anti-discrimination policy.

In many ways, Adolph Coors Company has acted to put its house in order since the labor confrontations of the '70s and '80s; the AFL-CIO lifted its endorsement of the Coors boycott in 1987. The company's response to our survey showed considerable progress on many fronts. Sexual orientation is not only included in Coors's anti-discrimination policy; it is also included in its diversity training. The company even has a lesbian and gay employee group—LAGER, Lesbian and Gay Employee Resource—which formed in February 1993 and is recognized as an official Coors diversity council. The company provides the group with facilities and internal publicity. In fact, in the company's 1992 annual report, an interview with CEO

Peter Coors mentioned the existence of the group. LAGER meets monthly, and members marched in the 1993 Denver PrideFest Parade along with a LAGER limousine. The group has sponsored showings of the videos "Pink Triangles" and "Marching for Freedom" at the company plant for interested employees. No company benefits have yet been extended to domestic partners, although Coors is reported currently to be studying the subject. All medical and disability benefits are available to people with HIV/AIDS. Coors responded to the disease quickly. It formed a company task force on AIDS in 1985 and announced a company policy in May 1986 that said AIDS would be treated like any other serious illness, that affected employees would be afforded privacy, and that efforts would be made to accommodate employees with HIV and enable them to remain productive. Since then, Coors has sponsored events for and made grants to numerous AIDS groups, including Los Angeles's Minority AIDS Project, the AIDS Library of Philadelphia, AIDS Walk D.C., and Project Angel Food. Nearly $275,000 has been contributed to AIDS groups since 1988.

As various groups began to forsake the Coors boycott in the late 1980s, the brewer moved aggressively to market its products toward the various constituencies whose leaders had called for them to boycott. Coors has made strong advertising pushes in women's and feminist magazines, publications serving African-American and Latino communities, and lesbian and gay media. The company also continually seeks events to sponsor in these communities. Coors sent us long lists of events it has sponsored for lesbian and gay organizations over the past five years. Events and organizations include the Gay Rodeo Association, Austin's Gay/Lesbian International Film Festival, the Boston Gay Bowling Tournament, Project Open Hand in San Francisco, and the Big Apple Gay and Lesbian Softball League. Coors and its distributors have given nearly $345,000 to lesbian and gay community programs since 1988, and its list of sponsorships has grown longer every year.

Coors's increased marketing toward lesbians and gays is consistent with its reported progress in employment practices and policies: While no benefits are yet available to employees' domestic partners, the presence of a long-standing anti-discrimination policy, Coors's AIDS policy, and the emergence of a lesbian and gay employees group indicate that the company has come a long way from its alleged questioning of employees' sexual orientation in polygraph tests. We congratulate Coors management on this progress. Unfortunately a comprehensive evaluation of Coors is not that simple. While the diverse range of Philip Morris's marketing and charitable activities left lesbians, gays, and people with AIDS with the impression that the company greeted them with one hand and shook hands with their enemies with the other, dealings with Adolph Coors Company leave them feeling like the brewer is helping them with one hand while the Coors family is throttling them with the other.

Several members of the family are prominent funders of the far right, including some of America's most persistent and vicious anti-gay groups. This fact could reasonably be ignored in our study if the Coors family did not also hold all of the voting stock in Adolph Coors Company. They control the company, and its profits are their profits. Family patriarch Joe, ex-wife Holly, and sons Joe Jr., Jeffrey, and Peter personally—as well as through the Coors Foundation and Coors Company PAC (Public Action Coors Employees)—contribute to numerous conservative and far-right political and religious organizations. The two organizations that have received the most Coors money are the Heritage Foundation and the Free Congress Foundation. In 1973 Joe Coors, Sr., provided the $250,000 first-year budget to start the Heritage Foundation, which has been a driving force behind the "new right" since its inception. In *Issues '88*, a suggested national election platform "for a stronger and healthier America," Heritage called for the reintroduction and enforcement of sodomy laws and routine HIV-testing for public employees and all institutional populations, including prisons, hospitals, and schools.

Issues '88 was co-published by the Free Congress Foundation, a group that sprang from the Committee for the Survival of a Free Congress, which also received its original funding, in 1974, from Joe Coors. The Free Congress Foundation, much further right than the Heritage Foundation, has received continual financial support from the Coors family, its primary funder. In 1988 alone, with Jeffrey Coors as chairman of its board, the FCF received $150,000 from the Coors Foundation. The FCF is one of America's leading distributors of frighteningly homophobic literature. Its "Senior Contributing Scholar" Father Enrique Rueda wrote a book in 1987 titled *Gays, AIDS and You*, which FCF distributes and which suggests that "once you understand the agenda of the homosexual movement, you will probably perceive it as a terrible threat—to ourselves, our children, our communities, our country." The FCF's order form for the book features a silhouette of a suited man working in an office; its caption reads, "This man wants his 'freedom' so bad he's ready to let America die for it. He fights like a warrior possessed, on the front lines of the Gay Rights movement. Our civilization stands in the path of his fulfillment as a freely promiscuous homosexual. And he's willing to sacrifice our freedom, our families, and even our lives to get his way."

It is impossible to square the virulently anti-gay politics of the Coors family with the newly progressive employment and AIDS policies and stepped-up, gay-targeted marketing of the Adolph Coors Company. The family's philanthropy and political involvement are channeled almost exclusively toward groups that espouse the anti-union, racist, sexist, and homophobic stances that allegedly characterized the atmosphere at the company in the early 1970s and before—an atmosphere that brought on a decade of strikes and boycotts as well as a 1975 lawsuit by the Equal Employment Opportunity Commission. Perhaps the only viable explanation for the gulf is a boycott-sharpened hypersensitivity to public relations. This sensitivity can be seen in a telling flaw of the company AIDS policy, as seen in its *AIDS in the Workplace* literature. Included is a section entitled "Public Concern" that says, "Although scientific evidence clearly shows that HIV or AIDS is not transmitted through the casual contact involved in a manufacturing process, the company has to be sensitive to the concerns and public confusion that still surround AIDS in the workplace. As a result, employees who are known to be infected will be assigned to positions that do not involve direct contact with the product."

In many cities, the lesbian and gay community has slowly relaxed or even abandoned the Coors boycott as the company has bought ads in their papers and sponsored their events. While we could gladly recommend a publicly held corporation with the Coors Company's recent record of progress on lesbian and gay issues and AIDS work, we cannot in good conscience recommend a Coors family-held Coors Company to workers, consumers, or investors who are concerned about the rights of lesbians, gays, and people with AIDS. Readers will have to weigh the company's recent record against the family's activities and make their own decisions. The Coors Company makes a strong case for its contention that its internal policies and outside support make it more progressive on AIDS and lesbian and gay issues than either of its major competitors: Anheuser-Busch and Philip Morris's Miller Brewing Company. Although all three aggressively court the lesbian and gay market, only Coors answered our survey and, to the best of our knowledge, only Coors has a lesbian and gay employees group and is actively considering domestic partner benefits.

It is unlikely that Coors, Philip Morris, or Anheuser-Busch would currently be advertising in lesbian and gay media if **Carillon Importers**, of Teaneck, New Jersey, had not jumped in first. Carillon's head Michel Roux had been advertising in many cutting-edge magazines and using the art of openly lesbian and gay artists in his ads for Sweden's Absolut vodka since gaining the account in 1979. But in the mid-1980s many thought he was taking a big risk by buying major spreads in lesbian and gay magazines. As a *New York Times* advertising columnist put it in an *Advocate* article in April 1994, "It was a big, big deal when Michel bought into the gay media. A lot of people saw him as a trendsetter. When the sky didn't fall in, they followed him." And follow him they did. Absolut was the first mainstream advertiser to enter the lesbian and gay media. Other alcohol marketers such as Hiram Walker & Sons, Schieffelin & Somerset Company, and William Grant & Sons then began to do the same. With its Miller Brewing Company already advertising, it was logical for Philip Morris to begin advertising its cigarettes, adding another product category to the advertiser base for lesbian and gay magazines. Mainstream advertisers in other fields, such as apparel (The Gap, Armani, Benetton), entertainment (Sony, Polygram, Time Warner, MCA), and computers (Apple) have since followed suit. Because Carillon Importers is not a Fortune 1,000 company (it's a 60-employee division of the British company Grand Metropolitan), it was not included in our original survey mailing, and the company did not complete one that was sent subsequently. A Carillon representative told us that their policies come from Grand Met but volunteered that the company has conducted AIDS education.

Brown-Forman, one of the few makers of hard liquor large enough to make the Fortune 1,000, began in late 1993 to advertise Southern Comfort in the lesbian and gay media but also did not respond to our surveys. New York's **Joseph E. Seagram and Sons** was the only Fortune 1,000 liquor distributor to do so. Seagram includes sexual orientation in its diversity training and added sexual orientation to its anti-discrimination policy in 1988. Gay and lesbian employees have not organized an employee group, but management said if one formed it would be recognized and supported. Bereavement leave is the only company benefit currently extended to include employees' domestic partners. The company does conduct AIDS education and has sponsored AIDS Walk New York. Seagram has sponsored events in the lesbian and gay community, including Labor Day L.A., events during Palm Springs's annual White Party weekend, and events for the Gay and Lesbian Alliance Against Defamation. Seagram has also been involved with New York's Hetrick Martin Institute, which supports and educates lesbian, gay, and bisexual youth. Seagram has also on occasion directly advertised several of its products in the lesbian and gay media: Chivas Regal scotch, Captain Morgan's and Myer's rums, and Godiva chocolates. People are now watching to see if Seagram makes much greater use of lesbian and gay media since Absolut moved its business from Carillon to Seagram in early 1994. Seagram has maintained the same ad agency for the brand and the same publicist, but since Roux himself was the driving force behind Carillon's heavy use of lesbian and gay media, it will be interesting to see if liquor-giant Seagram makes the same major commitment. Ad placement and sponsorships in the first half of 1994 indicate that it will.

Conversely, and more interestingly, advertising managers at lesbian and gay magazines around the country are holding their breath in anticipation of the possible effects of the other consequence of Absolut's split with Carillon: Carillon has been signed to market and distribute Stolichnaya vodka. More specifically, beverage and fast food giant **PepsiCo** has signed Carillon to handle Stoli. Pepsico's products and franchises include Pepsi-Cola, Mountain Dew, Frito-Lay snack foods, KFC, Pizza Hut, and Taco Bell. The Purchase, New York, company declined to participate in our survey but did send a letter and copies of its equal opportunity and sexual harassment policies, neither of which specifically include sexual orientation as a protected category for its 350,000 employees. PepsiCo did note that its divisions operate autonomously and so may have their own policies. For now, however, all eyes (at lesbian and gay publications, at least) are on PepsiCo's marketing. When asked by the *Advocate* about his advertising plans for his new vodka client, Carillon head Michel Roux declared, "We are planning on staying very close to the gay community. The investment will be in the same style and backed by the same dollars as before. You can count on it." People have been anxious to see if PepsiCo will give Roux free rein to execute that plan. Carillon informed us that its agreement with PepsiCo specifies that the beverage and fast food giant will have no control over Stoli's marketing, and Stoli's ad campaign through the first half of 1994 seems to be pure Roux. People are even more curious as to whether PepsiCo's approach to the gay market for Stoli might eventually spread to some of the company's other products. Leaving Stoli's marketing to Carillon allows PepsiCo the comfort of approaching the gay market indirectly with one of its products. But if Roux brings the same kind of success to Stoli that he brought to Absolut with a marketing campaign that embraces lesbians and gay men, wouldn't PepsiCo be tempted to approach gays and lesbians with some of its other products? We suspect that if the company would run some photos of 1950s spokesperson Joan Crawford sipping Pepsi in lesbian and gay publications, the soft drink would easily increase its market share. Dammit, Tina! No more wire hangers—*and no more Coke!*

None of PepsiCo's major beverage or fast food competitors completed our surveys, but we do have some information on most of them. Atlanta's **Coca-Cola Company** declined to participate in our survey, but a February 1993 *Business Week* cover story on companies' response to AIDS characterized Coca-Cola's AIDS education efforts as "paltry." Ann Arbor-based **Domino's Pizza** also did not complete our survey. We have no information on the employment policies, benefits, or marketing of the privately owned company, but we know that the actions of Domino's president and owner Tom Monaghan have angered women's and pro-choice groups. They urged a Domino's boycott in the 1980s because Monaghan supported his own opposition to abortion by giving generously to pro-life groups. It comes as no surprise, then, that in 1993 James Dobson, president of the notoriously homophobic Colorado Springs group Focus on the Family, was awarded the Domino's Pizza Humanitarian Award. On the opposite side of the charitable spectrum, in 1988 Joan Kroc, widow of company founder Ray Kroc and majority stockholder in **McDonald's**, gave $1 million to AmFar and $25,000 each to the San Diego AIDS Assistance Fund and the San Diego AIDS Project. Those gifts followed a 1987 gift of $10 million to finance an AIDS hospice, also in San Diego. McDonald's Corporation did not respond to our survey requests.

McDonald's major competitor in the U.S., Miami-based **Burger King**, is a unit of the British company Grand Metropolitan. Burger King fully completed our survey, pointing out that it is a franchise system with more than 7,200 restaurants in 50 countries. Corporate employment policies cover only the 14% of those restaurants that are owned and managed by the company. Burger King told us that sexual orientation is included in their harassment policy, but failed to mention whether or not it is included in their anti-discrimination policy. It is included in company diversity training. The company has not extended any benefits to include domestic partners and did not list a lesbian and gay employees group. Despite the focus of Burger King's philanthropic activities on education, it has contributed to AIDS groups via its contributions to the Dade County United Way and through the company's sponsorship of the 1994 International AIDS Walk Miami.

Burger King told us that it has placed advertising in programs that have positive portrayals of lesbians and gays, listing ads placed recently during the broadcast of the film *And the Band Played On*. However, this revelation is largely overshadowed by an incident that probably inspired it. In the fall of 1990, Burger King came under fire from several right-wing Christian groups because of its sponsorship of a number of television programs, including an adaptation of Dominick Dunne's *People Like Us*. A boycott of Burger King was proposed by Christian Leaders for Responsible Television and Donald Wildmon's American Family Association, which objected to the TV movie's portrayal of "homosexual lovers as caring, sensitive, rational men" and even complained because "a major part of the plot included a movie star committed to raising funds for AIDS research." In a desperate attempt to avoid the boycott, Burger King took the unprecedented step of placing ads titled "An Open Letter to the American People" in newspapers across the nation, which read:

> Burger King wishes to go on record as supporting traditional American values on television, especially the importance of the family.
>
> We believe the American people desire television programs that reflect the values they are trying to instill in their children.
>
> We pledge to support such programs with our advertising dollars.

Given Burger King's groveling response to the Christian right's attack on its advertising practices, we have to wonder how the company might respond if it received complaints because it employs lesbians and gays.

In January 1991 the management of **Cracker Barrel Old Country Stores**, of Lebanon, Tennessee, a restaurant chain with locations primarily in the Southeast, revised its employment policies to exclude lesbians and gay men from its workforce. A memo sent to all of its managers stated, "It is inconsistent with our concept and values, and is perceived to be inconsistent with those of our customer base, to continue to employ individuals in our operating units whose sexual preferences fail to demonstrate normal heterosexual values which have been the foundation of families in our society." The managers complied with the new directive, and within a short time 11 Cracker Barrel employees were fired for being lesbian or gay. According to a report in the May/June 1992 issue of *Mother Jones*, the general manager for a Cracker Barrel restaurant just outside of Atlanta filed a separation notice with the Georgia Department of Labor after firing a lesbian cook who had previously been awarded one of the company's "personal achievement awards." The separation notice read: "This employee is being terminated due to violation of company policy. The employee is gay." As amazing and frightening as that sounds, it is perfectly legal in most of America.

Cracker Barrel's policy and the subsequent firings drew a firestorm of criticism and protests from lesbian and gay activists and the mainstream press. In February 1991 Cracker Barrel rescinded its policy, calling it a "well-intentioned over-reaction," but made no move to reinstate or compensate the fired workers. In March the New York City comptroller and the Chairperson of the New York City Employees Retirement System (NYCERS), a major Cracker Barrel stockholder, wrote to Cracker Barrel CEO Dan Evins, taking exception to Cracker Barrel's characterization of the rescinded policy as "well-intentioned," demanding that the company clearly state its employment policies in relation to sexual orientation, and asking what was to be done for the fired workers. Cracker Barrel did not address any of these concerns. Over the summer, protests continued at Cracker Barrel restaurants throughout the South, with protesters arrested at several of the demonstrations; it was also alleged that more Cracker Barrel employees were quietly fired for being lesbian or gay. A boycott of Cracker Barrel was called. In November, a NYCERS representative raised the subject of the rescinded policy and firings at Cracker Barrel's annual stockholders' meeting. When no satisfactory response was given, NYCERS announced its intention of putting a resolution on the company's proxy statement for its 1992 stockholders' meeting that would have the company adopt an anti-discrimination policy with regard to sexual orientation. Cracker Barrel management refused to include the resolution on the 1992 proxy and forced NYCERS and its co-sponsors to file suit to secure its inclusion on the proxy form for the 1993 meeting. A U.S. District Court judge eventually ruled that the resolution had to be included, but it was voted down at the stock-holders' meeting.

Over the course of the controversy, major network and syndicated television shows, including *Larry King Live, The Oprah Winfrey Show,* and *20/20,* have all run stories on Cracker Barrel. Barbara Walters, host of *20/20,* concluded their segment by saying that, based on the information in their report, she would not eat in a Cracker Barrel restaurant. And neither would we. Of the companies we looked at, Cracker Barrel Old Country Stores is the most blatantly homophobic major company in the United States. While homophobia exists to some degree at virtually every company, only at Cracker Barrel has it been elevated to the status of official policy. Even though the policy was quickly rescinded, it is evident that there has been no change in the company attitude that spawned the policy. Cracker Barrel refuses to implement an anti-discrimination policy for sexual orientation. CEO Dan Evins has stated in a *Los Angeles Times* interview that each restaurant is free to decide whether or not it will employ lesbians and gays. The company has made no effort to reinstate or compensate the fired workers, and it has actively thwarted the efforts of major stockholders to shape company policy. Cracker Barrel is obviously not a safe place for lesbian and gay workers to seek employment. Nor is it a suitable company for investors who are concerned with lesbian and gay civil rights or who expect that a company will be responsive to its shareholders. Nor should it be a company that any of us patronizes.

FOOD, TOBACCO, BEVERAGES, AND FAST FOOD

Company	Survey Response	Policy	Date Added	Soft Benefits	Hard Benefits	AIDS Education	Diversity Training	G/L Group	Authors' Choice
Ben & Jerry's	♦♦	♦		♦	♦		none		♥
Burger King	♦♦						♦		
Cargill	♦					♦	NI		
Carillon Importers	♦					♦			
Coors	♦♦	♦	1/78	UC	UC		♦	♦♦	
Del Monte	♦	♦*				♦			
Kellogg	declined	♦							
McCormick & Co.	♦♦♦	UC					NI		
Nestlé Beverage Co.	♦♦♦	♦	1/91	♦		♦	♦	♦♦	
PepsiCo	♦								
RJR Nabisco	♦♦♦	♦	7/88	♦		♦	♦	♦♦	
Seagram	♦♦♦	♦	1/88	♦		♦	♦		
J.M. Smucker	♦♦						none		

* Del Monte does not include sexual orientation in its anti-discrimination policy, but does include the term in its equal opportunity policy.

Companies that declined to participate in our surveys: Anheuser-Busch, Brown-Forman, Coca-Cola, ConAgra, CPC International, Dean Foods, Dibrell Brothers, Dr. Pepper/Seven-Up, Dole, Domino's, Gerber, H.J. Heinz, Hershey, Hormel, Hudson, International Multifoods, Kellogg, Mars, Metromedia, Quaker

Companies that did not respond at all: American Brands, ARA Group, Archer Daniels Midland, Borden, Campbell Soup, Chiquita, Cracker Barrel, Dial, Fleming, General Mills, Land O'Lakes, McDonald's, Ocean Spray, Pet, Philip Morris, Ralston Purina, Sara Lee, Super Valu, Sysco, TW Holdings, Tyson Foods, Universal, UST, Wendy's, Wrigley

Key

Survey response	Sexual orientation included in anti-discrimination policy	Date sexual orientation added to anti-discrimination policy	Soft benefits (bereavement or family/personal/sick leave) extended to domestic partners	Hard benefits (health insurance) extended to domestic partners	AIDS education	Diversity training	Lesbian and gay employees group	Authors' choice
blank=None. ◆=Provided some information, but didn't complete survey. ◆◆=Completed one survey. ◆◆◆=Completed both surveys.	blank=No, it is not, or unknown. ◆=Yes, it is. UC=Under consideration.		blank=None known. ◆=Has bereavement or family/personal/sick leave for partners. UC=Company is actively considering extending bereavement leave or family/personal/sick leave to domestic partners.	blank=No. ◆=Yes, it is. UC=Company is considering extending health insurance to domestic partners.	blank=None known. ◆=Yes, company conducts AIDS education.	blank=Unknown if company has any diversity training. none=Company has none. NI=Company has diversity training, but sexual orientation is not covered. ◆=Sexual orientation is included in company's diversity training. UC=Company is actively considering including sexual orientation in its existing or proposed diversity training.	blank=None known at company. ◆=Company has a gay and lesbian employees group. ◆◆=Company has a gay and lesbian employees group that it officially recognizes.	♥=The authors feel the company has distinguished itself on lesbian/gay and AIDS issues within its industry.

12

HOUSEHOLD AND PERSONAL PRODUCTS

ADMITTEDLY THIS CHAPTER was set up as a catchall for makers of products ranging from detergents to computer disks to cosmetics to photographic supplies to furniture to toys. From several of those industries we received a very limited response to our surveys. **Herman Miller**, of Zeeland, Michigan, the only furniture company to respond, has a modestly good record. They have included sexual orientation in their anti-discrimination policy since 1990 and also include it in their diversity training. They do not yet have a gay and lesbian employees group but wrote that, if one did organize, it "would be fine." Herman Miller does conduct AIDS education for its employees. Toy maker **Fisher-Price** responded to our survey with a brief letter indicating that sexual orientation is not included in their anti-discrimination policy; in 1993 Fisher-Price was bought by Mattel, which, like the other toy companies, did not respond to our surveys. White Plains, New York–based **Tambrands**, maker of tampons and home pregnancy tests, declined to complete our full survey, but did tell us that sexual orientation is included in its anti-discrimination policy and is included in diversity training, which it is implementing this year.

We had no positive response at all from the independent cosmetics companies and would have no information if a significant portion of that industry were not controlled by one of the world's major household and personal goods companies. Cincinnati-based giant **Procter & Gamble** quickly became the largest cosmetics company in America (with 34% of the market) when its purchase of Max Factor in 1991 followed close on the heels of its 1989 acquisition of Noxell. P&G, the company behind products as recognized and varied as Bounce and Dramamine, Clearasil and Fixodent, and Hawaiian Punch and Crisco, added sexual orientation to its anti-discrimination clause on September 15, 1992, and includes sexual orientation in its diversity training. While the company does recognize employee organizations, it does not have a gay and lesbian employees group. The company indicated that its benefit plans provide coverage only to "couples whose marriages are recognized by law."

From its New York headquarters, **Colgate-Palmolive** goes toe-to-toe with industry leader P&G on supermarket shelves around the world, with brands such as Ajax, Fab, Mennen Speed Stick, and Softsoap. At the time of our original survey in July 1993, sexual orientation was not included in the company anti-discrimination policy, but since that time Colgate has included an anti-discrimination statement in its Code of Conduct, its employment application, and in its revised sexual harassment policy. Like its competitors who responded to our surveys, Colgate does not yet have a gay and lesbian employees group. Nonetheless, the company appears to be taking its gay and lesbian employees more seriously than other companies in this category, and Colgate management is developing some momentum on its own. Diversity training including sexual orientation has been implemented in 1994, and the company has established a Domestic Partner Task Force that is currently reviewing company policies. The Task Force is not only investigating extending benefits to include employees' domestic partners; it is also reviewing Colgate's general communications "to insure that they are conducive to an open, inclusive environment."

The sense of gathering momentum at Colgate stands in contrast to **Alberto-Culver** of Melrose Park, Illinois, which, in addition to its Alberto VO5 line of hair-care products, makes FDS Feminine Deodorant Spray, Static Guard, and Mrs. Dash seasonings. Like Colgate, Alberto-Culver was also considering adding sexual orientation to its anti-discrimination policy at the time of our original survey, and the provision was added when new employee handbooks were printed in November 1993. However, that appears to be the extent of Alberto-Culver's commitment to its gay and lesbian employees at this time; the company clearly indicated that it conducts no diversity training and is not currently contemplating any changes in its benefit policies.

Interestingly, none of the mega-advertisers discussed above completed our follow-up survey, which contained a section on the companies' advertising and marketing programs. Household product manufacturers place a significant portion of American advertising, but despite their deep historical ties to racy daytime television programming—these companies put the "soap" in "soap opera"—they are notoriously skittish about connecting their precious brand names to any other programming or media that might prove controversial. We are unaware of marketing initiatives by any of these companies toward gay men and lesbians, although an article in *Crain's Chicago Business* in September 1993 reported that industry leader Procter & Gamble has sought information from Overlooked Opinions, a marketing and research firm specializing in the gay and lesbian market. We are more familiar with stories of major advertisers pulling their ads from episodes of television shows with gay and lesbian themes. In 1992 the Gay and Lesbian Alliance Against Defamation called for a boycott of **Gillette** because it had yanked its ads from gay-themed episodes of *Golden Girls, L.A. Law,* and *Law & Order.* Gillette did not respond to our surveys.

Moving from the huge, diversified household products companies to those with more specific focuses, **H. B. Fuller Company**, which makes adhesives in Saint Paul, declined to answer our survey but did write to tell us that "sexual preference" is included in their anti-discrimination policy. **Corning Incorporated**, the glassmaker from the upstate New York town of the same name, today is also a leader in fiber optics and laboratory services. Corning did not complete our surveys but sent a letter accompanied by an armful of materials about their diversity initiatives. The company has been viewed by many as a model for corporate diversity programs; we received copies of their "Valuing Diversity" brochure, their Corporate Diversity Initiative outline, and reprints of two 1991 *Business Week* articles—including one cover story—focusing on Corning's diversity work. The company has made a concerted effort on these issues and began doing so in 1986, before diversity became a corporate buzzword. Unfortunately Corning's work has been deep but narrow. Nowhere in any of their materials was there a single mention of sexual diversity. In fact, the company admittedly has limited the scope of its diversity work and equal employment initiatives thus far to women and African-Americans. Sexual orientation is neither listed in Corning's anti-discrimination policy nor addressed in its diversity training. While we applaud the seriousness of their efforts as a whole, we are dismayed by their inability over eight years of work to grasp the full meaning of diversity. Company materials indicate that after the success of Corning's efforts for its female and African-American employees, "Asians and Hispanics will be targeted next." How many years will gays and lesbians have to wait?

They aren't waiting at **3M** (Minnesota Mining and Manufacturing Company), the Saint Paul manufacturing giant that's best known for Scotch™ brand tapes and Post-it® brand repositionable notes (yup, that's what they're called), but which also produces a vast array of products for industrial use, life sciences, and information and imaging technologies. Sexual orientation is included in the company's diversity training and was added to the anti-discrimination policy on January 1, 1992. The policy change came one year after 3M's gay and lesbian employee association (then known as EAGLE, but now called 3M Plus—People Like Us) approached the company's Human Relations Department about the issue. 3M recognizes 3M Plus and has provided the group with facilities and internal publicity. Since the addition of sexual orientation to the company anti-discrimination policy, no claims have been filed under the provision.

When company policy was amended to include sexual orientation in 1992, 3M management indicated that the self-insured company was not considering extending employee benefits to include domestic partners. That continues to be the case. 3M's performance on AIDS issues has been good but could be improved. By all accounts, the company has been very supportive of employees with HIV/AIDS; all benefits are available and every provision is made to allow affected employees to continue working. The company indicated that it does not conduct ongoing, formal AIDS education, but does have speakers and educational information available on World AIDS Day every year. Nevertheless the company newsletter, *3M Today*, has featured several articles on the subject. Addressing both the scientific and the personal aspects of the disease, articles have featured an interview with the director of 3M's Medical Department, dispelling rumors about how the virus is transmitted, and an interview with an HIV-positive employee, describing his experience working at 3M since his diagnosis. The materials have been thorough and thoughtful. Still, if 3M made formal, regular educational programs available to employees, it would be an improvement. The company has made sizeable donations to the Saint Paul chapter of the American Red

Cross for public AIDS prevention and education programs. These, however, are the only AIDS- or gay-related donations the company has made. It has made no attempts to market toward the gay and lesbian community.

The brightest spot for gay and lesbian concerns in our sprawling household goods category is at photographic companies. By purchasing Sterling Drug in 1988, Rochester, New York's **Eastman Kodak Company**—the world's leading producer of photographic equipment and supplies—acquired general household products like Bayer Aspirin, Mop & Glo, and Lysol, and helped us justify its placement in this chapter. Kodak has included sexual orientation in its anti-discrimination policy since June 1986 and also includes sexual orientation in its diversity training. In the fall of 1992 a gay and lesbian employees group, Lambda Network at Kodak, was formed. Kodak has provided facilities and internal publicity to the recognized group. Chuck Collins, a member of the network, says Kodak management has been supportive of the group since its inception. During a time of intense pressure from outside the company to disband the group, management and the company's other employee networks stood firmly behind Lambda.

In response to our survey, Kodak indicated that child-care and relocation benefits are available to employees' domestic partners. More importantly, bereavement leave and family/personal/sick leave have been extended to both opposite-sex and same-sex partners. Kodak has fought the extension of more significant benefits to domestic partners in the past. In 1990 John Wilkinson, a 16-year Kodak employee in Seattle, retained a lawyer in an attempt to gain health benefits for his partner of 20 years, David Davenport. His fight was chronicled in the *Advocate*, but no lawsuit was ever filed. Lambda's Collins says Kodak's human relations and benefits organizations are currently working hard with Lambda to further extend benefits to gay and lesbian employees, but Kodak objected to our characterization of the company as "actively considering" changes at this time. Because Kodak declined to complete our follow-up survey, we have no information on the company's marketing and advertising or charitable activities. Kodak does have a Corporate AIDS Task Force, which is working to develop a comprehensive AIDS educational program for all of its employees.

Polaroid, more specialized than Kodak, is the world's leading maker of instant cameras and film. The Cambridge-based company fully completed our surveys. Polaroid added sexual orientation to its anti-discrimination policy in January 1990; no claims have been lodged under the provision since then. Sexual orientation is also included in company diversity training. In 1992 the Gay, Lesbian, and Bisexual Polaroid Employee Association was formed, and in 1993 members participated as a group in the Boston Gay Pride Parade. The company provides the active group with facilities and company media coverage. Polaroid has been especially open to its gay and lesbian employees. Not only does the company library have a section devoted to gays and lesbians in the workplace; included in the Polaroid New Hire Orientation Package is a welcome letter to new gay, lesbian, or bisexual employees. Partner-related family and bereavement leave are available under Polaroid's Personal Time Off Policy. Further benefits have not yet been extended, but Polaroid's gay/lesbian/bisexual employees association has submitted a formal proposal to the company Benefits Committee requesting full coverage for same-sex and opposite-sex domestic partners and their children. Polaroid is actively considering the proposal. In May 1994, Polaroid's vice president for human resources announced to the Greater Boston Business Council (Boston's gay chamber of commerce) that he would be devoting his energy to securing spousal equivalent benefits at the company, leaving Polaroid's gay/lesbian/bisexual association members feeling confident that the company would extend benefits within the year. The company has not marketed toward gays and lesbians, but did point out that it has advertised on controversial television programs (including ones with AIDS or gay themes), despite threats of boycotts by conservative groups. When asked if it had advertised in gay and lesbian media, Polaroid promisingly answered "not yet." Polaroid later confirmed that it is currently researching the gay and lesbian market.

Beyond its exemplary efforts to accommodate and welcome its gay and lesbian employees, Polaroid has shone most brightly among American corporations in its AIDS work. In 1987 a company task force commissioned by the vice president for human resources recommended that Polaroid adopt an AIDS action program that was startlingly comprehensive by any standards. It included a company position statement, awareness training for all employees, the establishment of an in-house AIDS Information Office, participation in community groups surrounding AIDS, stepped-up AIDS philanthropy, promotion of employee community service in AIDS

HOUSEHOLD AND PERSONAL PRODUCTS

Company	Survey Response	Policy	Date Added	Soft Benefits	Hard Benefits	AIDS Education	Diversity Training	G/L Group	Authors' Choice
Alberto-Culver	◆◆	◆	11/93				none		
Colgate-Palmolive	◆◆	◆	1/94	UC	UC		◆		
Corning	◆						NI		
Eastman Kodak	◆	◆	6/1/86	◆			◆	◆◆	✔
H.B. Fuller	◆	◆							
Herman Miller	◆◆	◆	1/90				◆		
Polaroid	◆◆◆	◆	1/90	◆	UC	◆	◆	◆◆	✔
Procter & Gamble	◆◆	◆	9/15/92			◆	◆		
Tambrands	◆	◆					◆		
3M	◆◆◆	◆	1/92				◆	◆◆	

Companies that declined to participate in our surveys: Duracell, Estée Lauder, Gillette, Hasbro, International Flavors & Fragrances
Companies that did not respond at all: Avon, Clorox, Helene Curtis, Mary Kay, Mattel, Revlon, Rubbermaid, Tyco, Unilever

Key

Survey response	Sexual orientation included in anti-discrimination policy	Date sexual orientation added to anti-discrimination policy	Soft benefits (bereavement or family/personal/sick leave) extended to domestic partners	Hard benefits (health insurance) extended to domestic partners	AIDS education	Diversity training	Lesbian and gay employees group	Authors' choice
blank=None. ◆ = Provided some information, but didn't complete survey. ◆◆ = Completed one survey. ◆◆◆ = Completed both surveys.	blank=No, it is not, or unknown. ◆ = Yes, it is. UC=Under consideration.		blank=None known. ◆ = Has bereavement or family/personal/sick leave for partners. UC=Company is actively considering extending bereavement leave or family/personal/sick leave to domestic partners.	blank=No. ◆ = Yes, it is. UC=Company is considering extending health insurance to domestic partners.	blank=None known. ◆ = Yes, company conducts AIDS education.	blank=Unknown if company has any diversity training. none=Company has none. NI=Company has diversity training, but sexual orientation is not covered. ◆ = Sexual orientation is included in company's diversity training. UC=Company is actively considering including sexual orientation in its existing or proposed diversity training.	blank=None known at company. ◆ = Company has a gay and lesbian employees group. ◆◆ = Company has a gay and lesbian employees group that it officially recognizes.	♥ = The authors feel the company has distinguished itself on lesbian/gay and AIDS issues within its industry.

organizations, support groups for employees who are caregivers for people with HIV/AIDS, establishment of a circulating AIDS-related book and video collection in the Polaroid Library, regular employee communications about HIV/AIDS, and the availability of voluntary, confidential HIV antibody testing through the company Medical Department. Polaroid acted on all of the commission's recommendations. Today the company has an AIDS Awareness Office with a full-time manager; it oversees all of the programs proposed in 1987. AIDS information appears in the company newsletter frequently, and Polaroid's CEO has delivered speeches about AIDS education and AIDS in the workplace on numerous occasions. Furthermore Polaroid's educational efforts have continuously reached beyond employees to their families, and particularly to teenagers. Only two or three large American companies have AIDS education efforts that can compare with Polaroid's.

13

INSURANCE

WHEN ASSESSING THE PERFORMANCE of insurance companies on issues of interest to lesbians and gay men, there are two distinct areas that need to be addressed. One is how well they, like the rest of corporate America, have performed in assuring equal rights for lesbians and gays in the workplace. The other, particular to them and to the drug industry, is how they have reacted to the AIDS crisis that has so decimated our community.

As far as equal employment treatment is concerned, the insurance industry as a whole seems to do quite well in providing anti-discrimination guarantees. No company, however, has yet instituted domestic partnership benefits. Almost all of the insurance companies that we surveyed, whether they responded to the full questionnaire or not, have employment policies that prohibit discrimination on the basis of sexual orientation or preference. The major insurance companies that wrote to us that do not yet specifically include sexual orientation in their anti-discrimination policies are **General American Life Insurance Company, Jackson National Life Insurance Company**, and **Northwestern National Life Insurance Company**. We don't want to be too harsh on these companies, however. Unlike many other companies, they did respond to our requests, and we like to think that this will start them thinking about adopting this most basic of protections soon.

In fact, many of the insurance companies have only recently included sexual orientation in their anti-discrimination policies, most of them since 1990. **Allstate Insurance Company** added sexual orientation to its policy in 1992 and told us no claims have been filed under the provision since then. Sexual orientation will also be included in Allstate's diversity training, which is going to be launched in late 1994. The company does not have a lesbian and gay employees group and has not extended any benefits to domestic partners. Nor has Allstate conducted a regular AIDS education program for its employees, telling us it conducts training locally "on an as-needed basis." It places no job or insurance restrictions on employees with HIV/AIDS and has contributed money and volunteers from its senior management to national corporate AIDS efforts, such as the National Leadership Coalition on AIDS. Allstate has not marketed directly toward lesbians and gays.

Continental Insurance added sexual orientation to its anti-discrimination policy in July 1992 and has adopted what seems to be an innovative training module as part of its diversity training program. The company's Human Resources Department describes the training video as follows: "One of the eight vignettes depicted in this series deals with both gay and lesbian issues, centering around the performance review of an openly gay man who may have been viewed differently after disclosing his sexual orientation. The review is being defended by the gay employee's supervisor (who wrote it) to his manager, who we find out later is a lesbian who does not believe she should disclose this information for fear of the impact on her career. The classroom activities require the audience to articulate all sides of the situation and offer solutions. We are not aware of another video-based training vehicle like it and are proud of its inclusion in our diversity series."

Along with other insurance companies, Continental has a good record in funding AIDS causes; it has contributed to the New York's GMHC AIDS Walk, made in-kind donations to the Village Nursing Home, and sponsored a performance by the People with AIDS Theater Workshop.

New York Life is one of the few companies we have encountered in any industry that spells out explicitly what kinds of behavior it will not tolerate when it comes to sexual orientation: "It is New York Life's policy that an individual's sexual preference or orientation will not be considered when making any personnel decisions. One's sexual preference or orientation is strictly personal, and such information will not be used in any way by the Company or its employees. Harassment of an individual because of his or her actual or perceived sexual preference or orientation will not be tolerated. Such harassment can be described as unwanted verbal or physical abuse, including threats, destruction of property, graffiti, gossip, and any other such conduct or behavior." We think the policy is a model of its kind and that something similar should be adopted and enforced by other companies.

Likewise, **Penn Mutual** has an exemplary policy with regard to HIV-positive employees, people with AIDS, and people who are perceived as having AIDS or being at risk for it. It includes the following provisions: "If employees who share the same work environment with an employee with AIDS express concerns over their personal safety and health, supervisors or managers must explain that, based on guidelines issues by the United States Public Health Service and expert medical opinions, casual contact with a co-worker with AIDS poses no threat of transmission.... Refusal to work with a person with AIDS, or suspected of having AIDS, is not a valid excuse for refusal to fulfill assigned job responsibilities and may leave employees open to disciplinary action."

UNUM Life Insurance Company of America has instituted such "soft" domestic partnership benefits as letting the same-sex partner use the fitness facility and the Employee Assistance Program, but has not yet extended bereavement leave or family/personal/sick leave for domestic partners; it is looking at including health benefits as well, partly at the urging of the company's fledgling LGB Employee Group. In 1993 the company began offering an innovative policy to insure medical workers against the risks of becoming infected with HIV on the job.

The extension of soft benefits such as bereavement leave and family/personal/sick leave are also actively being considered by **Mutual of New York** (MONY). Sexual orientation is included in MONY's anti-discrimination policy but has not been specifically addressed in the company's diversity training. MONY does not have a lesbian and gay employees group. It does conduct AIDS education and places no insurance or job restrictions on employees with AIDS. In the past eight years the company has donated more than half a million dollars to AIDS service groups. While MONY has not marketed directly to lesbians and gay men, it has contributed to lesbian and gay groups, including New York's Lesbian and Gay Community Services Center and Senior Action in a Gay Environment (SAGE).

Soft benefits, including bereavement and family/personal/sick leave, have already been extended to employees with domestic partners at **Lincoln National Corporation**, in Fort Wayne, Indiana. Sexual orientation is included in both the company's diversity training and its anti-discrimination policy, which was amended in 1991. No claims have been filed under the provision since then. Although the company does not have a lesbian and gay employee group, it distinguished itself from virtually every other American company by reporting that it has placed employment ads in the *Advocate*. Lincoln National conducts AIDS education for its employees and places no job or insurance restrictions on employees with HIV/AIDS. It has a long history of contributing to AIDS organizations, such as the AIDS Research Center of Wisconsin, the San Francisco AIDS Foundation, and the People with AIDS Coalition. Since 1987 the company has contributed more than $218,000 to the Fort Wayne AIDS Task Force, including funding the group's entire operational budget in 1989. Lincoln National has also extended its giving to at least one specifically lesbian and gay group, Fort Wayne's New World Church.

We hate to spoil such a rosy picture, but when it comes to actually assuming insurance risks for AIDS, the news we have to report about the industry is much less cheery. In fact, we have the suspicion that the insurance companies are making a concerted effort to be more forthright in their support for gay equality and in AIDS charitable giving (areas that cost them relatively little) as a way of countering the large doses of negative publicity they have received about providing (oops! we mean *not* providing) insurance for people with AIDS.

There is a big financial reason why this has been the case. From 1986 to 1993 U.S. insurance companies paid out $4.9 billion to cover health and life insurance claims caused by HIV. They estimate that total claims will reach $10 billion to $14 billion by the year 2000. Of course, the industry has consistently overestimated this cost: Back in 1987 insurers were estimating that AIDS would cost them $50 billion by the end of the century.

Among insurance companies, **Aetna Life and Casualty Company** seems to be the best on gay and lesbian issues. Aetna has anti-discrimination protection based on sexual orientation, and it has a very active employees' group. In its guidelines on Women's Health

Care, it advocates physician education that includes dealing with lesbian health issues, probably a unique position in corporate America. The company is a *big* giver to AIDS causes. The list of organizations it has helped goes on for pages, totaling $1.4 million for 1990–1993.

Like all other insurers, Aetna screens individual life insurance applicants for HIV in states where it's legal to do so. In a controversial article in *The Advocate*, dated July 14, 1992, former Aetna employee Alyssa Peterson alleged that while she worked there from 1988 to 1991 "memos were written that under no circumstances were we to see people with AIDS as deserving all claims. They were seen only as liabilities." In a reply, which the magazine did not publish, the company furiously denied the charge: "There is no written or unwritten policy at Aetna aimed at denying AIDS and HIV-related claims."

The reply to *The Advocate* was written by Steve Moskey, Aetna's public affairs officer responsible for AIDS policy and program, who is openly gay. Moskey says, "I've been involved in shaping this company's policy on AIDS for nine years. If such a policy existed, I would have known about it." Moskey also points out that Aetna worked with several gay and AIDS organizations in the mid-1980s to write insurance industry guidelines for HIV.

Aetna will not issue group health insurance policies that exclude or put special caps on coverage for AIDS or HIV. It supports restrictions on "experience-rating" for small employers, i.e., being hit with huge charges because one employee has a major illness. Aetna has, however, stopped writing individual health insurance policies.

Aetna's role in the AIDS insurance crisis was highlighted by a fortuitous event. In 1992 when tennis star Arthur Ashe announced he had AIDS, there was much publicity about the fact that he served on Aetna's board of directors. Mark Scherzer, a New York attorney who specializes in health insurance claims, said at the time, "Obviously, Aetna is distancing itself from the bad people on the block. . . . I assume that Mr. Ashe had no problem with [Aetna's] pre-existing condition exclusion. I assume that he has not sought reimbursement for drugs not yet fully approved by the Food and Drug Administration."

Tom Stoddard, noted gay rights activist and former head of Lambda Legal Defense and Education Fund and the Campaign for Military Service, was quoted in the *Los Angeles Times* as saying, "Aetna may be the best of a bad lot, but it's a really bad lot."

As we said, Aetna is not alone in screening life insurance applicants. According to an investigative report in the *Miami Herald*, "It's routine for life insurers to blood-test applicants for individual policies over $100,000." **Prudential** surveys applicants in companies with less than 200 employees about their HIV status if they sign up after the initial enrollment period has passed. **Travelers** requires workers at companies with less than 50 employees to fill out a questionnaire that asks about their HIV status.

After the state of California enacted insurance regulations that outlawed screening blood for the HIV virus, in 1988 **New York Life Insurance** announced that it would test for the level of T-4 helper cells in the blood of applicants for life insurance policies over $100,000, even though this does not actually indicate the presence of the AIDS virus. Insurance companies throughout the nation have lobbied heavily to keep other states from enacting legislation similar to that of California's (the District of Columbia has similar provisions; New York's were overturned in court). **John Hancock Mutual Life Insurance Co.** and other insurers took the State of Massachusetts to court to prevent it from excluding HIV testing.

Benjamin Schatz, then of National Gay Rights Advocates, summed up the whole controversy succinctly in a 1988 article in the *Wall Street Journal:* "The AIDS crisis points out the fundamental flaw in our insurance system. Those who most need access to health insurance are least able to get it."

The most egregious examples of the efforts of insurance companies to avoid insuring HIV-positive individuals have been charges that certain areas (West Hollywood, Greenwich Village) and occupations (florists, hairdressers) have been "pinklined"—redlined on the assumption that they have high concentrations of gay men. One health maintenance organization was accused of pinklining the whole city of San Francisco. At various times, **HealthAmerica Corp., Guardian Life Insurance Corp.**, and **Great Republic Insurance Co.** have all been accused of pinklining. In 1990 Great Republic settled a California case out of court in which it was alleged to have enforced a 1986 policy of denying coverage to unmarried men in "occupations that do not require physical exertion . . . such as floral design, interior decorating, or jewelry and fashion design." Also in 1990, Great Republic dropped coverage for 10,000 Californians whom it was insuring through small-group health insurance policies. A month later those with no history of HIV benefits were reinstated.

We tend to agree with Evan Wolfson of Lambda Legal Defense and Education Fund. He described the behavior of the insurance industry by saying, "They take your money until you need them."

INSURANCE

Company	Survey Response	Policy	Date Added	Soft Benefits	Hard Benefits	AIDS Education	Diversity Training	G/L Group	Authors' Choice
Aetna	◆	◆	late 1990s	◆	UC	◆	◆	◆	♥
Allstate	◆◆	◆	1992				◆		
Chubb	◆◆	◆	10/93	◆		◆	◆		♥
CIGNA	◆◆	◆	1/90				◆		
Continental	◆◆	◆	7/92			◆	◆		
Equitable	◆	◆							
GEICO	◆	◆							
General American Life	◆								
Jackson National Life	*						NI		
Lincoln National	◆◆	◆	1991	◆		◆	◆		♥
Mass Mutual	◆	◆	9/5/91			◆	◆		
MONY	◆◆	◆		UC		◆	NI		
New York Life	◆	◆							
Northwestern Nat'l Life	◆◆						NI		
Penn Mutual	◆◆	◆	1/89				◆		
Prudential	◆◆	◆	10/17/91	◆			◆	◆◆	♥
UNUM	◆	◆	8/30/90	UC	UC		NI	◆◆	

* Jackson National declined to participate in our survey; information was supplied by employees and must be considered unofficial.
Companies that declined to participate in our surveys: Jackson National, John Hancock
Companies that did not respond at all: Hartford Life, IDS Life, Metropolitan Life, Nationwide Life, New England Mutual, Northwestern Mutual, Principal Mutual, State Farm, Travelers, USAA, Variable Annuity Life

Key

Survey response	Sexual orientation included in anti-discrimination policy	Date sexual orientation added to anti-discrimination policy	Soft benefits (bereavement or family/personal/sick leave) extended to domestic partners	Hard benefits (health insurance) extended to domestic partners	AIDS education	Diversity training	Lesbian and gay employees group	Authors' choice
blank = None. ♦ = Provided some information, but didn't complete survey. ♦♦ = Completed one survey. ♦♦♦ = Completed both surveys.	blank = No, it is not, or unknown. ♦ = Yes, it is. UC = Under consideration.		blank = None known. ♦ = Has bereavement or family/personal/sick leave for partners. UC = Company is actively considering extending bereavement leave or family/personal/sick leave to domestic partners.	blank = No. ♦ = Yes, it is. UC = Company is considering extending health insurance to domestic partners.	blank = None known. ♦ = Yes, company conducts AIDS education.	blank = Unknown if company has any diversity training. none = Company has none. NI = Company has diversity training, but sexual orientation is not covered. ♦ = Sexual orientation is included in company's diversity training. UC = Company is actively considering including sexual orientation in its existing or proposed diversity training.	blank = None known at company. ♦ = Company has a gay and lesbian employees group. ♦♦ = Company has a gay and lesbian employees group that it officially recognizes.	♥ = The authors feel the company has distinguished itself on lesbian/gay and AIDS issues within its industry.

14
OIL AND GAS COMPANIES

As ONE WOULD SUSPECT, companies in the petroleum industry have not been at the forefront of corporate America on gay and lesbian issues. In fact, as we will see, they have sometimes been the most problematical on questions of anti-gay and anti-AIDS discrimination. One company, Chevron, stands head and shoulders above its competitors in its positive response to its gay and lesbian employees and deserves recognition for that.

The country's fourth-largest integrated oil company, **Texaco** did not respond to our surveys. We do know, however, that the company, which normally sponsors programming on PBS, withdrew funding for the 1992 broadcast of a BBC-produced adaptation of David Leavitt's gay-themed novel *The Lost Language of Cranes*.

For an example of discrimination within the workplace, we can look at **Enserch Corporation**, a Dallas-based diversified energy company. In 1985 Enserch put the headwaiter of their corporate dining room on involuntary leave when they discovered he had AIDS. Terry Uhlrey, the headwaiter, says Enserch required him to take an HIV test after two hospitalizations had roused suspicion. After Uhlrey's test disclosed his condition, the company insisted that their 22 other food-service workers be tested. Furthermore, they announced an ongoing policy of requiring all of their food-service workers to be tested for HIV antibodies, even though the Centers for Disease Control had determined and announced that the AIDS virus could not be spread through handling food or casual contact.

Enserch did not respond to our original surveys, but did provide some information when asked to review our profile of the company. The company pointed out that Uhlrey's HIV test was not an isolated incident; at the time, the company had adopted a policy requiring all food-service handlers to be tested for communicable diseases because the State of Texas had no such regulations. Testing was reportedly also done for diseases such as urinary infections, kidney disease, tuberculosis, hepatitis, worms, and parasites. Enserch also emphasized that it had sent Uhlrey home on full pay and then paid for 100% of his medical benefits when the company policy was for employees to make 25% co-payments. The company says its thinking on AIDS has evolved since that first incident and that it has conducted AIDS education for its employees. Enserch sums up its policy on the disease this way: "In essence, today we treat an employee with AIDS the same way as we would treat an employee with a kidney disease." Enserch provided no information on its other employment policies or benefits.

Elsewhere in Texas in 1985, several of the largest companies in Houston worked to defeat a city law that would have banned discrimination based on sexual orientation. Among these companies was **Coastal Corporation**, another diversified energy company that focuses primarily on natural gas. During the drive to stop the gay rights ordinance, Coastal's irascible founder and chairman, 67-year-old Oscar Wyatt, sent a memo to all his employees, expressing concern about the ordinance's effect "on the future public image and economic climate of our community." Coastal declined to complete our surveys.

In one way, Wyatt was correct: Outlawing discrimination based on sexual orientation can have devastating economic effects, as **Shell Oil Company** discovered. In 1991 a California superior court judge ruled that a former employee who was fired because he was gay was entitled to $5.3 million in damages from Shell, including $2 million in punitive damages. Dr. Jeffery Collins had been fired from his job at a Shell subsidiary in 1985 after a sheet of safe-sex party rules, which he had inadvertently left in an office printer, was discovered. Although it was two months after the discovery of the safe-sex memo that Collins was fired and although Shell tried to cover up the reason for the dismissal, the judge found that Shell had fired Collins, a 19-year employee making more than $115,000 a year, "solely because he was a sexually active homosexual." California labor law prohibits the dismissal of an employee solely because of sexual orientation. Shell did not respond to our surveys.

Mobil Corporation did not complete our surveys but did respond with a letter. Their manager of equal employment opportunity compliance writes, "While you will note that sexual orientation, as well as other potential forms of discrimination, are not specifically mentioned, Mobil's broad policy of non-discrimination in employment has long been practiced and communicated both internally and externally." However, their policy *does* specifically mention all of the usual potential areas of discrimination, including race, color, religion, national origin, sex, age, handicap, disability, and status as a disabled veteran or Vietnam-era veteran. Apparently the policy is broad except when it's narrow. It should be noted, however, that in 1988, upon receiving a complaint from gay rights advocates, Mobil publicly apologized for the harassment of a gay man by the manager of a Mobil station in Lafayette, California. Reportedly a station attendant refused to sell gas to Todd Mangini and ordered him to leave, threatening to kick his "faggot ass." Mobil also promised to keep the complaint on file and to consider it when their relationship with the station owner came up for renewal.

Phillips Petroleum Company of Bartlesville, Oklahoma also declined to complete our survey but responded with an informational letter. The company admitted that it has not been active on "issues of sexuality." It conducts diversity training but did not say whether or not sexual orientation is included in the program. Similarly, Phillips told us it has an AIDS policy that encourages employees with HIV/AIDS to continue working as long as they are able, but did not mention an AIDS education program. Although its charitable giving traditionally focuses on education, the environment, domestic violence, and United Way organizations in the communities where it has facilities, Phillips has made some contributions to AIDS groups. It did donate the gray-and-black walkway material that is used around the country in displays of The Names Project's AIDS memorial quilt.

Panhandle Eastern, a natural-gas pipeline company based in Houston, and **Diamond Shamrock**, a San Antonio petroleum refiner and marketer, are not leaders on gay and lesbian issues, but the companies did answer our surveys. Panhandle Eastern informed us that they did not include, nor were they currently considering including, sexual orientation in their anti-discrimination policy, and they do not recognize any employee groups. Diamond Shamrock's response to our surveys was more extensive than Panhandle's, but similarly it does not display any measurable progress on issues of concern to gay men and lesbians. Their anti-discrimination policy does not include sexual orientation, and they offer no benefits for domestic partners. No AIDS education programs are in place for employees, but the company does provide diversity training; sexual orientation, however, is not specifically addressed. Diamond Shamrock did not disclose its charitable contributions, but volunteered that its matching-gift program is open only to contributions to the United Way.

The only company that could be called an industry leader on our issues is **Chevron**, the third-largest U.S. petroleum company and the only fully integrated oil company to complete our survey. Although not officially recognized (Chevron recognizes only groups that are "recreational in nature"), Chevron does maintain communications links with members of its vocal gay and lesbian employees association—the only one we could find at an oil company. Pressure from the Chevron Lesbian and Gay Employee Association (formed in October 1991) helped convince the company to add sexual orientation to its anti-discrimination policy in May 1993.

Jeff Stelmach, who was co-chair of the association at the time the anti-discrimination clause was amended, says that one of the ways they were able to achieve this was by being visible—showing the company just how many gay and lesbian employees it had had a noticeable effect on management. The employee group has had mixed results with its other efforts. Sexual orientation is specifically included in the company's diversity training. Stelmach complained, however, that, although they have been very vocal in their desire to do so, the gay and lesbian group itself has never been invited to be part of the diversity training program. Chevron has not extended any hard benefits to employees' domestic partners, but the company does offer bereavement leave. The gay and lesbian employees group has not made the push for more major benefits a focus of their activities as yet. However, one significant change that they were able to institute was to have the Chevron employees' federal credit union (which is a separate entity, not controlled by Chevron) extend membership to unmarried household members of employees. This helped the credit union by expanding its depositor base and helped gay and lesbian employees by giving them the chance to take out joint automobile loans and mortgages with their partners.

Stelmach feels that the atmosphere in his office (he works in the financial area) has been fairly tolerant of his openness about his sexuality and his activism in helping to get the gay and lesbian group

OIL AND GAS

Company	Survey Response	Policy	Date Added	Soft Benefits	Hard Benefits	AIDS Education	Diversity Training	G/L Group	Authors' Choice
Chevron	◆◆◆	◆	5/93	◆		◆		◆	◆
Diamond Shamrock	◆◆◆						NI		
Enserch	◆					◆			
Mobil	◆								
Panhandle Eastern	◆◆								
Phillips	◆								

Companies that declined to participate in our surveys: Amerada Hess, Coastal, Enron, Exxon
Companies that did not respond at all: Amoco, Ashland, Atlantic Richfield, Kerr-McGee, Occidental, Quaker State, Shell, Sun Company, Tenneco, Texaco, Total Petroleum

Key

Survey response	Sexual orientation included in anti-discrimination policy	Date sexual orientation added to anti-discrimination policy	Soft benefits (bereavement or family/personal/sick leave) extended to domestic partners	Hard benefits (health insurance) extended to domestic partners	AIDS education	Diversity training	Lesbian and gay employees group	Authors' choice
blank=None. ♦ =Provided some information, but didn't complete survey. ♦♦ = Completed one survey. ♦♦♦ = Completed both surveys.	blank=No, it is not, or unknown. ♦ =Yes, it is. UC=Under consideration.		blank=None known. ♦ =Has bereavement or family/personal/sick leave for partners. UC=Company is actively considering extending bereavement leave or family/personal/sick leave to domestic partners.	blank=No. ♦ =Yes, it is. UC=Company is considering extending health insurance to domestic partners.	blank=None known. ♦ =Yes, company conducts AIDS education.	blank=Unknown if company has any diversity training. none=Company has none. NI=Company has diversity training, but sexual orientation is not covered. ♦ =Sexual orientation is included in company's diversity training. UC=Company is actively considering including sexual orientation in its existing or proposed diversity training.	blank=None known at company. ♦ = Company has a gay and lesbian employees group. ♦♦ =Company has a gay and lesbian employees group that it officially recognizes.	♥ =The authors feel the company has distinguished itself on lesbian/gay and AIDS issues within its industry.

up and running. When his former partner died of AIDS in 1987, his co-workers were kind and supportive. It is a tradition in his work group for all the employees to get together for a shower for co-workers when they marry or have a baby. When Stelmach formalized his relationship with his new partner in October 1993 at a ceremony at San Francisco's First Unitarian Church, he was surprised and pleased that his office threw a shower for him. His only disappointment in the occasion was that while most of the women in the office attended, all of his male co-workers found an excuse to be absent that afternoon.

Chevron has been particularly active in AIDS issues. A long list of donations to AIDS groups includes the San Francisco AIDS Foundation, AmFar, the Shanti Project, and a $125,000 grant to Project Open Hand that enabled it to establish a permanent headquarters with kitchen facilities when it was about to lose the church kitchen facilities it had been using. In addition to funding researchers and service providers, Chevron has been unusual in its dedication to AIDS education. By the end of 1985 the company had produced a 20-minute videotape about AIDS for its employees, as well as a four-page brochure. Outside the company, Chevron funded two special programs on KPIX, the San Francisco CBS affiliate, which became part of a one-hour educational special called "AIDS Lifeline." The company has also contributed $25,000 for the production of an AIDS education video for use in the San Francisco school district.

We have seen throughout this book that factors such as being headquartered in a city that is gay-friendly and having a vocal gay and lesbian employee group play major roles in spurring a company's progress on AIDS and gay and lesbian issues. Chevron, the only oil company located in San Francisco and the only one with a gay and lesbian employee group, has certainly benefited from those circumstances. Nevertheless, it is the company's own attitudes and awareness that have contributed most significantly to its advances over its competitors. In a homophobic industry, Chevron deserves to be congratulated for its efforts.

15
PHARMACEUTICALS AND MEDICAL SUPPLIES

THE PHARMACEUTICAL INDUSTRY has been a particular target of AIDS activists, who have often accused drug companies of profiteering over the bodies of people suffering from HIV.

The most visible of all these companies has been **Burroughs Wellcome** because it holds the patent for the drug AZT, which was the first, and is by far the most used, drug approved by the Food and Drug Administration (FDA) for the treatment of HIV infection. Burroughs Wellcome is the U.S. subsidiary of Wellcome PC of Great Britain, which is organized as a charitable trust.

When AZT was first approved for use in 1987, Burroughs Wellcome cited high development costs in pricing the drug at about $10,000 a year for an average patient. In fact, the drug was developed by a U.S. government scientist for another purpose, and Burroughs Wellcome's costs were actually incurred in obtaining regulatory approval and marketing. In response to continued demands by AIDS activists, politicians, and others that the price be dropped to a more reasonable level, the company stonewalled. In 1989 members of ACT UP/New York (including one of the authors) traveled to the company's headquarters in Research Triangle Park between Raleigh and Durham, North Carolina. Three members of the group, led by activist Peter Staley, chained themselves inside one of the company's offices. They were quickly removed by local police who smashed down one of the office's walls to get to them.

In spite of the resulting negative publicity, Burroughs Wellcome refused to lower AZT's price. The same group of activists then invaded the New York Stock Exchange in March 1990, sounded fog-horns, and raised a banner reading "Sell Wellcome" before they were set upon by members of the exchange and security guards. Later that day, ACT UP/New York held a massive demonstration outside of the Stock Exchange. The demonstration took place on a Friday; the following Monday Burroughs Wellcome announced that it was lowering the price of the drug by 20%.

Following these confrontations, the two sides reached a *modus vivendi.* On June 31, 1992, Staley announced that Burroughs Well-come had agreed to donate $1 million to ACT UP and to AmFAR to carry out community research programs on AIDS.

It was around this time—specifically, on March 18, 1992—that Burroughs Wellcome adopted its policy barring discrimination based on sexual orientation. Not unexpectedly, the company pro-vides a high level of AIDS awareness and training to its employees. For example, in the fall of 1992 the company sponsored 22 sessions on AIDS awareness at its North Carolina headquarters that were attended by a total of 2,558 employees. Burroughs Wellcome con-ducts blood tests on all new hires as part of the medical history it works up for them; however, the company says that it does not screen for HIV or drug use.

In November 1990 Burroughs Wellcome began a series of AIDS awareness ads, which have appeared in several gay publications; it also has sponsored educational forums on AIDS that it has publicized in the gay press. The campaign was accepted by most publications that were approached and obviously did much good by referring people to an independent hot line for AIDS information. However, many people pointed out that if the informational campaign achieved its desired aim of getting high-risk people to test for HIV and begin early treatment, the end result would be increased sales of AZT.

In addition to its blockbuster grant to ACT UP and AmFAR, the company has been a notable giver to other AIDS organizations: "Burroughs Wellcome Co. has provided over 400 grants to organiza-tions providing services to people with HIV and AIDS since 1990. The mission of the Burroughs Wellcome Co. HIV Community Grants Program is to fund treatment-related education and services that are part of a comprehensive community-based approach to managing HIV disease. Funding is focused on the 20 highest incidence cities/ regions in the United States and on national programs. In addition, funding has been provided to AIDS organizations in North Carolina." The Community Grants Program totaled almost $6 million from 1990 to the end of 1993.

When lesbian and gay groups announced a boycott of Colorado following the enactment of Amendment 2, which denied fair treatment to homosexuals, Burroughs Wellcome canceled a sales meeting in that state "at significant expense." It should also be noted, however, that Burroughs Wellcome has contributed to the right-wing Heritage Foundation, which has been a notable supporter of "family values."

Bristol-Myers Squibb, America's second-largest drug company (after nonrespondent Johnson & Johnson), is the manufacturer of ddI, a member of the nucleoside analogue family that includes AZT. When initial test results showed that ddI might be effective against HIV, Bristol-Myers Squibb met with representatives of AIDS activist groups, at their request. They worked out an unprecedented arrangement, called expanded access, under which Bristol-Myers agreed to distribute the drug free to people with AIDS who were failing on AZT or could not reach the ddI clinical trials, pending final approval by the Food and Drug Administration, at which time it could put the drug on sale. As the result of this agreement, 25,000 people received a drug that may have prolonged their life during a time when it was otherwise unavailable. Since the drug has been approved for sale, Bristol-Myers has continued to supply it at no charge to those who cannot afford to pay for it.

Following the model it had established for ddI, in October 1992 Bristol-Myers released a new drug, d4T, in a "parallel track" program that allowed HIV-positive individuals to receive the medication free of charge while clinical trials were taking place. By the time the drug was approved by the FDA in September 1994, 13,000 people had participated in the program.

The Clairol subsidiary of Bristol-Myers helped in the promotion of the "Red Hot + Country" album that was marketed to promote AIDS research organizations and donated $200,000 to the Red Hot Organization, which has produced several benefit records for AIDS research. Clairol also has a program called "Color Can Make a Difference," sponsored by its Professional Division, which markets to beauty salons, that has donated more than $500,000 to AmFAR.

We were contacted by a lower-level management employee of Bristol-Myers in northern California who had been passed over for a promotion in 1991 after he seemed assured of the new position. Not knowing the reason, months later he was told by a friend that it was because management found out he was gay. In the conclusion to his letter, he writes, "BMS is homophobic at the top levels where it counts. Only at the bottom end of management is there any understanding and/or tolerance [for] those who dare to be different."

This is one man's story, and we have no way of knowing whether it is true or not. If so, it is definitely against company policy. Although Bristol-Myers did not complete our questionnaire, they did send a copy of their anti-discrimination policy, which does include sexual orientation, and a letter from the president and CEO, Charles A. Heimbold, Jr., in which he calls on "managers at every level to strive to create a working environment which accommodates diversity and is free from all forms of discriminatory harassment."

Another large pharmaceutical company that has been a frequent target of AIDS activists is **Hoffman-La Roche** of Nutley, New Jersey. Hoffman-La Roche did not respond to our questionnaires, but it has had a long history of interaction with the AIDS community. The company had developed a nucleoside analog, similar to AZT, called ddC, which had shown some promise as a treatment for AIDS symptoms, especially when used in combination with AZT. Unlike what Bristol-Myers Squibb had done with ddI, Hoffman-La Roche was unwilling to release the new drug on any kind of "expanded access" or "parallel track" basis, which would have allowed doctors and patients to obtain the drug before it received full FDA approval. (Part of the problem was that under such a program the company would have had to provide ddC free of charge since it could not legally be sold.)

In response to this reticence, ACT UP/New York interrupted a Hoffman-La Roche management meeting in August 1991, distributing leaflets demanding access to the drug. This began a long and involved series of dialogue and charges and countercharges between the company and AIDS activists. Finally, nine months later, Hoffman-La Roche set up an expanded access program for ddC. Activists were quickly disillusioned when they realized that the program had very restrictive criteria and required such a mass of paperwork that few doctors were willing to do the work necessary to enroll their patients. Faced with stonewalling on the part of the company, AIDS activists called for a boycott of Hoffman-La Roche.

The boycott was quite successful. The activists had done their homework and were able to distribute a list of drugs to doctors that told them about substitutes for Hoffman-La Roche pharmaceuticals. The company was furious, and Carl Owens, the activist who got the boycott going, said he was the recipient of many angry phone calls from corporate representatives. Eventually the company gave in and adopted what Owens calls "more humane entrance criteria" in September of 1992. At the same time, Hoffman-La Roche set up a Community Advisory Board to try to avoid such problems in the future. Owens says that it quickly became apparent, to him, at least, that the company intended to use the Board as a means of co-opting the activists.

At the meeting of December 12, 1992, the Community Advisory Board was the target of a fiery demonstration led by famed activist Larry Kramer, in which tables were overturned and shrimp cocktail thrown about the room. The new structure dissolved amidst recriminations on both sides. Out of frustration, ACT UP/New York led a large demonstration, which resulted in many arrests, against the New Jersey headquarters of the company in February of 1993. Since then, any possibility of dialogue has largely disappeared. Nor does the company seem to have learned from its past experience. It is currently testing a different kind of drug called a proteinase (or protease) inhibitor that it has named saquinavir, which has shown promise in initial tests. Activists say Hoffman-La Roche is dragging its feet, and the first 200-person study is not planned to start before the beginning of 1995. No access to the drug outside of the small clinical trial will be possible.

America's third-largest pharmaceutical company, New Jersey–based **Merck & Co.**, returned our survey, indicating that it includes sexual orientation in its anti-discrimination policy and that no claims have been filed under the provision. Sexual orientation is also included in Merck's diversity training, but the company does not have a lesbian and gay employees group. Merck is self-insured and reported that it is currently considering extending all company benefits to employees' domestic partners. The company does conduct AIDS education and places no job or insurance restrictions on employees with HIV/AIDS. Merck does not usually market its products directly to consumers and so does not have much opportunity to approach lesbian and gay customers directly, but said that it had advertised its hepatitis B vaccine in lesbian and gay publications. It frequently donates money to AIDS groups, including AmFar, the New Jersey

Community Foundation AIDS Partnership Program, and the Pediatric AIDS Foundation. In 1994 alone, $131,000 was earmarked for AIDS organizations.

More important, Merck has spent several hundreds of millions of dollars researching and attempting to develop AIDS drugs—so far without an approved and marketable product. The company's protease inhibitor, L-735,524, has been its most successful attempt to date. Initial results of trials showed a 99% decrease in patients' blood levels of HIV. Unfortunately, virus amounts returned to their original levels within six months, indicating the development of resistance to the drug. Testing continues, with a focus on higher dosages and combination therapies with other drugs. Merck's former chairman, Dr. Roy Vagelos, was well-respected in the AIDS community for his commitment to fighting the disease. The development of a useful anti-HIV agent is reported to have been both a corporate and a personal goal for him. He was instrumental in the founding of the Inter-Company Collaboration (ICC), an industry-wide effort to share information about AIDS drug development. Under Vagelos, Merck appeared to have its AIDS priorities—heavily funded research and shared information—in order.

One company that has been the particular focus of the anger of AIDS activists is **Abbott Laboratories**, headquartered outside of Chicago. In 1991, ACT UP chapters across the country threatened to lead a boycott of the company's HIV diagnostic tests if it did not release its drug clarithromycin on a compassionate-use basis. Clarithromycin is used against MAI, another opportunistic infection to which HIV-positive people are susceptible. The drug was manufactured by Abbott at a plant in Ireland and was sold there and in several other Western European companies. However, in 1991 the drug had completed only "Phase I" trials in the United States and could not be sold in this country. The activists were furious that Abbott would not follow the precedent set by Bristol-Myers and provide the drug without charge to AIDS patients who needed it and who were often reduced to importing it illegally through buyers clubs. James Driscoll of ACT UP was quoted as saying, "It's infuriating to us to see Bristol-Myers on the one hand spending millions for expanded access to its anti-viral drug, ddI, and Abbott on the other hand making money from AIDS diagnostics but unwilling to invest in expanded access."

In March 1991 members of ACT UP/Golden Gate in San Francisco occupied Abbott's San Francisco offices. On April 1, Abbott announced that it would make clarithromycin "available under a compassionate-treatment protocol." Continuing to dog Abbott, on July 7, 1992, the Golden Gate ACT UPpers took a leaf out of ACT UP/ New York's book and invaded the Pacific Stock Exchange in San Francisco, chanting "Save babies! Sell Abbott!" This time the reason for the protest was that Abbott refused to test (because of liability worries) a drug called HIV Immune Globulin that had shown promise in significantly reducing the spread of HIV from an infected woman to her unborn baby. Abbott did not respond to our survey.

Nor did the **Eli Lilly & Company** of Indianapolis. Lilly caused consternation when it announced that it was halting all research on treatments for AIDS, according to a company spokesperson quoted in the *New York Times* on January 17, 1994. He said the decision was made "in order for us to focus those resources where we feel we have a competitive advantage. . . . As you would expect, scientists who have put their heart and soul into trying to discover therapies for what they know is a very, very important medical need are disappointed that the company has to do this." The company was conducting research into one promising new AIDS drug that it said it would try to pass off to another company.

Genentech, the world's leading biotechnology company, located in South San Francisco, continues to devote a large portion of its research and development dollars (which represented an astounding 43% of sales in 1991) to treatments for AIDS. Like many Bay Area companies, it seems to be supportive of its lesbian and gay employees, offering company facilities for the meetings of Genentech Gay, Lesbian, Bisexual and Friends (GGLBF). At the time of our survey, a spokesperson from the company's Human Resources Department indicated that offering domestic partnership benefits was under active consideration. On June 1, 1994, full benefits were extended to employees' same-sex domestic partners.

Genentech requires a blood test of new hires, but this test specifically excludes HIV-testing, and "employees cannot request that it be done." The company has contributed to a number of AIDS causes, including its own company-sponsored benefit, the uniquely named AIDS Ho Ho, to raise money for local AIDS charities. It was one of the sponsors for the AmFAR benefit dance during the 1993 March on Washington, and it gives a 100% matching grant to the contributions of its employees to the San Francisco AIDS Walk.

Genentech's neighbor, **Syntex Corporation**, is a Palo Alto–based company that first came to public attention in the 1960s when it became one of the first developers and marketers of birth control pills. Since then, it has developed a large line of prescription drugs for a variety of ailments. It has been criticized by AIDS activists for trying to recoup the $40 million development costs for ganciclovir, a drug used to treat CMV retinitis that can cause blindness in people with AIDS, by charging $8,000 a year per patient. Activists have reportedly found the company to be receptive to their concerns.

Syntex provided us with its 1993 annual report and some information about ganciclovir, but declined to participate in our survey, which is unfortunate because the company appears to have a good record in the area of AIDS education and programs for infected employees. Part of the company's guidelines read, "Employees are asked to be sensitive to the needs of colleagues who have life-threatening or chronic illnesses. Co-workers are asked to recognize that continued employment for an employee who is ill is often beneficial. Through counseling and education, Syntex will attempt to alleviate concerns of employees who feel uncomfortable working with a colleague who is ill."

Moving away from San Francisco, we find a much less supportive climate. We are sorry to report that **American Home Products Corporation**, which manufactures such cushions against life's daily aches and pains as Preparation H and Advil and is headquartered in New York City, does not include sexual orientation in its anti-discrimination policy, and inclusion of the provision is "not under consideration at the present time." The company does diversity training, but its definition of diversity does not extend to sexual orientation.

American Home Products has been the source of much criticism from groups such as the Gay and Lesbian Alliance Against Defamation because it seems to be particularly susceptible to demands from "family values" groups, such as Donald Wildmon's American Family Association, that it pull its consumer-products advertising from any television show with a lesbian or gay theme. Among others, American Home Products has pulled ads from episodes of *L.A. Law, Golden Girls,* and *Dear John.* The company does not have a lesbian and gay employees group.

Baxter Healthcare Corporation, of Deerfield, Illinois, is the world's largest manufacturer of medical supplies, including intravenous systems, heart valves, and surgical instruments. It does not include

sexual orientation in its anti-discrimination policy and is not thinking about including it. We suggest that the Gay, Lesbian and Bi-
Sexual Employees of Baxter might want to make this a priority. The
company does, however, include sexual orientation in its diversity
training and has an AIDS awareness program. Baxter's offshoot,
Caremark, Inc., located in Northbrook, Illinois, a major supplier of
home nursing services to people with AIDS that became a separate
company on November 30, 1992, continues to use Baxter's benefits
programs and has many of the same policies. However, Caremark is
reevaluating its benefits package and indicates that domestic partnership benefits are under consideration.

American Cyanamid, headquartered in Wayne, New Jersey, is a
major manufacturer of vaccines and pharmaceuticals, including
Centrum brand multivitamins and FiberCon laxatives. Its major
pharmaceutical division is Lederle Labs. The company added
"sexual/affectional orientation" to its anti-discrimination policy at
the beginning of 1993. It conducts diversity training for its employees,
and includes material on lesbians and gays in its program.

PHARMACEUTICALS AND MEDICAL SUPPLIES

Company	Survey Response	Policy	Date Added	Soft Benefits	Hard Benefits	AIDS Education	Diversity Training	G/L Group	Authors' Choice
American Cyanamid	◆◆	◆	1/93				◆		
American Home Products	◆◆			◆			NI		
Baxter	◆◆◆					◆	◆	◆◆	
Burroughs Wellcome	◆◆◆	◆	3/18/92			◆	◆		
Caremark	◆◆	UC		UC	UC		◆		
Genentech	◆◆◆	◆		◆	◆	◆	◆	◆◆	➤
Hoffmann-La Roche	◆					◆	NI		
Merck	◆◆◆	◆		UC	UC	◆	◆		
Mylan Laboratories	◆								
Syntex	◆					◆			

Companies that declined to participate in our surveys: Abbott Labs, Allergan, Upjohn
Companies that did not respond at all: Bausch & Lomb, Bristol-Myers Squibb, Eli Lilly, Johnson & Johnson, Pfizer, Rhône-Poulenc Rorer, Schering-Plough, Smithkline Beecham, Warner-Lambert

Key

Survey response	Sexual orientation included in anti-discrimination policy	Date sexual orientation added to anti-discrimination policy	Soft benefits (bereavement or family/personal/sick leave) extended to domestic partners	Hard benefits (health insurance) extended to domestic partners	AIDS education	Diversity training	Lesbian and gay employees group	Authors' choice
blank = None. ♦ = Provided some information, but didn't complete survey. ♦♦ = Completed one survey. ♦♦♦ = Completed both surveys.	blank = No, it is not, or unknown. ♦ = Yes, it is. UC = Under consideration.		blank = None known. ♦ = Has bereavement or family/personal/sick leave for partners. UC = Company is actively considering extending bereavement leave or family/personal/sick leave to domestic partners.	blank = No. ♦ = Yes, it is. UC = Company is considering extending health insurance to domestic partners.	blank = None known. ♦ = Yes, company conducts AIDS education.	blank = Unknown if company has any diversity training. none = Company has none. NI = Company has diversity training, but sexual orientation is not covered. ♦ = Sexual orientation is included in company's diversity training. UC = Company is actively considering including sexual orientation in its existing or proposed diversity training.	blank = None known at company. ♦ = Company has a gay and lesbian employees group. ♦♦ = Company has a gay and lesbian employees group that it officially recognizes.	♥ = The authors feel the company has distinguished itself on lesbian/gay and AIDS issues within its industry.

16
PUBLISHING

Because most of the major book publishing houses have been swallowed up by larger, diversified entertainment companies, this chapter deals almost exclusively with newspaper and magazine publishers. As the owner of several television stations, **McGraw-Hill** could almost be considered a diversified entertainment company itself. The New York publisher did not complete our written surveys but did consent to a very brief phone survey. Sexual orientation is included in the company's anti-discrimination statement and reportedly has been for more than ten years. The company has not extended any benefits to domestic partners.

Another New York publisher that did not complete our survey is **K III Communications**, which includes *New Woman, New York, Premiere,* and *Seventeen* among its magazines. Nevertheless, we do know that K III helped raise money for AIDS groups in 1993 by helping to sponsor *Red Hot and Country,* the Red Hot Organization's country music follow-up to its previous fund-raising cassettes and videos. We also know that it took the involvement of the Gay and Lesbian Alliance Against Defamation in 1992 to reverse *New York* magazine's long-standing refusal to accept ads from bisexuals in its personal ads section. These two reports leave us curious about the publisher's internal policies.

Wall Street Journal publisher **Dow Jones & Company**, which is heavily involved in information services, also did not complete our survey, but did send an informational letter. Sexual orientation is included in both the company's anti-discrimination policy and its diversity training. Dow Jones extends no benefits to domestic partners but pointed out that all benefits must be determined through collective bargaining. Their employees' union raised the subject of domestic partner benefits in their last contract negotiations but did not push hard for the benefits, which were not included in the final contract. The New York company's matching-gifts program is limited to colleges and universities.

The world's leading supplier of marketing and business information, **Dun & Bradstreet** is also headquartered in New York and also declined to complete our surveys. It was not nearly as forthcoming as Dow Jones, however, telling us only that it added sexual orientation to its anti-discrimination policy "approximately five years ago, before it was popular to do so." We were appalled that the survey king wouldn't complete our simple questionnaire; if everyone responded to D&B's surveys the way they responded to ours, the information merchant would be out of business.

Moving from the sublime to the ridiculous, the **Enquirer/Star Group**, the Lantana, Florida, publishers of the *National Enquirer, Soap Opera Magazine*, and *Weekly World News*, could not respond to our surveys because it has no public relations staff. In August 1990 the *Advocate* reported that the editor of the *Weekly World News* apologized for a homophobic article that appeared in the tabloid's edition of July 3. The editor said that, given the decision to make again, he would not run the article "Jet Passengers Punch Out Pansies," which reported that four gay men who were publicly displaying affection on an airline flight were beaten by offended passengers. Describing the gay men as "kissing and moaning like a bunch of sex-starved seals" and making a "disgusting display of perverted passion," the article said that "after 20 tummy-turning minutes, an infuriated mom stomped up to the limp-wristed loudmouths and told them to knock off the crap." Other passengers then allegedly "beat the sissies silly." When the article came under fire for being so violently homophobic, the editor apologized profusely, saying: "I don't want to incite violence against any group. We value our gay readers. I know we have many gay readers in San Francisco. No one on our staff is homophobic, and we wouldn't hesitate to have a gay person on staff." The letter from *Enquirer/Star*'s Human Resources Department declining to participate in our survey confirmed part of this when the vice president who responded wrote that she knew some employees were gay because they "mentioned it in social conversation." Without a survey response, however, we have no information on how far the company goes to make its gay and lesbian employees welcome.

In addition to its namesake paper, the **Washington Post Company** publishes *Newsweek* and owns the Stanley H. Kaplan Test Preparation Centers. The *Post* did not respond to our survey, but gays, lesbians, and AIDS groups have had several run-ins with the company in the past several years regarding advertising policies at the *Post.* In December 1991 the *Post* refused to sell an ad in its "announcements" section to Jay Heavner, co-chair of the Washington chapter of the Gay and Lesbian Alliance Against Defamation. The section features announcements of weddings, anniversaries, and births, and Heavner wanted to place an announcement regarding his relationship with his lover. The *Post* said its policy was to accept ads only for "legally recognized ceremonies," therefore excluding gays and lesbians, who cannot legally marry. Defending the policy, the paper's legal counsel said, "There are many events in people's lives that one could advertise in a section like that if one were inclined to, but we are using a legal standard to make that judgment for us." One year later the *Post* drew heavier criticism when it refused to run an AIDS prevention ad showing two men embracing and holding a condom. The ad was sponsored by the District of Columbia's premier AIDS service organization, the Whitman Walker Clinic, whose longtime executive director, Jim Graham, called the *Post* "hypocritical, homophobic, and out of touch with the reality of AIDS prevention" for refusing to run the potentially life-saving ad. We have no information on The Washington Post Company's employment policies, benefits, or internal AIDS education efforts, but the above incidents are less than promising.

The *Post*'s neighbor in nearby Arlington, Virginia, the **Gannett Company** is the largest newspaper group in the United States. It's national newspaper *USA Today* is second in daily circulation only to the *Wall Street Journal.* A multimedia company, Gannett also owns ten television stations, fifteen radio stations, and the largest outdoor advertising company in America. Gannett fully completed our surveys. The company added sexual orientation to its anti-discrimination clause in July 1992 and reports no claims filed under the provision since then. Sexual orientation is also included in its diversity training. Management was unaware of any gay and lesbian employees group at Gannett at the time of our survey, but one comprised of *USA Today* and Gannett corporate employees has since formed at the company's headquarters. The self-insured company has not extended any benefits to domestic partners. It places no job or insurance restrictions on employees with HIV/AIDS and does conduct AIDS education.

The company's charitable giving is geared toward the many communities across the nation that its newspapers and radio and television stations serve. As a result, it has consistently given to a multitude of AIDS groups around the country, including the AIDS Project of the Ozarks, the Bronx's ASPIRA, Florida's Lee County AIDS Task Force, and the Metropolitan Washington Community AIDS Partnership. While the company listed no unilateral gifts to gay and lesbian groups, its matching-gifts policy allows employees to designate any 501(c)3 nonprofit as a recipient, and several such gay and lesbian groups have received funds accordingly. Gannett has not regularly advertised in gay and lesbian publications or sponsored community events, but at the 1993 National Lesbian and Gay Journalists' Association Conference, it both placed ads in the conference journal and co-sponsored one of the events. Perhaps Gannett's most significant contribution to the gay and lesbian community comes through its papers themselves. In 1992 Deb Price of Gannett's *Detroit News* launched a weekly gay issues column that was the first of its kind by a gay person in the mainstream media. The Gannett News Service offers the column to its subscribers and, through an agreement with the Los Angeles Times Syndicate, the column appears in about 25 Gannett and non-Gannett papers around the country.

The most advanced daily newspaper we located is the **Boston Globe**, which thoroughly completed our surveys. The *Globe* added sexual orientation to its anti-discrimination policy on July 1, 1987, and reports that no claims have been filed under the provision since its implementation. The company also includes sexual orientation in its diversity training but has no employee-organized groups. In June 1993 the *Globe* announced that effective July 1 of that same year it would extend medical benefits to the same-sex domestic partners of its management employees—the first daily newspaper in the country to do so. The *Globe*'s statement also announced the extension of bereavement leave and the services of its Employee Assistance Program to include same-sex partners and noted that by extending the benefits it was joining "a growing number of companies, universities and other organizations in recognizing the existence and significance of gay and lesbian relationships." Benefits have so far been extended only to partners of the company's 200 management employees. The rest of the company's 3,500 employees are unionized, and their benefits packages must be arrived at through collective bargaining. The *Globe* cannot implement benefits unilaterally.

Within months of the extension of domestic partner (DP) benefits by the *Globe*, the paper was purchased by the **New York Times Company**. In addition to the *New York Times*, the company publishes more than 30 other newspapers as well as a number of women's and sports and leisure magazines. The company also owns several television and radio stations and several paper companies. The *Times* completed the first of our surveys, telling us that sexual orientation was added to the company's anti-discrimination policy on August 1, 1993. Sexual orientation is included in its diversity training, and the *Times* has a gay and lesbian employees group that it recognizes and provides with facilities. Since its acquisition of the *Globe*, many eyes have begun to focus on the *Times*'s employee benefits package, which does not currently extend any benefits to domestic partners. The *Globe*'s DP benefits have been maintained since the purchase, and many are wondering how long the discrepancy between the *Times*'s own benefits and those at its subsidiary will continue to exist.

The first American company to add DP benefits was a publisher: V. V. Publishing, which puts out the **Village Voice**. New York's privately owned, progressive weekly paper, the *Voice* put its politics into practice by extending full benefits to employees' same-sex and opposite-sex domestic partners way back in 1982. The company, which fully completed our survey, had added sexual orientation to its anti-discrimination policy in January 1977. The *Voice* reports that no claims have been filed under the provision since then. The company has no diversity training but does have a Lesbian and Gay Caucus, which it provides with facilities and publicity. AIDS education is conducted by the *Voice*, which places no job or insurance restrictions on employees with HIV/AIDS. The paper contributes to God's Love We Deliver and has sponsored numerous AIDS events and fund-raisers. It has been a major sponsor of the GMHC AIDS Walk since the event's inception. The *Voice* does not advertise in gay and lesbian media but has researched its appeal to the gay and lesbian market. The paper's pages feature many ads that are designed to appeal to gay men and lesbians, including some of the *Voice*'s own ads. The *Voice* frequently covers issues that are of specific interest to gays, lesbians, and people with AIDS. Many of its regular columnists and staff writers are out gay men and lesbians.

Despite its early start at the *Voice*, industry pressure to add DP benefits has not been nearly as intense in publishing as it has been in the high-tech and entertainment industries, and progress has been slower. The exception to that rule has been the sector of the publishing industry that focuses on high-tech. Computer magazine publishers have ridden along with the industry they chronicle. In January 1993 **International Data Group**, of Framingham, Massachusetts, which publishes almost 100 computer magazines, including *Computer World*, extended its benefit plans to domestic partners of both same-sex and opposite-sex couples. IDG's major rival, New York's **Ziff-Davis Publishing**, did the same in June of that year. Ziff-Davis did not respond to our survey, but in an article in *PDQ*—the newsletter of the inter-company gay and lesbian high-tech employee association known as Digital Queers—Ziff employee Jeff Pittelkau described the process that resulted in the extension of benefits. His publisher responded to a letter he wrote inquiring about DP benefits by suggesting he raise the subject at an all-company meeting. When he did just that, Pittelkau says he was "floored by our chairman's queer-positive initial response." He then launched into basic research about DP benefits, including working with Ziff's benefits department to come up with questions to ask of companies that already had partnership benefits in place. With research completed, the benefits staff devised and submitted a proposal. Within months, Ziff's chairman announced the extension of full benefits to domestic partners.

PUBLISHING

Company	Survey Response	Policy	Date Added	Soft Benefits	Hard Benefits	AIDS Education	Diversity Training	G/L Group	Authors' Choice
Dow Jones	◆	◆							
Dun & Bradstreet	◆	◆	'88ish				◆		
Gannett	◆◆◆	◆	7/92			◆	◆	◆◆	
Boston Globe	◆◆◆	◆	7/87	◆	◆	◆	◆		►
Int'l Data Group		◆		◆	◆				►
McGraw-Hill	◆	◆							
New York Times	◆◆	◆	8/93	◆	◆	◆	◆	◆◆	
Village Voice	◆◆◆	◆	1/77	◆	◆	◆	none	◆◆	►
Ziff-Davis	◆	◆		◆	◆				►

Companies that declined to participate in our surveys: Enquirer/Star Group, Hearst, Knight-Ridder, E.W. Scripps
Companies that did not respond at all: Condé Nast, K III, Reader's Digest, Times Mirror, Tribune, Washington Post, Ziff-Davis

Key

Survey response	Sexual orientation included in anti-discrimination policy	Date sexual orientation added to anti-discrimination policy	Soft benefits (bereavement or family/personal/sick leave) extended to domestic partners	Hard benefits (health insurance) extended to domestic partners	AIDS education	Diversity training	Lesbian and gay employees group	Authors' choice
blank = None. ◆ = Provided some information, but didn't complete survey. ◆◆ = Completed one survey. ◆◆◆ = Completed both surveys.	blank = No, it is not, or unknown. ◆ = Yes, it is. UC = Under consideration.		blank = None known. ◆ = Has bereavement or family/personal/sick leave for partners. UC = Company is actively considering extending bereavement leave or family/personal/sick leave to domestic partners.	blank = No. ◆ = Yes, it is. UC = Company is considering extending health insurance to domestic partners.	blank = None known. ◆ = Yes, company conducts AIDS education.	blank = Unknown if company has any diversity training. none = Company has none. NI = Company has diversity training, but sexual orientation is not covered. ◆ = Sexual orientation is included in company's diversity training. UC = Company is actively considering including sexual orientation in its existing or proposed diversity training.	blank = None known at company. ◆ = Company has a gay and lesbian employees group. ◆◆ = Company has a gay and lesbian employees group that it officially recognizes.	♥ = The authors feel the company has distinguished itself on lesbian/gay and AIDS issues within its industry.

17
RETAIL AND CLOTHING

O F ALL THE CORPORATIONS in the United States, one that immediately comes to mind when you say "gay positive" is **Levi Strauss & Co.** In February 1992 Levi Strauss became the largest company to that date to institute domestic partnership (DP) benefits, when the company extended them to all of its 23,000 employees. Levi Strauss has also been particularly progressive in its AIDS policies in the workplace and in supporting AIDS organizations nationwide.

Levi Strauss produced a first AIDS awareness video for its employees in the early 1980s. This tape was criticized as being geared too much to the mind-set of the San Francisco–based headquarters staff. A new 18-minute video, "Talk About AIDS," was produced that was more culturally sensitive to all of the company's workers, including those in the South and Southwest, where most of Levi Strauss manufacturing plants are located. In the tape, which has also been made available to other companies, workers in factories in Mississippi, Arkansas, and California talk about their worries. A recently divorced woman, for example, asks what she should do to protect herself now that she's dating again. The concerns are answered by medical experts who continually stress that AIDS cannot be transmitted by casual contact. The video was made part of a mandatory one-hour AIDS awareness seminar for all employees.

The present chairman and CEO of the company, Robert D. Haas, great-great-grandnephew of company founder and jeans inventor Levi Strauss, volunteered to help hand out AIDS information at an employee information booth back in 1983. His commitment has continued, and in November 1991 he was the first recipient of the

National Leadership Coalition on AIDS award for "pioneering work in shaping the business sector's response to AIDS."

According to the company's response to the NGLTF questionnaire, "Levi Strauss & Co. has played a leadership role in the global corporate community with regard to HIV/AIDS since the early 1980s. Our CEO and others have been involved both internally and publicly. HIV support groups and employee involvement teams have been in existence for several years. Our Health Promotions (E[mployee] A[ssistance] P[rogram]) staff provides extensive assistance to employees affected by HIV. HIV training has been delivered to employees on a worldwide basis. Levi Strauss Foundation support has been generous over the years." By the end of 1993 Levi Strauss had donated more than $5.7 million to AIDS organizations.

On February 21, 1992, Levi Strauss announced that it would make full medical and dental benefits available to the domestic partners of its employees, including heterosexual employees; the new policy went into effect on June 1, 1992. The company has long been an innovator in personnel matters; it was also one of the first large companies to institute flex time and telecommuting. As is usually the case, Levi Strauss put in DP benefits after it was "nudged" in that direction by the company's lesbian and gay employees. Spearheading the campaign was Cynthia Bologna, a corporate communications assistant and co-founder of Levi Strauss's Lesbian and Gay Employee Association. Bologna needed benefits for her partner and worked to make Levi Strauss aware of a need that she shared with others. The company's senior vice president of human resources, Donna Goya, was quoted as saying, "This is really a discrimination issue. We realize that family structures are changing and want to respect this diversity."

Levi Strauss created a stir in 1992 when it refused to cave into pressure from the right wing, as the Bank of America had done, to recommence funding of the Boy Scouts of America. Along with several other large corporations, Levi Strauss had stopped contributions to BSA in 1992 in response to that organization's policy of discrimination on the basis of religious beliefs and sexual orientation. In response to Levi Strauss's action, 53 conservative members of Congress wrote a letter to Haas, saying "You and your corporation are now partners in a vile attack against a cherished American institution." Haas and Levi Strauss did not back down in their support for equitable treatment for everyone in every "cherished American institution."

In 1992, when the California legislature passed a bill banning job discrimination based on sexual orientation and sent it to Governor Pete Wilson for signature (he had vetoed the measure the previous year), Levi Strauss was forthright and public in its support for the measure.

Levi Strauss's Lesbian and Gay Employee Association was formed in July 1990. Under the company's guidelines for employee groups, it is not allowed to deal with issues of benefits and compensation, so the group was not formally involved in the company's decision to institute domestic partnership benefits two years later. What the group has concentrated on is ensuring that the company's diversity training programs pay attention to lesbian and gay issues. Some lesbian and gay employees who attended the company's initial diversity training sessions objected to the fact that among such subjects as gender, race, and ethnicity it did not include sexual orientation. Following representations made to it by these employees, the company approached the Lesbian and Gay Employee Association, which provided seven volunteers to appear in a video discussing sexual orientation in the workplace. The video is an integral part of the company's diversity training sessions, which is a four-day program in the San Francisco area.

The Lesbian and Gay Employees Association has undertaken other projects as well. Under the direction of Michele Dryden, one of the group's facilitators, it sponsored art exhibits in June 1993 and 1994 in the company's magnificent Plaza Atrium that featured works by emerging lesbian and gay artists. In April 1994 the group's Task Force on Confronting Homophobia conducted a survey of employees to try to gauge the level of acceptance of gay employees and to see if anyone had witnessed or suffered from acts of discrimination based on sexual orientation.

Levi Strauss is the largest apparel manufacturer in the United States. At the opposite end of the spectrum in many ways is **Milliken & Company**, also a privately owned company, which is the largest textile manufacturer in the United States. It manufactures a number of products, including carpets and various synthetics. Probably its best-known product is the trademarked VISA fabric, a line of "easy care" synthetics. Milliken did not respond to our survey, so our information is secondhand, but it seems damning enough to be worth repeating anyway.

The company has been led since 1947 by the redoubtable curmudgeon Roger Milliken, the grandson of the company's founder. Milliken and his wife are notable contributors to conservative causes. By 1988 their foundation, the Romill Foundation, had contributed $500,000 to the Free Congress Foundation, which has long supported "anti-sodomy" laws. Milliken itself has purchased full-page, full-color advertisements in publications of the John Birch Society. One does not find diversity training in place at Milliken & Company's Spartanburg, South Carolina, headquarters or at any of its other plants in North Carolina and Georgia.

A clothing retailer that seems to clothe all of gay America (okay, all of America), **The Gap**, through its affiliate Banana Republic, has advertised extensively in the gay press. One typical advertisement for Banana Republic that appeared in *Out* magazine shows five racially diverse (but all young and beautiful) models lying on the lawn with their eyes closed in dreamy reverie. The boys are holding hands with the boys, and the girls are holding hands with the girls. The caption is "My chosen family." This seems to be fairly out of the closet to us, but The Gap has declined to answer *any* questions about its marketing strategy. The *New York Times*'s Stuart Elliott, in his "Advertising" column about the gay market on September 1, 1992, writes, "And others involved in the [gay] market, like Gap, Inc., refuse to discuss it." Nevertheless, the company has been nominated by GLAAD to receive an award for its portrayal of lesbians and gays in its advertising. The company declined to complete our survey but did send a letter with some valuable information. Most important, its benefits department and an employee committee are currently investigating the possible extension of company benefits to domestic partners. The Gap is slated to introduce AIDS education for its employees in June 1994 and has contributed to numerous AIDS groups, including the AIDS ward at San Francisco General Hospital, the San Francisco AIDS Foundation (which has honored the company for its leadership on AIDS), and Housing Works and Hispanic Community Services, both in New York. The Gap has also made contributions to lesbian and gay groups, including New York's Lesbian and Gay Community Services Center and the Human Rights Campaign Fund.

Other retail operations are discovering the value of marketing to the gay community. **Dayton Hudson Corporation**, for example, announced on February 16, 1994, that it would test-market a line of gay-themed greeting cards at its Marshall Fields department stores in Chicago and at Dayton's in Minneapolis.

This represents quite a turnaround for Dayton Hudson. In October 1991 Target Stores, one of Dayton Hudson's operating units, lost a case before the California State Court of Appeal when the court ruled that private employers could not discriminate against homosexuals in job applications. Target had been sued by three applicants for security jobs at a San Francisco store who objected to a question on a psychological screening test that asked for a reaction to the statement, "I am very strongly attracted by members of my own sex." Dayton Hudson and all of its divisions (which also includes Mervyn's stores) now include sexual orientation in their anti-discrimination statements and diversity training. Bereavement leave and family/personal/sick leave have been extended to include domestic partners, and Dayton-Hudson has even said that it would consider placing employment ads in the lesbian and gay press. It was one of only two major department store companies to answer our surveys.

Dayton Hudson has quite a good record in terms of corporate giving. It has donated to many AIDS groups, including $100,000 to the Minnesota AIDS Project, and has sponsored the Minnesota AIDS Pledge Walk. The company specializes in grants to arts and social action groups and has funded programs that include mentoring young lesbian and gay writers, supporting the Minneapolis annual gay/lesbian/bisexual/transgender film festival, and sponsoring gay-themed plays at Minneapolis theater companies.

Retailing giants **Walgreen's, Wal-Mart**, and **Kmart** caused much adverse editorial comment in July and August 1992 when they refused to stock Magic Johnson's book, *What You Can Do to Avoid AIDS*, in their stores because it contained street slang in describing body parts and had a diagram on how to put on a condom. A Walgreen's spokesperson said that some of the material in the book was "inappropriate," while a Wal-Mart representative said they were not carrying the book "for obvious reasons." A Kmart spokesperson was quoted in the *Chicago Tribune* as saying the book "doesn't fit the family orientation of a Kmart shopper." None of the three companies responded to our survey. Dallas's **J. C. Penney** declined to complete our survey but did send a letter that said the company "conducts its business under a policy that requires each of our associates . . . to comply with all applicable laws and regulations. This policy certainly applies to any laws that prohibit discrimination on the basis of sexual orientation." It is safe to conclude from this that Penney does not specifically include sexual orientation in its antidiscrimination policy. Nor does Atlanta-based specialty retailer **Home Depot**, but the company indicated that it is currently considering adding the provision. Home Depot did not specify whether or not sexual orientation is included in its diversity training. **Toys 'R' Us**, based in Paramus, New Jersey, did not complete our survey but did write to tell us that sexual orientation is included in its diversity training program.

We suspect from our own shopping experiences that the gay population may be disproportionately represented among retail salesclerks. Not so coincidentally, therefore, there have been a number of instances of alleged employment discrimination against America's retailers.

In December 1989, **Woodward & Lothrop** was accused by a gay employee of being laid off for five days after he filed a union grievance because the company would not give him a spouse's discount card for his lover (the company said that he was suspended for failing to use a designated employee entrance and for misuse of his time card). As a result of the controversy, gay groups threatened to boycott the Washington, D.C.–based department store chain (which also owns Philadelphia's John Wanamaker stores). Under threat of a boycott proposed by lesbian and gay activists, set to begin during the big Presidents Day sales weekend, "Woodie's" caved in and agreed to start issuing the cards to gay domestic partners; it also amended its anti-discrimination policy to include sexual orientation. John Culver, a senior vice president, was quoted in the *Advocate* as saying, "There's no question that the intensity and number of letters we got from the gay community caused us to step back and realize that this issue was more important than we had originally thought."

Other department stores have had AIDS-related disputes. **Macy's**, which did not respond to our surveys, was sued in 1991 by HIV-positive employee Mark Woodley, who said that he was fired from his job as a Christmas-season Santa Claus when the company discovered that he was taking AZT and Prozac. Seattle-based **Nordstrom** was sued in 1990 by a former salesclerk who said that he was fired in 1988 because he was HIV-positive. But details in the case are far from conclusive. In a *Wall Street Journal* interview, a Nordstrom representative maintained that the employee, Sean Mulholland, had been fired "as a direct result of not coming to work," adding that Mulholland "was physically unable to handle the demands of a full-time sales position" and that Nordstrom had repeatedly offered him work in other parts of the company. The lawsuit has since been settled to the satisfaction of both parties, and the Northwest AIDS Foundation has called the retailer exemplary in its support of employees with AIDS. No insurance or job restrictions are placed on employees with HIV/AIDS, and the company has conducted more than 300 AIDS training sessions since beginning AIDS education in 1987. Nordstrom has contributed to numerous AIDS groups across the country.

Nordstrom was the other department store company (with Dayton Hudson) to complete our survey. It added sexual orientation to its anti-discrimination policy in 1991. Unfortunately, the policy relegates sexual orientation and several other classifications to a secondary level of vigilance, refusing to go beyond existing laws: "Nordstrom is committed to providing equal employment opportunities to all applicants for employment regardless of sex, race, color, creed, national origin or religion; or to the extent provided by law, age; marital status; pregnancy; physical, mental or sensory disability; or sexual orientation." Many of the company's employees work in jurisdictions where discrimination based on sexual orientation is prohibited, but all of the company's employees deserve that protection—regardless of where they work. The self-insured retailer has no lesbian and gay employee group and has not extended any benefits to domestic partners. Nordstrom's commitment to its lesbian and gay employees has lagged behind its commitment to (and interest in) its lesbian and gay customers. Nordstrom is the only major department store we located that has advertised directly to lesbians and gay men. It placed a two-page ad in the District of Columbia's largest gay newspaper, the *Washington Blade*, welcoming the hundreds of thousands of participants in the 1993 Lesbian and Gay March on Washington. The store also carried at least one T-shirt designed specifically for the march during that period. Beyond its marketing aims, the company has also done some political good for lesbians and gay men by publicly denouncing Colorado's Amendment 2.

Focusing on a much smaller retailer, one of the most notorious examples of AIDS discrimination in recent years was the case of Jack McGann and the **H & H Music Company** of Houston. McGann was diagnosed with AIDS in December 1987. He submitted claim forms for his HIV-related treatment to H & H's insurer, General American Life Insurance Co. In March 1988 company officials met with McGann to discuss his disease. Soon thereafter, the company announced that it was going to provide health benefits through self-insurance, to be administered by General American. When the new plan went into effect on August 1, 1988, it specifically limited lifetime claims for AIDS, alone among all diseases, to $5,000. McGann quickly ran through his benefits and was unable to get insurance anywhere else. For the last three years of his life he was treated through Medicaid and the charitable contributions of Houston doctors. He died in June 1991.

McGann sued H & H, and the lawsuit was continued following his death by Frank Greenberg, the executor of his estate, working with Lambda Legal Defense and Education Fund. Lambda was joined in its brief by several other organizations, including the American Medical Association, the American Public Health Association, and the American Association of Retired Persons. The courts ruled that, under the federal Employee Retirement Income Security Act (ERISA) of 1974, the company had the right to self-insure, that is, to collect premiums and pay benefits themselves, and that if they did so they were exempt from state regulations concerning health insurance. Texas state law would have prohibited the company from cutting off McGann's insurance if H & H had used an outside insurance company. By self-insuring it was subject only to the federal law. Partially as a result of this ruling, the number of workers covered by self-insurance plans went from 5% in 1974 to 60% in 1992.

The U.S. 5th Circuit Court of Appeals ruled against the McGann estate on November 4, 1991. The case was appealed to the Supreme Court. The Court asked the Solicitor General under the Bush administration, Kenneth Starr, for his opinion. He wrote that H & H had an entirely lawful purpose: "to avoid the expense of paying for AIDS treatment." On November 9, 1992, the Supreme Court voted 7–2 (Justices Blackmun and O'Connor dissenting) not to take up the case, thereby letting the Appeals Court decision stand. Cases like this fueled the growing demand for national health insurance.

While H & H was limiting HIV-related claims on its health insurance, convenience store giant **Circle K Corporation** was trying to eliminate them altogether. In December 1987 the Phoenix-based company reacted to the doubling of its medical costs in 1987 by brazenly amending its policies so that employees "proven to suffer illness and accidents that result from the use of alcohol, drugs, self-inflicted wounds and AIDS" would be dropped from the company's self-insured health plan. In September 1988, after nine months of criticism from AIDS groups and members of Congress, Circle K announced it was suspending the new policy for review. We do not know if the policy has since been reinstated or what the company's other policies and benefits are since Circle K did not respond to our surveys. Dallas-based **Southland Corporation**, which operates 7-Eleven stores, did respond with a letter, although it declined to complete our survey. The letter did not specify any of the company's employment policies with regard to sexual orientation, suggesting to us that such a provision is not actually included in any written policies. Southland told us that none of its benefits are currently available to domestic partners, although they did promise to consult with other companies on the matter to investigate the possibility. In 1988 Southland refused to sell an issue of *Spin* magazine that contained—in addition to a message encouraging readers to practice safer sex to prevent the spread of AIDS—a free condom. Southland informed us that, at that time, condoms were stocked behind counters at their stores and that prospective purchasers had to specifically ask for them. Since then, Southland assures us, its position on condoms has been completely reversed to focus on access. Condoms are now visible and readily available to all customers.

Oakland-based supermarket giant **Safeway** also refused to sell the condom-carrying issue of *Spin*. Safeway did not answer our surveys. In fact, only one major supermarket chain did cooperate with our project. **Supermarket General Holdings**, which is located in Woodbridge, New Jersey, and operates Pathmark supermarkets and drugstores in the Northeast, answered our first survey. The company has included sexual orientation in its anti-discrimination policy since June 1984, but it does not include sexual orientation in its diversity training. Supermarket General told us that it is happy to make accommodations for employees with HIV, when requested. A major competitor for Pathmark drugstores in the Northeast is **Rite Aid**, based in Shiremanstown, Pennsylvania. Rite Aid completed our first survey, telling us that it has no diversity training and is currently considering adding sexual orientation to its anti-discrimination policy. Rite Aid also told us that it extends family/personal/sick leave to include domestic partners.

Mail-order catalogs for many types of merchandise have proliferated in the past decade, making it impossible for us to write about retailers without considering catalogs. In fact, several catalog companies have arisen in recent years that focus exclusively on the lesbian and gay market, including **Shocking Gray** ("the catalog of gay and lesbian family values"), which in its survey response estimated that 99% of its customers are gay. As for DP benefits, Shocking Gray says that "we are a small start-up company and do not have many benefits available at this time but will as growth allows." Within its means, the company gives extensively to gay and AIDS programs.

Other catalog companies are also notable givers, including the **Lillian Vernon Corporation**. The eponymous founder of the company has been named to the President's Council of the Gay Men's Health Crisis (GMHC) for her work for that organization, including serving on the organizing committee for GMHC's annual charity auction at Sotheby's. Contributions to AIDS organizations are a fairly safe bet for any corporation. However, Lillian Vernon has been one of the rare companies that has given to specifically gay and lesbian organizations as well, including both the New York and Los Angeles gay and lesbian community centers, Metropolitan Community Church, and the Campaign for Military Service. Lillian Vernon offers no diversity training for its employees. Sexual orientation is slated to be added to the company's anti-discrimination policy in January 1995.

The granddaddy of catalog companies, **L. L. Bean**, has had a somewhat troubled reputation in the gay community—not so much for what the company itself has done (which seems to be fairly positive), but for the reputation of Linda Bean Jones, granddaughter of the company's founder, part owner, and member of the board of directors. Jones is a rabid conservative who made a number of homophobic statements during her campaign for Congress in 1992 (she lost!). Jones had herself photographed in front of the well-known L. L. Bean store in Freeport, Maine, for one of her campaign commercials. In response to a complaint from the New York office of the Gay and Lesbian Alliance Against Defamation, L. L. Bean disavowed any

RETAIL AND CLOTHING

Company	Survey Response	Policy	Date Added	Soft Benefits	Hard Benefits	AIDS Education	Diversity Training	G/L Group	Authors' Choice
Dayton Hudson	◆◆◆	◆		◆		◆	◆		
The Gap	◆			UC	UC	◆			
Home Depot	◆◆◆	UC							
Lands' End	◆◆			◆			none		
Levi Strauss & Co.	◆◆	◆		◆	◆	◆	◆	◆◆	◆
Lillian Vernon	◆◆◆	◆	1/95			◆	none		
Nordstrom	◆◆◆					◆	◆		
J. C. Penney	◆								
Rite Aid	◆◆	UC		◆			none		
Shocking Gray	◆◆◆								
Southland	◆								
Supermarket General	◆◆	◆	6/84				NI		
Toys 'R' Us	◆						◆		

Companies that declined to participate in our surveys: Brown Group, Bruno's, Circuit City, Costco Wholesale, Dillard, Jack Eckerd, Fieldcrest Cannon, Fruit of the Loom, Gitano, Great Atlantic & Pacific Tea, Hartmarx, Home Shopping Network, Kroger, The Limited, Melville, QVC, Spiegel, Stop & Shop, West Point–Pepperell

Companies that did not respond at all: Albertson's, American Stores, L. L. Bean, Burlington, Carter Hawley Hale, Circle K, Federated, Food Lion, Giant Food, H & H Music, Kmart, Leslie Fay, Liz Claiborne, Lowe's, R. H. Macy, May, Milliken, Montgomery Ward, Nike, Publix, Reebok, Safeway, Sears, Service Merchandise, Springs Industries, Tandy, VF, Vons, Wal-Mart, Walgreen's, Winn-Dixie, Woolworth

Key

Survey response	Sexual orientation included in anti-discrimination policy	Date sexual orientation added to anti-discrimination policy	Soft benefits (bereavement or family/personal/ sick leave) extended to domestic partners	Hard benefits (health insurance) extended to domestic partners	AIDS education	Diversity training	Lesbian and gay employees group	Authors' choice
blank=None. ◆=Provided some information, but didn't complete survey. ◆◆= Completed one survey. ◆◆◆= Completed both surveys.	blank=No, it is not, or unknown. ◆=Yes, it is. UC=Under consideration.		blank=None known. ◆=Has bereavement or family/personal/sick leave for partners. UC=Company is actively considering extending bereavement leave or family/personal/sick leave to domestic partners.	blank=No. ◆=Yes, it is. UC=Company is considering extending health insurance to domestic partners.	blank=None known. ◆=Yes, company conducts AIDS education.	blank=Unknown if company has any diversity training. none=Company has none. NI=Company has diversity training, but sexual orientation is not covered. ◆=Sexual orientation is included in company's diversity training. UC=Company is actively considering including sexual orientation in its existing or proposed diversity training.	blank=None known at company. ◆=Company has a gay and lesbian employees group. ◆◆=Company has a gay and lesbian employees group that it officially recognizes.	♥=The authors feel the company has distinguished itself on lesbian/gay and AIDS issues within its industry.

connection with the candidacy and publicly reaffirmed its policy of anti-discrimination on the basis of sexual orientation. In this, L. L. Bean is one step ahead of its direct competitor, **Lands' End, Inc.**, which does not even include sexual orientation in its written non-discrimination policy.

18
SOFTWARE

On September 3, 1991, a new era in the struggle for gay and lesbian rights began when the **Lotus Development Corp.** of Cambridge, Massachusetts, became the first publicly traded company in the United States to offer what it called "spousal equivalent benefits." This achievement was the result of an internal lobbying campaign carried out by three lesbian employees (Margie Bleichman, Polly Laurelchild-Hertig, and AnnD Canavan). Their efforts were the outgrowth of an informal E-mail network of gay and lesbian employees begun by Canavan when she first started working at Lotus in 1984. In early 1989 she sent out an E-mail letter convening a group of employees interested in working on a proposal for domestic partnership (DP) benefits—the Lotus Extended Benefits Group. After the initial enthusiasm, the group dwindled down to the core three.

The three women argued that the company's employment policy guaranteed equal treatment regardless of sexual orientation, but that gay and lesbian employees were patently not being treated equally because their partners had no access to benefits extended as a matter of course to spouses of married employees. The company bought this line of argument with relatively little difficulty. While there was some reticence from the Human Resources Department, Jim Manzi, president and CEO, said that he was in favor of the idea. Bryan Simmons, the openly gay manager of corporate relations for Lotus, was quoted as saying, "One of our operating principles is to value diversity and encourage it. We assume that there are gay men and lesbians among the best people available. If offering benefits gives us an edge, we want that."

Although the management at Lotus was fairly quickly convinced of the equity of the proposed provision, it took much longer to convince the re-insurance company that assumed the risks for catastrophic health coverage for Lotus's self-insured health benefits plan. Without quite admitting it, the re-insurer was clearly concerned about the risks associated with the catastrophic costs of AIDS. Lotus's management hired Andrew Sherman of the Segal Company, an employees' benefits consulting firm, to help put the package together.

Together with the employees group, Sherman did research to show that the costs connected with AIDS were no greater than those for such other major illnesses as cancer and heart disease (which was, after all, the point of having a re-insurer in any case). They also found anecdotal evidence from associations (such as the American Psychological Association) and small companies (such as the Village Voice and Ben & Jerry's) that had already instituted same-sex DP benefits that showed that there was no difference in health-care costs for same- and opposite-sex partners. With this information, Lotus was able to convince the re-insurance company to accept the new policy. The re-insurerer initially added a 2% surcharge to the company's health-care policy for a period of two years. Experience showed that the surcharge was unwarranted, and it was dropped.

Lotus did not, however, go as far as the Extended Benefits Group had originally wanted. In the spirit of fair play, the group had proposed that both homosexual and heterosexual couples be included in the plan. The company instead opted to include only same-sex partners (a policy since followed by some of the other corporations offering domestic partner benefits). The reasoning was that opposite-sex partners could get married if they wanted to, an option legally denied to same-sex couples.

At Sherman's suggestion, the qualification for benefits was an affidavit signed by both same-sex partners stating that they lived together, planned to continue living together, and that they shared financial responsibility. Once the policy had been agreed upon, Russ Campanello, Lotus's vice president of human resources, announced the decision to the company's employees. He opened his memo by writing, "Since early in its history, Lotus has had a stated policy prohibiting discrimination based on sexual preference. Lotus recognizes that lesbian and gay employees do not have the choice to legalize permanent and exclusive relationships through marriage; thus, they cannot legally share financial, health and other benefits with their significant partners. For this reason, in the interest of fairness and diversity Lotus will recognize the significance of such relationships by including them in our policies and benefits. . . . This new policy is further evidence of our firm commitment to value differences and provide fair and equal access to benefits for all Lotus employees. I wholeheartedly endorse this policy and am proud to be part of a company in which such policies are possible." Campanello's memo started a potential revolution in the way gay and lesbian employees are treated in corporate America.

Laurelchild-Hertig says that the adoption of the DP benefits strengthened the company's already strong commitment to diversity and equal rights for all employees. Lotus's diversity training includes sections on gay and lesbian issues, and there is a speakers' bureau from the gay and lesbian group that is often asked to speak to other employee groups. She says that no one she knows "has ever had any negative repercussions in their careers after they came out," but she adds that that does not mean that there still aren't some of her colleagues who are in the closet.

Lotus's competitors in the software business have been in the forefront of treating gay and lesbian employees fairly. All of the major ones include clauses in their personnel policies that prohibit discrimination on the basis of sexual orientation. Many have followed Lotus's lead in offering DP benefits: Microsoft Inc. of Redmond, Washington, extended medical and dental benefits to both same- and opposite-sex unmarried partners of its employees in April 1993, while Quark Inc. of Denver, Colorado, did so on July 1, 1993. **Word-Perfect** of socially more conservative Salt Lake City, Utah, has yet to do so. **Oracle Corporation** of Redwood Shores, California, initially offered DP benefits only to the employees of its Canadian subsidiary before extending them to the much larger number who work in the United States on June 1, 1993. Oracle has slated the launch of its diversity training program for June 1994; the training will include sexual orientation issues.

Interestingly, **Microsoft**, the largest software company of them all, has been reluctant to give out any details of its DP policy, saying that it is the company's practice not to announce benefit changes, especially those that might prove to be competitively advantageous. It strongly denied rumors that the company's reticence was based on a desire not to offend certain of its clients.

Randy Massengale, Microsoft's diversity manager, says that the new policy was signed off on personally by Bill Gates, the legendary founder and CEO of the company. Gates's support illustrates one of the major themes of companies that have successfully implemented DP benefits—get the CEO's endorsement and anything's possible, but don't expect the Human Resources Department to push very hard. Microsoft's policy was adopted after the company completed studies that showed that the change would have a minimal impact on the bottom line and after it was reviewed by several focus groups that included members of GLEAM, Microsoft's gay and lesbian employees group. GLEAM members were notified of the new policy the day before it was announced to all employees in an intracompany memo.

The infamous Colorado referendum of November 3, 1992, on Amendment 2, which foreclosed any state legislation extending equal rights to gays and lesbians and invalidated local equal rights laws, caused several software executives to take public stances in favor of justice. A small company, XChange Inc. of San Francisco, canceled its planned move to Fort Collins, Colorado, when Amendment 2 was approved by Colorado voters. The company's president, William Buckingham, was quoted in *Business Week* as saying, "I view it as a backward step in a state I had thought was progressive."

Tim Gill, chairman of **Quark, Inc.**, which makes the best-selling desktop publishing package Quark Xpress, not only came out publicly against Amendment 2 and donated $40,000 of his own money to fight it, but he joined with his employees to donate even more money, computer equipment, and software to the groups who organized to fight the discriminatory ploy. As of February 1994, the company had donated $145,000 in cash and equipment to gay and lesbian causes within Colorado—$486,000 nationwide—and both figures *exclude* the company's donations to AIDS organizations.

Gill's response to the initiative should not cause too much surprise since he is probably the most outspokenly gay chief executive of a large American company. (He holds 50% of company stock and is chairman of the board; his heterosexual business partner, Fred Ebrahimi, holds the other half of the stock and is president. Gill is also vice president in charge of research and development.) Ranked by *Forbes* magazine as one of the 400 richest people in the United States, Gill started his company in 1981 with his former lover after several computer companies told him he didn't have adequate technical skills. By Christmas of that year, he was employing 13 people in his one-bedroom apartment. Officially incorporated in December

1982, Quark currently has sales of $120 million annually and employs about 450 people.

Gill estimates that about 10% of the employees of Quark are gay or lesbian, largely, he says, because the company is headquartered in Denver, about a half mile from Denver's main gay neighborhood. When he first started out, he advertised for employees in gay publications, but says that it is more efficient to advertise in the mainstream newspapers. He now makes it a pre-condition for any media interview that, if the interviewer would normally mention the marital status of an interviewee, they mention explicitly that he is gay and has a lover. Gill is a member of Quark Queers, the gay and lesbian employees group. It is largely a social group, but it did work on the campaign against Amendment 2. After the amendment passed, Quark Queers published the home addresses of all the state's elected officials and the prominent combatants on both sides of the issue, including the board members of Colorado for Family Values. Ironically, two major "family values" lobbying organizations, Colorado's Focus on the Family and the Oregon Citizens Coalition, use Quark Xpress software to publish their newsletters.

Gill's gay activism has extended to threatening his bank (NorWest) with withdrawing Quark's business if they did not adopt a sexual orientation anti-discrimination clause. He has requested all of his suppliers to do the same. Not too surprisingly, most of them have agreed (with the notable exception of Federal Express!). Quark holds an annual customers meeting in Denver every year. After Amendment 2 passed, Gill made an impassioned speech to the group, urging them to vote to hold the next meeting outside of Colorado. The vote to move elsewhere was almost unanimous and an alternate site was selected, but when the state supreme court declared Amendment 2 to be unconstitutional, the meeting was moved back to Colorado.

Gill faults himself for not being the first to institute DP benefits. He says that he had always assumed that the insurance companies would never allow it, and that he wanted to kick himself when Lotus Development beat him to the punch.

SOFTWARE

Company	Survey Response	Policy	Date Added	Soft Benefits	Hard Benefits	AIDS Education	Diversity Training	G/L Group	Authors' Choice
Borland		◆		◆	◆				◆
Lotus	*	◆		◆	◆			◆◆	◆
Microsoft	◆◆	◆	6/90	◆	◆		◆	◆◆	◆
Oracle	◆◆◆	◆	9/15/86	◆	◆		◆	◆◆	◆
Quark	◆◆◆	◆	1/83	◆	◆	◆	none	◆◆	◆

* Lotus declined to participate in our surveys. Information listed was given by members of their gay and lesbian employees group and was widely available in the press, but is unofficial.

Companies that declined to participate in our surveys: Aldus, Computer Associates, Lotus

Companies that did not respond at all: Adobe, Borland, Novell, Software Publishing, WordPerfect

Key

Survey response	Sexual orientation included in anti-discrimination policy	Date sexual orientation added to anti-discrimination policy	Soft benefits (bereavement or family/personal/sick leave) extended to domestic partners	Hard benefits (health insurance) extended to domestic partners	AIDS education	Diversity training	Lesbian and gay employees group	Authors' choice
blank=None. ◆=Provided some information, but didn't complete survey. ◆◆= Completed one survey. ◆◆◆= Completed both surveys.	blank=No, it is not, or unknown. ◆=Yes, it is. UC=Under consideration.		blank=None known. ◆=Has bereavement or family/personal/sick leave for partners. UC=Company is actively considering extending bereavement leave or family/personal/sick leave to domestic partners.	blank=No. ◆=Yes, it is. UC=Company is considering extending health insurance to domestic partners.	blank=None known. ◆=Yes, company conducts AIDS education.	blank=Unknown if company has any diversity training. none=Company has none. NI=Company has diversity training, but sexual orientation is not covered. ◆=Sexual orientation is included in company's diversity training. UC=Company is actively considering including sexual orientation in its existing or proposed diversity training.	blank=None known at company. ◆=Company has a gay and lesbian employees group. ◆◆=Company has a gay and lesbian employees group that it officially recognizes.	♥=The authors feel the company has distinguished itself on lesbian/gay and AIDS issues within its industry.

19

TELECOMMUNICATIONS

SOUTHWESTERN BELL declined to complete our survey, but it did send a letter saying, "For more than 10 years, SBC has had a policy not to question an individual's sexual orientation and that does not permit sexual orientation to become a criterion for becoming . . . or remaining an employee," suggesting that it has included sexual orientation in its anti-discrimination policy since the incorporation of the Baby Bells and the break-up of AT&T in 1984.

Our research indicates that the first of the Baby Bells to add sexual orientation to its anti-discrimination policy was **Pacific Telesis** (in the form of one of its pre-AT&T break-up constituents, Pacific Bell) in 1980. Unfortunately, this early start cannot be attributed to forward thinking on the part of the company or to the fact that it is headquartered in San Francisco. The addition was more likely the direct result of pending litigation. In December 1986, as the culmination of a lawsuit against Pacific Bell begun in 1975, Pacific Telesis agreed to set up a $3 million fund to pay damages to former employees and job applicants who claimed they were the targets of anti-gay discrimination. At the time, this was the largest settlement ever in a gay discrimination lawsuit in the United States. Pacific Telesis maintained that the settlement was not an admission of guilt, but the lawyer for the plaintiffs said that until 1976 Pacific Bell actually had a *written policy* that it would not hire open homosexuals. In a *Wall Street Journal* article announcing the settlement, a PacTel spokesperson asked about the policy said, "There was something written that was not applied."

Pacific Telesis did not complete our survey but did forward some information in response to our draft profile. Bereavement leave has been officially extended to domestic partners, and the company includes sexual orientation in its diversity training. Pacific Telesis has and recognizes its Gay and Lesbian Employee Association. We also know that PacTel conducts AIDS education and sponsors support groups for its employees. As with the reactive addition of sexual orientation to its anti-discrimination policy, this laudable work may have arisen out of an incident in the early 1980s when a Pacific Bell crew in Los Angeles refused to install phone lines in an AIDS foundation office for fear of infection. The pattern of transgression followed by reactive (rather than pro-active) protection of gay, lesbian, or HIV-affected employees is one that crops up in the telecommunications industry repeatedly, as we shall see.

NYNEX, the Baby Bell that serves New York and New England, completed both of our surveys. The company, which conducts a significant portion of its business in areas such as Massachusetts, Vermont, Connecticut, and New York City, which have laws protecting gays and lesbians from employment discrimination, has included sexual orientation in its anti-discrimination policy since October 1987—before most of those localities adopted those protections—and also includes sexual orientation in its diversity training. NYNEX is self-insured and has no job or insurance restrictions for employees with HIV/AIDS. AIDS education is aggressively conducted within the company, and has been since NYNEX had an AIDS-related controversy in the mid 1980s. In 1987 an employee who claimed he had been dismissed after his supervisor discovered he had AIDS was reinstated to his job as part of an out-of-court settlement. It was then that NYNEX leapt to the forefront of companies implementing progressive AIDS policies. Nonetheless, in 1992 a Massachusetts man formerly employed by the New England Telephone division of NYNEX filed suit against the company, contending that he was fired after revealing that he was HIV-positive. The company gives to many AIDS organizations, including the National Association of People with AIDS, the Children's Hope Foundation, and God's Love We Deliver. It also matches the pledges of its employees in the GMHC AIDS Walk, although its matching gifts policy normally restricts its giving to educational or cultural institutions and selected environmental groups. NYNEX is also one of very few companies to go beyond AIDS giving to contribute directly to the lesbian and gay community—in 1992 it gave $10,000 to the Hetrick Martin Institute, New York City's comprehensive, community-based, lesbian and gay youth services organization that operates the Harvey Milk High School for lesbian and gay teens.

Gays and Lesbians for Corporate Diversity is the name of NYNEX's employee group, which it recognizes and provides with facilities and publicity. The group is active and vocal. It is surprising, then, that NYNEX listed itself as offering no benefits that include its employees' domestic partners—not even the "soft" benefits like bereavement leave and partner-related family/personal/sick leave, which many companies have already officially extended. The company has done no marketing directed at its lesbian and gay customers, and in fact has tangled with those customers in the past. In 1987 Heritage of Pride, the group that organizes New York City's annual Gay Pride Parade and Rally, asked NYNEX to create a subheading of "Gay and Lesbian Organizations" in its yellow pages directories, because at that time all listings under "Social Services Organizations" or "Human Services Organizations" were simply lumped together alphabetically. NYNEX at first refused to create the subheading and further enraged its lesbian and gay customers by suggesting that if Heritage of Pride wanted its listing to be found by lesbians and gays it might consider listing itself under "Escort Services" or "Nightclubs." Only after the Gay and Lesbian Alliance Against Defamation organized a petition drive and enlisted the help of elected officials and the New York State Consumer Protection Board weighed in on Heritage of Pride's side did NYNEX agree to create the subheading. Today, as the Baby Bells scramble to get in on the ground floor of the dawning interactive media age, there are rumors that NYNEX has begun discussing with the company's lesbian and gay employee group the possibility of marketing toward lesbians and gays. Similarly, although it has never advertised job listings in the lesbian and gay press before, the company indicated in our survey that it may consider doing so in the future.

An exception to the pattern of reactive policymaking on lesbian and gay issues among the Baby Bells is **US West**, which serves 14 states in the Northwest, the Rockies, and the Pacific Northwest, including Colorado, Washington, Arizona, and Minnesota. US West added sexual orientation to its anti-discrimination policy in 1988 (Northwestern Bell, one of the three regional telephone companies that was combined to form US West after the AT&T break-up, had added sexual orientation to its policy in 1986). Since then, 18 claims have been filed under the policy, and US West described the actions taken in response to the claims as "policy coverage, training, [and] discipline up to and including dismissal." Sexual orientation is included in the company's diversity training, and US West has an active lesbian and gay employees group, EAGLE—Employee Association for Gays and Lesbians, which it recognizes and provides with facilities and publicity. Soft benefits—child care, relocation assistance, and adoption assistance, in addition to bereavement leave and family/personal/sick leave—are available to employees with same-sex domestic partners. In July 1991, Drew Hansen became the first gay employee to take advantage of the extended child-leave benefits when he and Chris Benngstton, a lesbian employee of the company, became parents. In its survey response, US West also indicated that the addition of health care benefits for same-sex and opposite-sex partners has been researched and is currently being reviewed by its "senior team." No decision has been made.

Self-insured, US West places no job or insurance restrictions on employees with HIV/AIDS; however, the company lags behind its peers in AIDS education, which it says it conducts "informally." It has been responsive to the needs of employees with HIV; when some employees who had AIDS or partners or family members with AIDS had trouble locating doctors willing to treat people with AIDS, US West began to compile and maintain a list of those who would do so, as well as other resources. In response to our survey, the company did not indicate that any significant unilateral donations had been made by the US West Foundation to lesbian and gay or AIDS groups. Rather, it suggested that contributions to such groups (unspecified) had been made as part of the company's matching-gifts program, which covers any IRS-recognized 501(c)3 organization. Consequently this policy has also obligated the company to match employee gifts to anti-gay groups, such as Concerned Women for America, the Family Research Council, Focus on the Family, and the Eagle Forum, which have been increasingly active in states where US West operates, such as Colorado and Washington. The company has not consistently marketed toward lesbians and gays but indicated in its survey response that it did run one local support ad in lesbian and gay media in Minnesota.

Moving on to the big long-distance service companies, the pattern of reactive policymaking that we have seen in several of the regional Baby Bells continues. Washington-based **MCI Communications** did not respond to our surveys, but we are aware of one discrimination claim and its resolution. David Gatten, a former employee of MCI, filed a complaint with the New York City Human Rights Commission, alleging that he was fired from his job in January 1988 because he is gay. Gatten said that, despite an excellent performance record, a supervisor dismissed him and told him it was because co-workers objected to working with a homosexual. New York City law prohibits employment discrimination based on sexual orientation. With the help of the Lambda Legal Defense and Education Fund, Gatten pursued his case and in December 1988 reached a settlement with MCI. As part of the settlement, although it admitted no wrongdoing in the case, MCI agreed to an undisclosed financial award to Gatten, who had taken another job and did not return to the long-distance giant. MCI also agreed to amend its company-wide anti-discrimination policy to include sexual orientation. So, as a result of a local ordinance protecting gay rights, a large national corporation agreed to amend its policy to cover all of its employees, regardless of whether local laws protect their particular work site.

Interestingly, MCI was the first long-distance carrier to market its services directly to lesbians and gays. In November 1993 many lesbian and gay households around the country received a direct-mail piece from MCI promoting its "Friends and Family" long-distance program. Given the dearth of advertisements by American companies crafted specifically to appeal to lesbians and gays, the mailer deserves close analysis. Without using the words "lesbian" or "gay," it is nevertheless a cornucopia of queer codes and images. Its envelope features a photograph of almost a dozen vibrant, multiracial, twenty- and thirtysomethings running up a beach holding hands. Eschewing gender parity—and the possibility of perfect heterosexual pairing-off—the group consists of four women and seven men. In defiance of the disparity in numbers, however, the photo almost manages to avoid same-sex touching. With boys on both ends of the line—and one boy mysteriously lurking behind it (and behind a woman)—the models are arranged boy-girl-boy-girl, except for two men next to each other in the center.

But exactly who are these projections of the target audience? Three of the women have a glamorous appearance, wearing trendy skirts or dresses with serious hair and makeup, while the fourth woman, who wears baggy jeans and a T-shirt, has a shaved head (stereotypical lesbian, anyone?). The men are all gym-bodied and well-coiffed and they, too, look as if they are dressed not for the beach but rather for nightclubbing. In jeans and shorts, they sport T-shirts and tank tops. One wears a button-down shirt with the sleeves cut off, and one is shirtless. Most wear boots—even combat boots or work boots on the men wearing shorts. The suggestive but restrained photograph is captioned with the more direct slogan "When your friends are family."

Inside, the copy continues its "nontraditional family values" tack but gets slightly more obtuse: "Long-distance lovers, friends who are important to you but live far away. Some of the closest families today don't necessarily share the same house, same area code, or even the same state," and "MCI is the best way for you, your friends, family and lover [*singular!*] to stay close . . ." But there is also another picture of our models on the beach, and now the rigidity of the pose on the envelope has collapsed. The 11 are piled on top of each other now, grinning for the camera, and the restraints on same-sex touching are dramatically relaxed. Three of the four women are lumped together—which consequently guarantees more contact between the larger number of men. And, for the men at least, there is a lot of contact. The women are lying on top of one another's backs, but most of their arms are out of view. The men are also piled on top of each other's backs, but now hands are everywhere—touching each other's arms and shoulders and chests. The homoeroticism that was mostly suggested by physique and dress on the cover of the mailer is explosively actualized inside at the top of MCI's appeal. At the end of the letter there is one last blatant queer reference. Below the post-script, MCI's satisfaction guarantee appears—in a large triangular box. Even if we didn't know that the piece had been sent out to rented "lesbian and gay" mailing lists, the mailer itself was obviously designed to appeal not just to a young, hip, urban market but to a young, hip, urban, lesbian and gay market. In a sea of mass-market-directed appeals, this mailer stands out.

Unfortunately, despite all the tense suggestion of MCI's mailer, it is a closeted piece. Why actively seek out lesbian and gay dollars without ever coming out and addressing them as lesbian and gay? All the energy that apparently went into market research, symbolism, and design to finely calibrate the mailer to appeal to—even titillate—lesbians and gay men could have been better devoted to working up the courage to approach us openly. Marketers who want to reach lesbians and gays should realize that we are sophisticated consumers who bridle at such dishonest and oblique approaches. Having lived through the tyranny of the closet, lesbian and gay consumers are definitely not in Kansas anymore.

But **Sprint Corporation** is. Sprint, of Westwood, Kansas, is the only major telecommunications company since the breakup of AT&T to operate both long-distance service and local telephone companies, which it operates in 17 states. Sprint completed the first of our surveys, indicating that it has included sexual orientation in its anti-discrimination policy since March 1990. Sexual orientation is also included in the company's diversity training. Sprint does recognize employee-organized groups, but a lesbian and gay group is not among them. We, however, were able to locate one such group within the company.

We have received troubling reports of a homophobic atmosphere in at least one Sprint facility. Former employee Julie Boyea reports that she and other lesbians and gays at Sprint's Relay Texas/Colorado division (they do voice/computer interfaces for deaf customers) in Austin, Texas, were subject to ridicule and harassment by members of a group of "Christian" co-workers and that management refused to take any action. Boyea was dismissed on charges of having sexually harassed two women colleagues in August 1993. She categorically denies that any such harassment (involving sexually suggestive touching) ever took place and says that she was the victim of a campaign to eliminate a visible lesbian presence from the plant. Her dismissal was, however, upheld at a state employment hearing.

The company's point of view is different. Jill Ferrel, a lawyer and assistant vice president for human resources for Sprint, talked to us extensively about the Boyea case, which seems to have created a number of waves within the corporation and to have become something of a *cause célèbre*. Ferrel acknowledges, with Boyea, that there were a large number of lesbians and gays in the Austin facility and says that Sprint not only tolerated but welcomed their presence and strove to make sure that it was a conducive environment. She and Boyea both seem to agree that Boyea went out of her way to see just how welcoming that environment could be. The company drew the line at allowing employees to wear sexually explicit or politically controversial T-shirts. Once that ruling had been made, Boyea worked hard to test the limits. The example they both referred to was a T-shirt with interlocking pink triangles. Although knowledge of the T-shirt seems to have reached far beyond Austin, Texas, the company's decision was that it did not violate the guidelines.

Ferrel says that rather than being the object of harassment from Christian co-workers, she felt that it was more likely that Boyea was the source of such harassment. She says that Boyea was constantly being counseled about inappropriate behavior and was the subject of numerous complaints from her colleagues, although she also seems to have had a number of friends within the facility. It was the fact that self-professed friends of Boyea made the sexual harassment charges against her that led Sprint to give them immediate credence and, following extensive interviews with the three complainants, to ultimately dismiss Boyea.

We are in no position to make a judgment as to whether the accusations in this "she said/she said" case are true. However, we think that it is highly illustrative of where the front lines of personnel policy are. Human resources managers use the mantra of "managing diversity" as though it were a be-all and end-all for conducting human relationships. The problem is that once you have a diverse workforce there is inevitably going to be friction between people based on those differences, and there are no easy answers. If Boyea is allowed to wear T-shirts proclaiming her sexuality, at what point do the rights of people who are offended by that sexuality take precedence? Is a T-shirt with two women kissing permissible? What if they are having sex? Maybe these are not common situations, but there are always going to be people like Julie Boyea who want to test the limits. In cases like this, ready-made and pat answers are not going to be adequate.

MCI in its closeted mailing rented gay mailing lists and went directly to lesbian and gay mailboxes themselves. Sprint has managed to selectively reap lesbian and gay dollars without actually even making the approach themselves. Sprint sold its service in bulk to Chicago's Overlooked Opinions, which then marketed that service to lesbians and gays as its "Community Spirit" program. The indirect arrangement allowed Sprint to cash in on the market without ever having to own up to actively doing business with the lesbian and gay community, going MCI one better (or worse).

McCaw Cellular Communications, of Kirkland, Washington, the country's largest cellular telephone company, responded to our original survey. They indicated that they have included sexual orientation in their equal opportunity policy since the policy's inception in the 1980s. McCaw also includes sexual orientation in its diversity training. Patterned after its maverick chairman and CEO, Craig

McCaw, the company stresses innovation and individual empower-ment, as is reflected in the name of the company's human resources department, People Development. It will be interesting to see if those characteristics can survive the company's impending merger of its own 8,000 employees with AT&T's 300,000. In the summer of 1993 the telecommunications supergiant announced its purchase of Mc-Caw. Final details of the merger have yet to be hammered out and regulatory approval is not certain, but if all goes according to plan, the sale should be completed by early 1995.

Even after the federally mandated divestiture from its local phone companies in the early 1980s, **AT&T** is today the largest service company of any kind in the United States and is also a leading manufacturer of computers. The long-distance supergiant did not originally respond to our survey requests but did forward ample information to us after reviewing our draft profile of the company. AT&T was one of the first U.S. companies to add sexual orientation to its anti-discrimination policy, which it did in March 1975. Sexual orientation is included in the company's diversity training, and it conducts AIDS education. AT&T developed a progressive response to the disease early in the pandemic, including hosting support groups for affected employees and pledging to treat AIDS like any other life-threatening disease long before 1990s Americans with Dis-abilities Act made that the law of the land. In 1985 the AT&T Founda-tion contributed $10,000 to a New York City AIDS information line. By the summer of 1993, the Foundation had awarded $1.7 million to 85 different organizations that provide a variety of AIDS-related services and programs throughout the country.

LEAGUE—Lesbian, Bisexual and Gay United Employees at AT&T—was formed by a group of AT&T employees returning home inspired by the 1987 March on Washington; the group's original chapter was officially recognized by the company in 1988. Recognized as a national employee group in 1992, the group currently has more than 30 chapters around the country. Every year it conducts a three-day professional development conference that is held during the business week; members are encouraged to attend as a legitimate diversity training activity on company time. LEAGUE is a model for nascent lesbian and gay resource groups at other companies. Both within the company and at major lesbian and gay events around the country, it distributes glossy brochures featuring quotations from its members and a summary of the group's mission and history. It is evident from their brochures and from speaking with members of the group that many employees are very comfortable being lesbian or gay at AT&T and in most areas feel that the company is very supportive.

Sharply characterizing AT&T's work environment for lesbians and gays in many minds, however, the strength and activity of LEAGUE are frequently viewed against one incident: AT&T's involvement in a highly publicized federal discrimination lawsuit. Sandra Rovira and Marjorie Forlini met in 1976 when Rovira was a divorced law student at New York University raising two sons. In 1977 the two women exchanged rings in a commitment ceremony and proceeded to raise Rovira's sons together. In 1980 Forlini went to work for AT&T, where she continued to work until her death from uterine cancer in 1988. At that time Rovira asked AT&T to recognize her 12-year relationship with Forlini by paying her surviving-spouse benefits. When the company refused, Rovira filed suit in federal court, alleging that, in violation of New York City and state human rights laws and of its own long-standing anti-discrimination policy, the company had discriminated against her by treating her differently from other employees' spouses. AT&T continually maintained that it is up to legislators, not companies, to decide who qualifies as a spouse. In an *Advocate* cover story in 1990, AT&T spokesman Burke Stinson summed up the company's position this way: "I can apologize for any mistreatment to Ms. Rovira, but it's simply tough to claim benefits as a spouse when you are not a legal spouse." In 1993 the federal court sided with AT&T on exactly those grounds.

While many of the companies profiled in this book have been allowed the comfort of gradually moving toward recognition of their lesbian and gay employees—first through reforming their policies and then by putting their money where their PR is through gradually extending benefits—the Rovira suit placed AT&T, an early leader on policy, in the unenviable position of being called upon in federal court to summarily match its benefits to its rhetoric and leap to full recognition. At the time of the filing of the lawsuit, many may have found Rovira's demand to be outlandish, but in light of the subsequent rollout of full same-sex domestic partner benefits at companies as large and prominent as Microsoft, Levi Strauss, Apple, MCA, Viacom, and HBO (which are all, admittedly, considerably smaller than AT&T), AT&T's reticence is being viewed in an increasingly negative light. LEAGUE's prominence and success at the company have made it hard for many to accept AT&T's resistance on the key lesbian and gay workplace issue of domestic partner benefits.

Moving from the workplace to the marketplace, AT&T has just recently displayed a level of commitment to lesbians and gays that surpasses that of its competitors by becoming the first of the big three long-distance carriers to directly approach lesbians and gays as a market. For tens of thousands of lesbians and gay men across the country who had received MCI's closeted mailer, it looked like *déjà vu* all over again in May 1994 when they pulled from their mailboxes a letter from AT&T in a lavender envelope with a rainbow-colored phone cord pictured snaking across its front. The glossy piece inside enticing them to join AT&T's True USA service looked like a slightly more professionals-oriented version of MCI's mailer: assorted, attractive twentysomethings (now in suits and dressy casual clothes, instead of beach- or club-wear) are clumped together in various groups, touching each other to suggest lesbian or gay relationships.

To the tactics of the MCI mailer, AT&T adds another dimension by putting words in the models' mouths through captions, making the suggested relationships even more obvious. A polo-clad man rests his arm on the shoulder of another man in a suit, who remarks, "When David's away on business we like to stay close. I love to know what he's doing and what's on his mind." Elsewhere a lone, short-haired woman is pictured, saying, "Saving money on long distance is important to me. I don't know who talks to my grandmother longer, me or Claire." The mailer's lesbian and gay recipients cannot know exactly who David or Claire are, but the suggestion that they are the lesbian and gay lovers of the people depicted is unmistakable. The crafty long-distance giant also uses at least one model who has appeared on the cover of a gay magazine—New York City's *Homo Xtra*, a guide to gay nightlife that every week reaches 30,000 of the kind of prospects AT&T is no doubt hoping to attract with its mailer.

AT&T polishes and perfects the language and symbolism of suggestion and innuendo that MCI used in its mailer. And, like the MCI letter, AT&T's glossy brochure manages to speak to its targeted lesbian and gay audience without ever calling them by name. But then AT&T takes the approach one step further—and out into the open. A separate letter is enclosed that begins: "At AT&T, we believe it's important for you to feel good about the company you do business with . . ." and continues, "In fact, AT&T has an environment in which gay, lesbian and bisexual people feel comfortable in the workplace—and has a longstanding nondiscrimination guideline regarding sexual orientation." With that one sentence, AT&T enables lesbians and gay men to feel comfortable about doing business with them in a way that the MCI mailer and Sprint's relationship with "Community Spirit" never could. AT&T went to a professional gay marketer, Howard Buford, and his company, Prime Access, to create the ad and used other gay professionals, including the photographer and mailing list broker, in producing it.

In what must be a first, the marketing letter was signed not only by AT&T's long-distance service manager but also by the two national co-chairs of LEAGUE, and another insert in the envelope details LEAGUE's mission and history. The company is trading on the goodwill it hopes will be generated with knowledge of its support of its lesbian and gay employee group—and the group is fully cooperating. By actively helping the company to reach lesbian and gay customers, LEAGUE has raised its level of cooperation with management to an unprecedented level among lesbian and gay employee groups. Let's hope AT&T soon matches that level of cooperation with its lesbian and gay employees by extending full domestic partner benefits.

TELECOMMUNICATIONS

Company	Survey Response	Policy	Date Added	Soft Benefits	Hard Benefits	AIDS Education	Diversity Training	G/L Group	Authors' Choice
AT&T	◆◆◆	◆	3/75			◆	◆	◆	
McCaw Cellular	◆◆	◆	1980s				◆		
MCI		◆	12/88						
NYNEX	◆◆◆	◆	10/87			◆	◆	◆◆	
Pacific Telesis	◆	◆	1980	◆		◆	◆	◆◆	
Southwestern Bell	◆	◆							
Sprint	◆◆	◆	3/90				◆	◆	
US West	◆◆◆	◆	1/88	◆	UC	◆	◆	◆◆	♥

Companies that declined to participate in our surveys: None
Companies that did not respond at all: Ameritech, Bell Atlantic, BellSouth, GTE, MCI

Key

Survey response	Sexual orientation included in anti-discrimination policy	Date sexual orientation added to anti-discrimination policy	Soft benefits (bereavement or family/personal/sick leave) extended to domestic partners	Hard benefits (health insurance) extended to domestic partners	AIDS education	Diversity training	Lesbian and gay employees group	Authors' choice
blank = None. ♦ = Provided some information, but didn't complete survey. ♦♦ = Completed one survey. ♦♦♦ = Completed both surveys.	blank = No, it is not, or unknown. ♦ = Yes, it is. UC = Under consideration.		blank = None known. ♦ = Has bereavement or family/personal/sick leave for partners. UC = Company is actively considering extending bereavement leave or family/personal/sick leave to domestic partners.	blank = No. ♦ = Yes, it is. UC = Company is considering extending health insurance to domestic partners.	blank = None known. ♦ = Yes, company conducts AIDS education.	blank = Unknown if company has any diversity training. none = Company has none. NI = Company has diversity training, but sexual orientation is not covered. ♦ = Sexual orientation is included in company's diversity training. UC = Company is actively considering including sexual orientation in its existing or proposed diversity training.	blank = None known at company. ♦ = Company has a gay and lesbian employees group. ♦♦ = Company has a gay and lesbian employees group that it officially recognizes.	♥ = The authors feel the company has distinguished itself on lesbian/gay and AIDS issues within its industry.

20
TRAVEL AND TOURISM

It is often suggested that gay men and lesbians travel more frequently than the average American. Sociologists might explain this
phenomenon by pointing out that gay men and lesbians comprise the
only minority group whose members do not find themselves automatically born into families who are members of that same minority; gay
men and lesbians have to actively seek out communities of similar
individuals.

Other people might address an observed predisposition toward
travel for gay men and lesbians with more practical explanations.
Many of those practical reasons would stem from one reason: Because they don't pair off into procreative couples, gay men and
lesbians are much less likely to have children. The effects of this
simple fact on the travel and tourism industry are numerous and
their cumulative impact staggering. Without children to raise and
their attendant costs (food, shelter, clothing, tuition), gays and lesbians have more discretionary income. Furthermore, because gay
and lesbian couples are more likely than heterosexual couples to be
childless, both members of the couple are much more likely to be
employed, thus increasing household income even before savings on
child care are considered. So discretionary income for childless gays
and lesbians is doubly boosted above the levels of their parenting,
straight counterparts, regardless of socioeconomic level. At the same
time, barriers to travel are relaxed. Without children to include in
travel plans or to make other care arrangements for, gay men and
lesbians are freer to travel and to travel more frequently.

While gays and lesbians may not out-travel the average American to
the degree that some studies have suggested (that they are seven

times as likely to travel, in some), it is reasonable to believe that all these factors do lead to a significant increase in travel by gay men and lesbians.

When gay men and lesbians do travel, they quickly and continually come up against the travel industry's unique emphasis on "family." While queer Americans can buy toothpaste or software, or fill up at the gas station, or watch their favorite television shows without declaring or even thinking about their sexual orientation, travel and tourism are unique among American industries because they repeatedly provoke gay men and lesbians to come out. Airlines' frequent flier programs offer companion tickets that are often available only to "family" members; car rental agencies have rules for registering additional drivers that either exclude unmarried partners, charge them more than "family" members, or require them to declare their status as domestic partners to escape additional charges. And when the hotel clerk asks, "Will that be a room with two twin beds or one queen-size, ladies?" the question truly hits home for all involved.

For good or bad, travel has a strong "family" subtext that gay and lesbian travelers confront at every ticket counter and front desk. When this "family" fixation is combined with higher traffic levels by gay men and lesbians, the opportunities for incidents—homophobic or homo-friendly—are dramatically increased within the travel and tourism industry. As a result, while most chapters in this book measure companies' commitment to gay men and lesbians and AIDS primarily by focusing on their interactions with employees, this chapter will also be strongly shaped by the companies' involvement with customers.

Marriott Corporation, of Bethesda, Maryland, responded to our full survey. Marriott does not include sexual orientation in its anti-discrimination policy but does include the term in its non-harassment policy. Sexual orientation is also included in its diversity training. The corporate respondent to our survey knew of no gay and lesbian employees group or instances of Marriott placing job ads in the gay and lesbian press, but hastened to add that because Marriott has operations all over the world and is highly decentralized it may be unaware of an action or program occurring at the field-operations level. Marriott said it would consider placing employment ads in gay and lesbian media. The company is self-insured and places no job or insurance restrictions on employees with HIV/AIDS. It extends no benefits to employees' domestic partners but has recently added a terminal-illness benefit to the company's term life insurance plan that enables participants diagnosed with terminal illnesses to receive "a part of their life insurance benefits at no additional cost." Marriott has had an AIDS education program for its associates in place for more than four years. To the best of its knowledge at the corporate level, Marriott has not done any marketing directed at gays and lesbians nor did it list any charitable donations to gay and lesbian or AIDS groups.

The survey response from Marriott's competitor, Beverly Hills–based **Hilton Hotels Corporation**, whose worldwide holdings include the Waldorf-Astoria, was amazingly similar to Marriott's. Once again, sexual orientation is not included in the company's equal employment opportunity policy but is included in its anti-harassment policy and the company's diversity training. Hilton has no gay and lesbian employees group and said that, while there had been no corporate-placed ads in gay and lesbian media, local hotels may have placed such ads. The company is self-insured and has no job or insurance restrictions for employees with HIV/AIDS. No benefits have been extended to employees' domestic partners. Beyond policy and benefits issues—which the two hoteliers are likely to have compared and deliberately matched for the sake of competitiveness in recruiting and retaining employees—Hilton also mirrored Marriott in saying that it would consider placing job advertisements in the gay and lesbian press. AIDS education varies in frequency and format at Hilton's many locations but is conducted throughout the company. Like Marriott, Hilton corporate knows of no company marketing to gays and lesbians or of any charitable contributions to gay and lesbian or AIDS organizations.

Going beyond our surveys, Hilton has recently found itself distinguished from Marriott and its other competitors in one unfortunate incident. In 1993 in a case brought by three same-sex couples seeking to be legally married, the State Supreme Court of Hawaii ruled that the state must show compelling reasons why same-sex marriages cannot be permitted. Soon after, two bills were introduced in the Hawaii legislature to permanently exclude such marriages. When hearings were held on the bills in February 1994, Hilton regional senior vice president Dieter Huckestein testified that "allowing gay marriages in Hawaii could hurt tourism," and claimed that he had received 50 letters from concerned travelers in support of that assertion. It must be noted that Huckestein was testifying at the hearing not as a representative of Hilton, but rather as the elected chairman of the Hawaii Visitors Bureau.

Pressed for comment on Huckestein's testimony, Hilton officials first pointed out that Huckestein was unaware that the mainland's *Catholic Journal* and *Chicago Tribune* had opposed Hawaiian same-sex marriages and encouraged their readers to write letters to Hawaii expressing those sentiments, thus skewing the balance of the Visitors Bureau's mail on the subject. Two weeks after Huckestein's testimony, the Visitors Bureau officially backed Huckestein's testimony, but also offered to pass along all correspondence on the subject to the legislature. By that time, letter-writing campaigns by the International Gay Travel Association and in the gay and lesbian press had yielded many more positive letters to the Hawaii Visitors Bureau (as well as complaints to Hilton about Huckestein's testimony), giving a more balanced view. Hilton pointed out repeatedly that Huckestein was not speaking as a representative of the company during the hearing and expressed regret at any misinterpretation of his testimony. Hilton has taken no stand on the prospect of same-sex marriages being legalized in Hawaii. The company says it simply believes that the issue needs to be explored if it is likely to impact tourism.

No car rental companies responded to our surveys, but privately held **Alamo Rent a Car** has an informal gay and lesbian employee group, and, when Alamo's Family Wellness Department (responsible for personnel, training, reservations, and customer service) declined to cooperate with our survey, the group's members shared some basic information with us. Alamo, which is headquartered in Fort Lauderdale, conducts AIDS education for all of its employees and, in response to a management employee's death from the disease, sponsored a panel for the AIDS memorial quilt that featured the company name and logo. The employees we spoke with told us that the company has been uniformly supportive of its employees with AIDS, accommodating their needs so that they may continue working.

Alamo holds annual forums for its management and non-management employees where workers are encouraged to voice concerns, suggestions, and observations about the company. The employee group formed in 1993 after one of these forums (with more than 700 employees attending) at which a gay employee challenged management to add sexual orientation to company policies and to extend family benefits to domestic partners. At the time of our survey, the employee group called itself the Alamo Gay and Lesbian Alliance (AGALA), but Alamo has since informed the group that it may not use the company name, so the group has been re-christened the Gay and Lesbian Employee Alliance (GALEA). Alamo refuses to recognize GALEA or deal with it as a representative body of a group of employees, preferring to deal with individual employees. Nevertheless, sexual orientation was added to the company's anti-discrimination policy on September 20, 1993. Still, based on their interactions with management, GALEA members don't expect much movement from Alamo beyond the policy change. As one GALEA member put it, "although the Alamo corporate closet has been cracked, they have the wood filler out and are busy applying the putty."

With no response from and no known gay and lesbian employee groups at the other car rental companies, we have no information on their employment policies, benefits, marketing, or charitable work. Luckily the companies' additional driver policies, which were the subject of an article in Chicago's *Windy City Times* in December 1993, lend a clear insight into their thinking about gays and lesbians. Because car rentals with more than one driver present an increased liability for the companies, most agencies charge a fee for each additional driver. However, competition has driven the companies to waive those fees for spouses. The question, then, is who qualifies as a spouse. The answer varies from agency to agency. On September 7, 1993, employee-owned **Avis** endeared itself to gay and lesbian drivers as well as opposite-sex domestic partners when it advised its U.S. employees that the fee waiver would be extended to "couples without benefit of clergy or legality" if they simply declared themselves to be a couple at the time of the rental. So, if it's not too much commitment, come out: It will save you money. Alamo is almost equally fair to consumers because it doesn't even waive the additional driver fee for legal spouses (although it does waive the fee for employees' legal spouses). **National** clings to some semblance of officialdom by waiving the fee only for unmarried couples with proof of government-sanctioned domestic partnership status, so only couples from the handful of American cities with registries are eligible. **Hertz** and Chrysler-owned **Thrifty** have made no movement on the issue, claiming they have not received any complaints about their additional driver policies.

Best known for its yellow trucks, Miami's **Ryder System** is the nation's largest provider of commercial truck rentals, its leading transporter of new cars and light trucks, and the world's top independent distributor of new aviation supplies and parts. The company added sexual orientation to its anti-discrimination policy in 1993 and includes sexual orientation in its diversity training. It has no gay and lesbian employees group. Self-insured, Ryder provides no benefits to domestic partners. The company places no job or insurance restrictions on employees with HIV/AIDS but conducts no AIDS education. It has not marketed toward lesbians and gay men, but reports that it has contributed to several south Florida AIDS groups.

Like the car rental agencies, airlines have a number of special areas—involving both customers and employees—in which sexual orientation and domestic partnership become issues. Like most major airlines, **USAir Group**, based in Arlington, Virginia, issues passes that allow employees' spouses to fly for free. In 1993 flight attendant Todd Barr applied for a spouse pass for his lover, Jonathan. USAir first issued a pass with Barr's lover listed as his spouse; then, realizing his spouse was a man, requested that the pass be returned and issued another one without Barr's lover's name. Barr proceeded to fight the decision through the airline's internal appeals process, also requesting health benefits for his lover. In 1992 USAir issued four "buddy" passes to each employee—passes that allow travel at only 10% of the regular fare and that can be given to anyone. Many, including a Miami employee who contacted us, saw this as an attempt to appease the airline's gay and lesbian employees. Our Miami contact also reports that, despite USAir's corporate fight against domestic partner benefits, on the local level he finds the company to be comfortable to work for and even gay-friendly. USAir did not respond to our surveys.

Nor did **Trans World Airlines**, which is based in Mount Kisco, New York, and has also had its share of controversy over eligibility for free flights—this time involving customers. The year 1988 saw two incidents at the airline that resulted in lawsuits claiming discrimination. In the first of these, in the summer of 1988, TWA refused to issue a companion ticket to the lover of William Johnson, a gay lawyer in New York and frequent flier on TWA. In 1986 the airline had issued a new policy for its frequent flier program restricting the use of companion tickets to blood relatives and spouses of those enrolled in the program. With this restriction, the airline hoped to prevent people from trading or selling tickets earned under the program, but in the process seriously inconvenienced the program's members with unmarried domestic partners. Reportedly a TWA ticket agent had even suggested that Johnson claim that his lover was his cousin, but Johnson refused to lie and instead filed a suit under federal aviation law, alleging discrimination in access to air travel. Under pressure, in July 1989 TWA reversed its policy, allowing frequent fliers to designate anyone they wish as recipients of companion tickets. In a letter to one man who had complained about the restrictions, TWA sweetened the victory by declaring that it had reversed itself because "we are aware of the non-traditional life-styles prevalent in our society, and our sole interest is the promotion of travel, not social commentary."

The second incident of alleged discrimination by TWA focuses on yet another "family"-based policy common to airlines. In November 1988 gay San Franciscan Tony Hurd purchased a nonrefundable ticket for a flight to Washington, D.C. When Hurd's lover suffered a heart attack and was hospitalized on the day of the flight, Hurd remained at his side and missed the plane. TWA, like most major airlines, will grant refunds on nonrefundable tickets if ticket purchasers can show that an emergency within their immediate family caused them to miss the flight. But when Hurd requested a refund and provided proof of his lover's illness, the refund was denied because Hurd's lover was not considered to be a member of his immediate family. Hurd sued the airline for the refund, and when National Gay Rights Advocates threatened to file its own suit, TWA granted Hurd the refund. The resolution of the two discrimination lawsuits seems to show a grudging acceptance of the concept of domestic partnership by TWA. In the absence of a survey response, however, we have no idea whether the company's internal policies and benefits reflect that tenuous acceptance.

Phoenix-based **America West Airlines** did not respond to our original survey request but did submit information after reviewing a draft of this chapter (which made no mention of the company). America West added sexual orientation to its anti-discrimination policy in September 1991. The company also has included sexual orientation in its diversity training and conducts AIDS education. A video on AIDS was produced and distributed within the company by its corporate communications department. America West has extended no benefits to domestic partners, including flight benefits. The company does give its employees guest passes that can be used by unmarried partners, but it frankly admits that those are not at the same reduced fare available to spouses.

Even without a completed survey, it is easy to conclude that Atlanta's **Delta Air Lines** has developed no level of acceptance whatsoever for domestic partners, gays and lesbians, or people with AIDS. Delta's record may be corporate America's worst.

Where to begin? Starting with the truly outrageous, in 1985 Delta amended its contract of carriage to exclude passengers with AIDS. After protests and threats of lawsuits, Delta removed the clause ten days later, but the reprehensible tone of Delta's response to the disease had been set at the highest levels of management and would continue to be displayed in incident after incident. In August 1986 Mark Sigers, a person with AIDS, informed Delta of his condition and his need for oxygen in-flight and then flew Delta from San Francisco to Atlanta to visit his family. As Delta had requested, he flew with companions who were familiar with the administration of the oxygen, but he did not need any during the flight. When Sigers boarded his return flight without a companion (assuming that he would not need oxygen administered), a flight attendant reportedly recognized him, told his supervisor that Sigers had required constant care as well as oxygen on his flight to Atlanta, challenged his decision to make the return flight unaccompanied, and had Sigers removed from the plane. After protests, Delta apologized for Sigers's treatment, pledged to educate its employees about AIDS and its transmission, and declared that it welcomed people with AIDS on its flights.

Nevertheless, in October 1987 two straight men on a Delta flight from Washington, D.C., to Orlando noticed something less than welcoming. The flight also carried passengers wearing paraphernalia from the preceding weekend's gay and lesbian March on Washington; after an in-flight snack was served, the flight attendants donned rubber gloves to pick up the passengers' refuse. When questioned about the irrational, AIDS-phobic incident, a Delta spokesperson said he did not know why flight attendants would wear protective gloves while collecting refuse from passengers, but said he guessed it was up to individual discretion whether or not to do so.

Meanwhile, Delta corporate continued to demonstrate an amazing level of AIDS-phobia—and now added outright homophobia to its message. In November 1986 lawyers for Delta's insurer were negotiating compensation for passengers killed in a crash of a Delta plane. The lawyers actually argued that since one of the victims was a known homosexual, he probably had AIDS and would not have lived much longer anyway. They reasoned, therefore, that compensation for his family should be less because his lifetime earnings would have been greatly reduced. When Delta's lawyers' shameless tactic became known, AIDS organizations called for a boycott of the airline. True to form, after emphasizing that the airline did not closely supervise the handling of damage cases, Delta once again apologized, said it would adopt a policy prohibiting discrimination against passengers with AIDS, and repeated its pledge to educate its employees about AIDS. In spite of this, as recently as 1993 a *Business Week* cover story on corporate responses to AIDS said Delta's education efforts were inadequate and quoted a Delta spokesman's ludicrous statement: "We don't have any specific program. We haven't seen a need."

It should come as no surprise that Delta has also made headlines about alleged homophobia and AIDS-phobia in its employment practices. In his book, *Delta Air Lines: Debunking the Myth,* former Delta vice president and assistant general counsel Sidney F. Davis describes a time in the late 1970s when the airline was under close scrutiny by the Labor and Justice departments because of alleged discrimination against African-Americans and women. He was shocked, then, to be called to a meeting with another lawyer and Delta chief executive Tom Beebe where Beebe suggested the airline ". . . no longer hire any more male flight attendants, because they get restless, and restlessness creates unions. Besides, they are as gay as a three-dollar bill, and we don't need any fags in the Delta family." The incident is old and Beebe has long since retired, but a *Smithsonian* article in January 1994 revealed that today only 5% of Delta flight attendants are male. The company employs about 16,500 flight attendants.

Turning to a specific employee's case of alleged discrimination, in 1986 Gary Matthews, who had been a ramp worker and reservations agent for Delta since 1971, fell while at his job at Delta's reservations office in Rockville, Maryland, permanently damaging nerves in his right arm. During the course of his treatment, Delta's worker's compensation insurer, Wausau, directed Matthews to another doctor to get a second opinion about his injury. During that examination, Matthews discovered that the second doctor was not a neurosurgeon, but rather a psychiatrist who Matthews says proceeded to ask him, among other things, if he was gay, if he had a lover, if they had sex with other people, and if they had been tested for HIV. Matthews later completely lost the use of his right arm and hand, and was declared

75% functionally disabled by the Maryland Workers Compensation Commission. Delta transferred him to Atlanta, where his job was to sort bags of mail. By transferring Matthews to Atlanta, Delta moved Matthews from a jurisdiction that prohibits employment discrimination based on sexual orientation (Montgomery County, Maryland) to one that does not. Matthews was fired by Delta in 1990.

Unprotected by anti-discrimination laws based on sexual orientation, in 1992 Matthews filed suit in U.S. District Court charging that the airline failed to inform him that he could continue to receive medical benefits for an on-the-job injury. His case was dismissed. But, believing he was harassed and fired because he is gay and has AIDS, Matthews has since encouraged a boycott of Delta, urging "If you value your privacy, if you think your personal life is nobody's business but your own and if you support equal rights for gays and lesbians, don't fly Delta."

And don't apply for a job with Delta. In 1991 another uproar arose, this time about Delta's hiring practices. In August of that year Delta purchased New York–based European routes and a shuttle service from soon-to-be-defunct Pan Am Airlines and pledged to hire as many Pan Am employees as possible. By early November 200 to 300 employees and former employees of Pan Am complained to their union that during job interviews Delta had asked personal, inappropriate, and illegal questions. It was reported in *New York Newsday* that Delta's interviews included asking interviewees if they had roommates, if they were divorced, why they were not married, their sexual preference, what types of birth control they used, and if they were on medication—including drugs for AIDS and antidepressants. New York City and State law prohibits employers from asking prospective employees about marital status, sexual orientation, birth control, specific age, living arrangements, and disabilities. Employers are forbidden to seek such information even if they have interviewees sign a waiver; as part of its hiring practices, Delta asked all prospective employees to sign a waiver authorizing Delta to inquire into their "character, general reputation, personal characteristics, and mode of living." But an employer cannot legally ask an employee to waive his or her rights under New York's human rights law, and early in 1992 the New York City Human Rights Commission served Delta with more than 300 formal complaints of discrimination.

Delta attributed any "mistakes" in the interviewing process to the hectic nature of interviewing 10,000 applicants in two months. It emphasized that Delta was the only thing standing between thousands of Pan Am employees and unemployment. In August 1992 Delta settled one of the complaints, agreeing to hire and to give $13,958 in back pay to a man who had alleged that Delta had refused him a job because he was gay and HIV-positive. The airline also agreed to work with New York's Human Rights Commission to review its employment policies and interview practices. Delta said it had no intention of settling on any of the several hundred other complaints.

Delta's history of AIDS-phobia and discrimination continues to this day. In October 1992, Joseph Sullivan, who had been a Delta reservations agent and manager for 13 years, filed suit against the airline, alleging that he was fired from his job in 1991 because he has AIDS. Delta insisted that he was fired because he was unreliable and unable to perform his job. Delta's attorney said: "Alcohol, drug and sexual addiction problems were the root problems of all his difficulties. . . . Delta gave him a chance to succeed time and again. . . . In the end, Mr. Sullivan's chances simply ran out." Sullivan had taken two leaves of absence—in September 1990 and May 1991—for alcohol rehabilitation and, during a three-month period, missed 31 days of work due to illness. He had never been reprimanded for alcohol-related behavior on the job, and the absences cited by Delta were all health-related, including bouts of severe diarrhea and shingles. Sullivan had been promoted to a position supervising 200 other employees in 1989 and received a job evaluation in December 1990 (between his two rehabilitation leaves) that rated him at or above expectations in all nine performance categories.

Sullivan had informed his supervisor of his HIV status in November 1990. According to court records, prompted by one employee's nosebleed and other employees' resulting concerns, Delta managers met in April 1991 to discuss employees in the San Francisco office who were known or suspected to be HIV positive. Under the categories "documentation of HIV positive diagnosis," "advised management of HIV positive diagnosis," and "recurring illnesses/suspect AIDS related," one manager, Donna O'Leary, compiled a list of 13 employees, their physical appearance, known medical problems, and attendance records. The list (which included Sullivan) and descriptions, which were used as evidence in the trial, were forwarded to Delta headquarters. Delta maintained that the list was medically necessary so that supervisors could handle any medical emergencies the employees might have and accommodate any HIV-related attendance problems. The airline also said that the employees' privacy was not invaded because the list never left Delta management.

In April 1994 Sullivan's case went to Superior Court in California. During the trial, Delta lawyers repeatedly proposed to the court that prospective jurors in the case be required to complete a questionnaire that would have revealed their HIV status. At the trial's conclusion in May, Sullivan was awarded $275,000 on the grounds that Delta had violated his right to privacy and had broken a California law protecting employees who enter substance abuse programs. The jury deadlocked on the issue of whether or not Delta had discriminated against Sullivan because he was HIV-positive. Seven jurors voted that it had and five disagreed. The presiding judge declared a mistrial on the point because in a civil trial at least nine jurors must agree in order to reach a verdict. Given Delta's history, we find the facts to be more conclusive than that.

Delta declined several requests to participate in our survey, including a personal request to its equal employment opportunity director. Georgia's largest employer finally responded with some information only after reviewing a draft of this chapter. Although Delta did not say when the protection was added, sexual orientation is currently included in its anti-discrimination policy. While it conducts no formal AIDS education, information about the disease has appeared in the company newsletter on several occasions in the past several years, and Delta has made contributions to AIDS groups, including the Atlanta AIDS Fund, the National Community AIDS Partnership, Project Open Hand, DIFFA, and the Atlanta Interfaith AIDS Network. In June 1993 the airline modified its frequent flier program to extend the program's spousal benefits to government-registered domestic partners (in the handful of cities that register partners). We have no other remotely positive information to share.

We did receive some information from **American Airlines**, of Fort Worth, Texas. Although they declined to complete our surveys, the airline was happy to send us a copy of their equal employment opportunity statement, which had just been revised on June 1, 1993, to include sexual orientation, making American the first U.S. airline to officially add sexual orientation to its list of protected categories. Sexual orientation is also included in the company's diversity training.

Unfortunately 1993 also saw American take several pages from Delta's playbook. In April an American plane carrying many gay and lesbian passengers home from the March on Washington landed in Dallas and, once the passengers had deplaned, the flight crew requested a complete change of the plane's blankets and pillows—a highly unusual request that suggested homophobia and AIDS-phobia. Gay rights and AIDS activists quickly attacked the airline for having learned nothing from Delta's almost-identical offense during the previous March in Washington six years earlier. American's chairman, Robert Crandall, immediately apologized for the incident, and the employees responsible were reprimanded and educated about HIV transmission. It did not help American's defense of the incident when it became known that a week prior to the march the airline had specifically barred flight personnel from wearing the red ribbons that some had begun to wear as a symbol of AIDS awareness. American was simply enforcing its policy against flight personnel wearing any non-airline insignia on their uniforms, but the conjunction of the two incidents brought bad feelings and bad press. The airline has since made a major departure from its policy by allowing and even encouraging employees to wear red ribbons on World AIDS Day every year.

But shortly before that milestone arrived, American enraged not only gay rights and AIDS activists but also several members of Congress when it ejected a man with AIDS from one of its flights. On November 14, 1993, San Franciscan Timothy Holless boarded an American flight home from Chicago. He was dragged screaming from the plane and arrested by Chicago police for disorderly conduct after he allegedly refused flight attendants' requests to cover his Kaposi's sarcoma lesions and remove an IV bag that he had hung above his seat in violation of American regulations. The Washington, D.C. chapter of ACT UP immediately called for a boycott of American. Twenty-two members of Congress sent American chairman Crandall a letter decrying the incident, questioning the airline's compliance with federal anti-discrimination laws, and demanding that American clearly state a policy of anti-discrimination.

American maintained that it had been acting in the best interests of Holless and his fellow passengers by asking him to delay his flight while the airline evaluated his medical needs. Still, a settlement with Holless and his supporters was quickly reached, in which the airline agreed to conduct more sensitivity training for its attendants, ticket agents, and reservations people, and to reframe its corporate policy on disability. By 1991 American had already given Red Cross training about blood-born pathogens to more than 60,000 of its employees.

The airline has also made contributions to several AIDS groups, including the AIDS Foundation of Chicago, AIDS Legal Council, and The Names Project, for whom American transported the AIDS memorial quilt from San Francisco to the airline's base in Fort Worth at company expense. It has also agreed to air public service announcements produced by the Arthur Ashe Foundation on its flights in June and July 1994, in conjunction with its popular Wimbledon tennis tournament updates.

Although presaged by Delta's outrages, American's homophobic and AIDS-phobic actions came as a surprise because the airline had previously made some overtures to the gay and lesbian and AIDS communities. We received letters from several American employees chronicling their attempts to get American management to extend travel benefits to employees' domestic partners and their frustration at the airline's intransigence. But in 1989 American showed some sensitivity to gay and lesbian and AIDS concerns when it directed its insurer, Prudential, to accept new and previously rejected claims for AIDS treatment with then-experimental aerosolized pentamidine (most insurers will not cover claims for treatments that have not been fully approved by the FDA). Furthermore, at the same time that American was flagrantly displaying homophobia and AIDS-phobia to its customers, it was actively marketing to gay men and lesbians. In May 1993 American was one of 45 exhibitors at a consumer trade show for gay and lesbian travelers in San Francisco. American also serves as the official airline of the San Francisco AIDS Foundation. Since our survey, American has taken an unusual stand by being the only company we know of that is investigating the formation of a gay and lesbian employees group—specifically, how to encourage one.

American is not the only airline attempting to capture the gay and lesbian market. Houston's **Continental Airlines** participated in four of the 1993 gay and lesbian travel expos produced in different cities by the same company that held the San Francisco expo in which American participated. A story in the *Chicago Tribune* quoted the head of agency sales at Continental as saying the expos had brought the airline "a lot of bona fide sales leads." Continental may now be moving aggressively into the gay and lesbian market. It lined up the plum gay and lesbian event of 1994 by acting as the official airline for Gay Games IV in New York City in June. The week-long athletic competition and cultural festival brought more than a half million lesbians and gay men to New York from all around the world. Unfortunately Continental did not move as aggressively to respond to our surveys, so we do not know if any of the airline's policies or benefits have been reshaped to recognize Continental's gay and lesbian employees. We do know that in 1990, in what has become a familiar industry story, a gay Atlanta man had to sue the airline for refusing to issue a free companion ticket to his domestic partner. Continental and American are both going to have to bring their public and private policies into line with their marketing if they ever hope to be embraced by the politically aware gay and lesbian market.

Chicago's **United Airlines** has its own politically aware gays and lesbians. GLUE (Gay/Lesbian United Employee) Coalition is one of the most vocal employee groups we located. Formed at the end of 1992 in San Francisco, GLUE Coalition has members from almost every job classification at the airline, which operates in Latin America and Europe as well as the United States. When United did not respond to our surveys, some members of GLUE agreed to offer their insights; they cautioned, however, that United has several different unions and employees around the world, so their input should be viewed as skewed to the perspective of North America–based flight attendants. GLUE reported that United added sexual orientation to its official anti-discrimination policy on July 1, 1993. On January 1, 1993, United's chairman and president, Stephen Wolf, had issued a statement that included "sexual preference" as an area in the airline's commitment to equal opportunity. GLUE was then instrumental in having the phrase changed to "sexual orientation" and incorporated into official policy.

GLUE has been assigned a human resources representative by United but is not officially recognized. The coalition notes that it has not yet applied for official recognition because group members consider confidentiality to be a major issue, and they fear official recognition might jeopardize members' confidentiality. United has allowed the group to use facilities and has provided some in-house publicity. Unfortunately an announcement about GLUE in a company newsletter was met by a strongly negative reaction, and United chose to ban all announcements pertaining to social groups from the newsletter rather than defend GLUE's right to be included. According to GLUE, United's diversity training does not specifically include sexual orientation and spousal travel benefits on the airline are not available to domestic partners. Three-day bereavement leave is available to domestic partners, but while the three-day leave is paid for spouses, it is unpaid for domestic partners. GLUE is preparing a proposal to the airline for extension of all spousal benefits to domestic partners.

GLUE puts out a bi-monthly newsletter called *Friendly Persuasion*, which has discussed DP benefits, estate planning, and coming out, and has reported homophobic incidents at the airline and United's response. It holds a yearly central conference for its members and has snazzy T-shirts that members wore when they marched as a group in the 1993 Gay and Lesbian March on Washington. Marching in the 1993 San Francisco Lesbian and Gay Freedom Day Parade, GLUE members chanted "2-4-6-8, United Airlines ain't so straight!" and "6-5-4-3, Marry me and fly for free!" Many delighted spectators flashed their United Mileage Plus frequent flier membership cards in support of GLUE and the airline as the contingent passed. At the time of our survey, GLUE told us the airline has promised them the use of an inflatable United 747 (which requires 30 people to carry it) in the 1994 New York City march to commemorate the 25th anniversary of the Stonewall riots. Afterward, however, United changed its story, saying that it would only allow the inflatable plane to be used in events that are officially sponsored by UAL. We are unaware of any United marketing initiatives toward gays and lesbians.

As a final note, it was reported by Atlanta's gay paper, *Southern Voice*, in 1993 that Minneapolis/Saint Paul–based **Northwest Airlines** said it was considering adding sexual orientation to its anti-discrimination policy. Northwest did not respond to our surveys, and we were unable to discover any relevant information about the airline.

TRAVEL AND TOURISM

Company	Survey Response	Policy	Date Added	Soft Benefits	Hard Benefits	AIDS Education	Diversity Training	G/L Group	Authors' Choice
American	◆	◆	6/93			◆	◆		
America West	◆	◆	9/91			◆	◆		
Delta	◆	◆							
United	*	◆	7/93				NI	◆◆	
Alamo	declined*	◆	9/20/93			◆		◆	
Ryder	◆◆◆	◆	1993						
Hilton	◆◆◆					◆	◆		
Marriott	◆◆◆					◆	◆		

* United and Alamo did not complete our surveys. Information was provided by members of their lesbian and gay employees' groups and is unofficial.
Companies that declined to participate in our surveys: Alamo, Avis, Budget, Carnival Cruise, Circus Circus, Promus
Companies that did not respond at all: Continental, Northwest Airlines, Southwest, TWA, US Air, Hertz, U-Haul, Carlson Companies, Hyatt

Key

Survey response	Sexual orientation included in anti-discrimination policy	Date sexual orientation added to anti-discrimination policy	Soft benefits (bereavement or family/personal/sick leave) extended to domestic partners	Hard benefits (health insurance) extended to domestic partners	AIDS education	Diversity training	Lesbian and gay employees group	Authors' choice
blank=None. ◆=Provided some information, but didn't complete survey. ◆◆=Completed one survey. ◆◆◆=Completed both surveys.	blank=No, it is not, or unknown. ◆=Yes, it is. UC=Under consideration.		blank=None known. ◆=Has bereavement or family/personal/sick leave for partners. UC=Company is actively considering extending bereavement leave or family/personal/sick leave to domestic partners.	blank=No. ◆=Yes, it is. UC=Company is considering extending health insurance to domestic partners.	blank=None known. ◆=Yes, company conducts AIDS education.	blank=Unknown if company has any diversity training. none=Company has none. NI=Company has diversity training, but sexual orientation is not covered. ◆=Sexual orientation is included in company's diversity training. UC=Company is actively considering including sexual orientation in its existing or proposed diversity training.	blank=None known at company. ◆=Company has a gay and lesbian employees group. ◆◆=Company has a gay and lesbian employees group that it officially recognizes.	♥=The authors feel the company has distinguished itself on lesbian/gay and AIDS issues within its industry.

21
UTILITIES

IN RESPONSE TO our survey, western Michigan's **Consumers Power Company** sent a letter respectfully declining to participate. The letter did suggest that sexual orientation is not included in their anti-discrimination policy, saying "Our Company does not discriminate for or against anyone based on sexual orientation/preference in any of its employment practices but has also chosen not to raise this as an issue for any special Corporate consideration."

Consumers Power Company's statement is of particular note not because of its informational content but rather because it couches company policy (or lack thereof) in the language of recent and widespread initiatives by the religious right to repeal or prevent legislation protecting the civil rights of lesbians and gay men. These campaigns have yielded new success for anti-gay zealots in the 1990s. A significant factor in the advance of these initiatives has frequently been their proponents' ability to frame the discussion in their own terms, labeling lesbian and gay civil rights protections as "special rights." Gay activists in the states and cities where anti-gay initiatives have been launched are seeing fewer posters that quote scripture or command "Die, Sodomites." Instead they are confronted with a sea of posters, and even billboards, that say, "No special rights for gays." With the growing realization by the right of the limited persuasiveness of flagrant bigotry, the word "special" has become a popular stealth weapon when it comes to lesbians and gays, whether in "special rights" or "special Corporate (capital C) consideration." It is disturbing to see it creep into official correspondence from a major utility.

Michigan's other major utility, **Detroit Edison**, did answer our survey, supplying a copy of their anti-discrimination policy, which does not include sexual orientation. The company also told us that adding sexual orientation to the policy is not currently under consideration. Detroit Edison does have diversity training and told us that the session facilitators are trained to introduce any common mode of diversity that does not naturally arise in a specific session's discussion—including sexual orientation and disabilities. Employee groups are recognized by the company, but it does not have a lesbian and gay group. AIDS education has been conducted by Detroit Edison. In 1991 a 20-page educational brochure that the company had selected to be suitable for teens and adults was mailed to the homes of all employees. A cover letter suggested that employees share the information with their families and also promised that the company would supply additional copies of the brochure to employees who requested them for use in other organizations or groups to which they might belong. Detroit Edison has also contributed to AIDS service organizations, specifically identifying Detroit's Simon House, a support organization and shelter for PWAs.

Rounding out our responses from Midwestern utilities is **Commonwealth Edison**, headquartered in Chicago. In response to our survey, Commonwealth Edison indicated that it includes sexual orientation in its anti-discrimination policy, parenthetically noting "see reference to local ordinances." Upon inspection, however, we found that the policy, which includes race, color, religion, sex, age, national origin, disability, and Vietnam veteran status, does not list sexual orientation. The statement, "Additionally, Commonwealth Edison Company supports the principles and purposes of any and all state, municipal and city ordinances related to Equal Employment Opportunity," seems to indicate that in localities with anti-discrimination laws protecting lesbians and gay men the company adheres to those laws—which we would expect. This, unfortunately, falls short of efforts by many companies surveyed that protect all of their employees from discrimination based on sexual orientation, regardless of where the employees are located. Commonwealth Edison officials estimate that 40% of their operations are in localities that prohibit employment discrimination based on sexual orientation.

Commonwealth Edison's response on benefits was similar. They indicated that child care, adoption assistance, relocation assistance, and travel benefits are available to employees regardless of the gender or existence of a partner (and, we suppose, the partner does benefit). Life insurance is also available, in the sense that it is possible to name anyone as the policy's beneficiary. More significantly, though, the company indicated that family/personal/sick leave is available to opposite-sex as well as same-sex partners and that bereavement leave is available on a "case by case" basis. Significant steps like these indicate that the company is making more progress than its waffling answers about its anti-discrimination policy and other benefits might suggest. Diversity training is currently being researched by the company. If training is implemented, it will be interesting to see if sexual orientation, not specifically addressed in the anti-discrimination policy, is included.

In early 1993 former White House chief of staff Sam Skinner took over as president of Commonwealth Edison and reportedly shook things up at the utility during his first year on the job. Outside of the office, Skinner and his wife, Honey Jacobs Skinner, have been working hard with the Illinois Federation for Human Rights to have sexual orientation added to state anti-discrimination law. It is surprising, then, to find out that Commonwealth Edison has not provided the same protection. Belying the company's uninspiring policy and slowly expanding benefits, Greg Ward, head of the Commonwealth Edison Gay & Lesbian Employee Association, feels that the winds of change are blowing at the Chicago utility and have been accelerated since Skinner's arrival. The employee group formed two years ago and has been largely supported by management. Although the group has not officially applied for company recognition, management frequently meets with Ward and other group members to discuss issues of concern to lesbian and gay employees. Furthermore, Commonwealth Edison has funded a float, T-shirts, and hats for the group in the Chicago lesbian and gay pride parade for both years since the group's formation, and in 1993 publicized the company's parade participation in the company newsletter. The utility even allows the group to use one of its "Louie the Lightning Bug" company mascot costumes in the parade, which Ward says adds great camp flair to the company float. Ward also mentioned that company officials had recently approached him to discuss the possibility of the utility placing ads in the *Windy City Times,* Chicago's lesbian and gay newspaper, during the city's 1994 pride celebrations. AIDS education has been conducted for all human resources staff and has also been held for other employees at most company locations.

Only two eastern utilities responded to our surveys. Northeastern and central New Jersey's **Public Service Electric and Gas** declined to complete our survey, but did send copies of their equal employment opportunity and anti-harassment policies, both of which include sexual orientation. Miami's **Florida Power and Light** also declined our survey, but sent copies of materials from their equal employment opportunity and diversity programs. Sexual orientation is not included in their policies or programs.

Sexual orientation is included in the anti-discrimination policy of Arizona's **Pinnacle West Capital Corporation** and has been since 1988. The company also includes sexual orientation in its diversity training.

California is home to the two largest electric companies in America, both of which fully completed our surveys. **Southern California Edison Company** has included sexual orientation in its anti-discrimination policy since April 1993. Since then, no sexual orientation–based claims have been filed under the policy. Self-insured, SCE has no job or insurance restrictions on employees with HIV or AIDS. The company conducts both AIDS education and diversity training that addresses sexual orientation. Although SCE has not done so to date, they indicated that they would consider placing employment ads in the lesbian and gay press. They have not otherwise advertised in lesbian and gay media or marketed specifically toward lesbians and gay men. The company has a foundation, but it did not elaborate on its giving. SCE matches the charitable contributions of its employees only to educational institutions.

The largest gas and electric company in the United States is northern California's **Pacific Gas & Electric**. PG&E should be congratulated for adding sexual orientation to its anti-discrimination policy way back in 1982. It reports that claims have been filed under the provision but that confidentiality concerns prevent it from discussing their handling or disposition. Sexual orientation is specifically addressed in the company's diversity training. PG&E also conducts AIDS education, has had an AIDS anti-discrimination policy since 1987, maintains HIV support groups as part of its Employee Assistance Program, and has neither job nor insurance restrictions for employees with HIV/AIDS. No "hard" benefits have yet been extended to domestic partners of employees, but bereavement leave is available. Non-spousal joint pension benefits are available, but PG&E was forthcoming enough to note that the benefit level involved is "different from spousal pension" (and, we presume, lower).

PG&E has an active and vocal Lesbian, Gay and Bisexual Employee Association (LGBEA), which the company recognizes and provides with facilities, funding, and coverage in company media. In June 1988 the LGBEA marched in the San Francisco Freedom Day Parade under a PG&E banner—the first corporate group ever to do so in San Francisco's parade. Knowing that PG&E had always provided a float for the company's Asian employees group in the Chinese New Year Parade, LGBEA requested and was given the use of a truck for the Freedom Day Parade. Since then, the company has provided LGBEA with the use of a flat-bed truck in the parade annually.

When pictures of the group marching in the 1991 parade were published in *PG&E Week*, the company newsletter, management's support for the group was sorely tested. The photos elicited a storm of hate mail over the company's E-mail bulletin board. Reaction was so violently negative that vice president for human resources Russ Cunningham made a tour of company facilities to talk to employees about the incident. He was shocked at the level of hatred and promised LGBEA that diversity training would be accelerated and that employees making homophobic slurs would be disciplined. Cunningham sent a note to all of PG&E's 26,000 employees, reminding them that discrimination is against company policy; the company's CEO, Richard A. Clarke, issued a public statement emphasizing that the company would not tolerate discrimination of any kind.

PG&E is one of only a handful of companies outside the tobacco, beverage, and clothing industries that have advertised in lesbian and gay media, where they have advertised their energy-efficiency and customer-assistance programs. At LGBEA's suggestion, the company has also operated an information booth at San Francisco's Folsom Street Fair, a community fair celebrating the leather community, since 1989. Lia Shigemura, an equal employment opportunity and affirmative action representative, speaking of the company's different employee associations, says, "The reason we have these groups is that they represent not only our employees, but the communities we serve. . . . It's part good corporate citizenship and part enlightened self-interest. . . . If we didn't have LGBEA, we wouldn't have entrée into the [gay and lesbian] community."

PG&E has supported not only its lesbian and gay employees, but also the community at large. Contributions to AIDS groups include the San Francisco AIDS Foundation, the AIDS Task Force, the Black Coalition on AIDS, Project Open Hand, and the Shanti Project, which in October 1992 gave PG&E its Corporate Award for community involvement. PG&E not only contributes to Shanti but also encourages employees to volunteer for them. And PG&E is also one of only a few companies in the nation that, in addition to their AIDS giving, have contributed to lesbian and gay organizations, notably to the Lavender Youth Recreation Center. The company is a member of the Golden Gate Business Association, San Francisco's gay business association, and was one of the sponsors of the National Gay and Lesbian Task Force's Lesbian and Gay Workplace Issues Conference at Stanford University in October 1993. PG&E joined its LGBEA in funding two scholarships for gay or lesbian high school students through the Bay Area Network of Gay and Lesbian Educators. It has a corporate record equaled by few other companies in the United States.

UTILITIES

Company	Survey Response	Policy	Date Added	Soft Benefits	Hard Benefits	AIDS Education	Diversity Training	G/L Group	Authors' Choice
Commonwealth Edison	◆			◆		◆	UC	◆	
Detroit Edison	◆◆					◆	◆		
Florida Power & Light	◆								
Pacific Gas & Electric	◆◆◆	◆	1/82	◆		◆	◆	◆◆	◆
Pinnacle West Capital	◆◆	◆	1/88				◆		
Public Service Electric & Gas		◆							
Southern California Edison	◆◆◆	◆	4/93			◆	◆		

Companies that declined to participate in our surveys: Consolidated Edison, Consumers Power, Dominion Resources, Duke Power, Entergy, Houston Industries

Companies that did not respond at all: American Electric Power, Pacificorp, Philadelphia Electric, Southern Company, Texas Utilities

Key

Column	Key
Survey response	blank = None. ♦ = Provided some information, but didn't complete survey. ♦♦ = Completed one survey. ♦♦♦ = Completed both surveys.
Sexual orientation included in anti-discrimination policy	blank = No, it is not, or unknown. ♦ = Yes, it is. UC = Under consideration.
Date sexual orientation added to anti-discrimination policy	
Soft benefits (bereavement or family/personal/sick leave) extended to domestic partners	blank = None known. ♦ = Has bereavement or family/personal/sick leave for partners. UC = Company is actively considering extending bereavement leave or family/personal/sick leave to domestic partners.
Hard benefits (health insurance) extended to domestic partners	blank = No. ♦ = Yes, it is. UC = Company is considering extending health insurance to domestic partners.
AIDS education	blank = None known. ♦ = Yes, company conducts AIDS education.
Diversity training	blank = Unknown if company has any diversity training. none = Company has none. NI = Company has diversity training, but sexual orientation is not covered. ♦ = Sexual orientation is included in company's diversity training. UC = Company is actively considering including sexual orientation in its existing or proposed diversity training.
Lesbian and gay employees group	blank = None known at company. ♦ = Company has a gay and lesbian employees group. ♦♦ = Company has a gay and lesbian employees group that it officially recognizes.
Authors' choice	♥ = The authors feel the company has distinguished itself on lesbian/gay and AIDS issues within its industry.

Appendix I
GAY & LESBIAN
EMPLOYEE GROUPS

Contacts listed are correct as of June 1994, but may change. If the listed contact cannot be reached, employee groups can often be reached through a company's diversity or human resources departments.

3M
3M PLUS—People Like Us
3M Center,
Mail Stop #224-6N-03
St. Paul, MN 55144-1000
Contact: Ms. Janice E. Ross, 612-736-9706, or Mrs. Steven P. Brinduse, 612-736-1007

Abbott Laboratories
Abbott laboratories Lesbian, Gay & Bisexual Employees Organization
P.O. Box 57844
Chicago, IL 60657 *[home address]*
Contact: Ms. Laura Rissover, 312-794-5218

Aetna Life & Casualty
ANGLE—Aetna Network of Gay, Lesbian & Bisexual Employees
151 Farmington Avenue
Hartford, CT 06156
Contact: Workforce Diversity, 203-273-0123

Air Products and Chemicals
GLEE—Gay & Lesbian Empowered Employees
Electronics-A5225
7201 Hamilton Boulevard
Allentown, PA 18195
Contact: Mr. Dale Miller, 215-481-8212

Alamo Rent A Car, Inc.
GALEA—Gay and Lesbian Employee Alliance
455 N.E. 16th Avenue, #3
Fort Lauderdale, FL 33301-1379
Contact: Mr. Bradley R. Behnke, 305-760-7890

Aldus
AQuANet—Aldus Queer Association Network
411 First Avenue South
Seattle, WA 98104
Contact: John McMullen, 206-343-3380

Apple Computer
Apple Lambda
No address
Contact: Mr. Brad Zaller, 408-996-1010

AT&T
LEAGUE—Lesbian, Bisexual & Gay United Employees at AT&T
4 Campus Drive
Parsippany, NJ 07054
Contact: Ms. Kathleen Dermody, 908-658-6013

Baxter Healthcare
BAGLE—Baxter Association of Gay & Lesbian Employees
Mail Stop #MPA-1A
1430 Waukegan Road
McGaw Park, IL 60085
Contact: Mr. John Hnilicka, 708-578-6682

Boeing
BEAGLES—Boeing Employee Association of Gays and Lesbians
P.O. Box 1733
Renton, WA 98057
Contact: Resource Coordinator, 206-781-3587

Chevron
Chevron Lesbian & Gay Employees Association
c/o Kate Howard
Building A, Room 4212
6001 Bollinger Canyon Road
San Ramon, CA 94583
Contact: Ms. Gabrielle McKayle, 415-894-5865, or Mr. Kirk Nass,
    510-242-3932

Coors
LAGER—Lesbian and Gay Employee Resource
Mail Stop #NH420
Coors Brewing Company
Golden, CO 80401
Contact: Mr. Earl Nissen, 303-277-5309

Corestates Financial
MOSAIC—Corestate's Gay & Lesbian Employee Association
Mail Stop #1-9-19-1
510 Walnut Street
Philadelphia, PA 19106
Contact: Mr. Ben Garcia, 216-973-5970

The Walt Disney Company
LEAGUE
500 South Buena Vista Street
Burbank, CA 91521-5209
Contact: Mr. Garrett Hicks, 818-560-1000

DuPont
BGLAD—Bisexuals, Gays, Lesbians and Allies at DuPont
Nemours Building
Wilmington, DE 19898
Contact: Mr. Robert L. Hill, 302-774-1845

Eastman Kodak
Lambda Network at Kodak
P.O. Box 14067
Rochester NY 14614
Contact: Steering Committee, 716-234-4388

Fannie Mae
FLAG—Fannie Mae Lesbians and Gays
Mail Stop #3H-3N
3900 Wisconsin Avenue N.W.
Washington, DC 20016
Contact: Mr. Herb Moses 202-752-6011

Hewlett-Packard
GLEN—Gay, Lesbian and Bisexual Employee Network
P.O. Box 700542
San Jose, CA 95170
Contact: Mr. Kim Harris, 415-857-7771, or Mr. Greg Gloss, 408-447-6123

Honeywell
Honeywell Pride Council
Mail Stop #MN12-5258
P.O. Box 524
Minneapolis, MN 55440
Contact: Mr. Dan Lyden, 612-951-2057

Johnson & Johnson
RWJPRI
700 Route 200
Raritan, NJ 08869
Contact: Ms. Cheryl Vitow, 908-704-5607

Levi Strauss & Co.
Lesbian & Gay Employee Association
1155 Battery Street
San Francisco, CA 94111
Contact: Ms. Michele Dryden, 415-544-7103

Lockheed Missiles and Space
GLOBAL—Gay, Lesbian, Or Bisexual at Lockheed
LMSC Management Association—Bay Area Chapter
Department 27-62, Building 599
P.O. Box 3504
Sunnyvale, CA 95088-3504
Contact: Mr. Frederick Parsons, 408-255-4936, or Mr. Patrick Miller,
408-369-1713

Lotus Development
55 Cambridge Parkway
Cambridge, MA 02142
Contact: Ms. Polly Laurelchild-Hertig, 617-693-1737

Microsoft
GLEAM—Gay, Lesbian & Bisexual Employees at Microsoft
1 Microsoft Way
Redmond, WA 98052
Contact: Mr. Jeff Howard, 206-936-5581

Nestlé Beverage Company
Gay & Lesbian Associates of Nestlé Beverage Company
345 Spear Street
San Francisco, CA 94105
Contact: Mr. Jim Ahlers 415-546-4840

The New York Times Company
Gay & Lesbian Caucus
229 West 43rd Street
New York, NY 10036
Contact: Mr. David Dunlap, 212-556-7082

NYNEX
Gays & Lesbians for Corporate Diversity
4 West Red Oak Lane, 1st Floor
White Plains, NY 10604
Contact: Ms. Aggie Medige, 914-644-3853

Oracle Systems Corporation
Lambda
MD659412
500 Oracle Parkway
Redwood Shores, CA 94065
Contact: Mr. Kevin Mallory, 415-506-6168

Pacific Gas & Electric
Lesbian & Gay Employee Association
P.O. Box 191311
San Francisco, CA 94119
Contact: Ms. Cindy Collins, 415-695-3557

Polaroid
Polaroid Gay, Lesbian & Bisexual Association
575 Technology Square-4
Cambridge, MA 02139
Contact: Dr. Richard Williams, 617-577-2285

Prudential
EAGLES—Employee Association of Gay men & LESbians
P.O. Box 1566
Minneapolis, MN 55440-1566
Contact: Ms. Cathy Perkins 612-557-7918

Silicon Graphics, Inc.
Lavender Vision
2011 North Shoreline Boulevard
Mountain View, CA 94043
Contact: Ms. Ann Mei Chang, 415-390-4441

United Airlines
GLUE Coalition—Gay & Lesbian United Employees
2261 Market Street #293
San Francisco, CA 94114 *[group address]*
Contact: Mr. Tom Cross, 800-999-3448

US West
EAGLE—Employee Association for Gays & Lesbians
1600 Bell Plaza, Rm 2013
Seattle, WA 98191
Contact: Ms. Dawn Tubbs 206-346-7483

The Village Voice
Lesbian & Gay Caucus
36 Cooper Square
New York, NY 10003
Contact: Mr. Richard Goldstein, 212-475-3300

Time Warner
Lesbians & Gay Men at Time Warner
c/o HBO
1100 6th Avenue #515
New York, NY 10036
Contact: Mr. Rich Mayora, 212-512-5909, or Mr. Bill Hooper, 212-522-1063

Wells Fargo
Mail Stop #MAC 0188-133
111 Sutter Street, 13th Floor
San Francisco, CA 94104
Contact: Ms. Barbara Zoloth, 415-396-2767

Xerox
GALAXE—Gays and Lesbians at Xerox
P.O. Box 25382
Rochester, NY 14625
Contact: Mr. David Frishkorn, 716-423-5090

Appendix II

NATIONAL GAY & LESBIAN TASK FORCE POLICY INSTITUTE
Equal Employment Opportunity for Lesbian, Gay, and Bisexual Employees

Please take a moment to answer these questions on the corporate policy of your company with regard to lesbian, gay, and bisexual employees. Before July 30, 1993, fax us your response or mail it to us in the envelope provided. The results of this survey will be published. Thank you.

Name of Employer:_____

CEO:_____

Address:_____

Vice President, Human Resources:_____

Phone:_____ Fax:_____

Your Name:_____

E-Mail Address:_____

Title:_____

Address:_____

1a. Does your company have a written non-discrimination policy?   Y   N

1b. If yes, does it include sexual orientation?   Y   N

1c. If yes, when was this protection adopted?_____/_____/_____
    (Please attach a copy of your policy)

1d. If your company has no such policy for sexual orientation, is one under consideration?   Y   N

Please provide a copy of the most significant public statement that your CEO has made regarding your company's commitment to equal employment opportunity for gay, lesbian, and bisexual employees.

2a. Indicate whether your company provides any of the following benefits for employees' partners of the Opposite Sex (OS) or Same Sex (SS) partners. Check each question "OS" or "SS" for every category. (Leave *blank* if the category does not apply to your company.)

OS   SS

_____ _____   Medical Insurance

_____ _____   Dental Insurance

_____ _____   Other Insurance

_____ _____   Adoption Assistance

_____ _____   Child Care Benefits

_____ _____   Health Club Membership

_____ _____   Relocation Benefits

_____ _____   Employer-paid Travel (partners included)

_____ _____   Family/Personal/Sick Leave (partner care)

_____ _____   Bereavement Leave

_____ _____   Eligibility for Housing/Special Interest

_____ _____   Other:_____

_____ _____   Other:_____

2b. At what level is ultimate approval required for Same Sex (SS) benefits?

Board of Directors:_____

CEO:_____

VP, Human Resources:_____

Manager:_____

Supervisor:_____

Other:_____

2c. Are employees' unmarried partners of spousal equivalents invited to company events when married couples are invited?   Y   N

3a. Does your company provide any diversity training?   Y   N

3b. Does the diversity training include sexual orientation issues?   Y   N

3c. Does your company provide a specific training program on
     sexual orientation discrimination for your company's human
     resource professionals?   Y   N

     For your company's managers?   Y   N

     For your company's executives?   Y   N

     For your company's supervisors?   Y   N

     For line employees?   Y   N

4a. Does your company recognize any employee-organized
     groups?   Y   N

4b. Do they include a Lesbian/Gay/Bisexual (LGB) employee
     group?   Y   N

4c. If yes, please provide us with the following information:
     Name of LGB Association:_____

President:_____

Address:_____

Telephone Number:_____

4d. Is the LGB group allowed to utilize company facilities for special func-
     tions?   Y   N

4e. Does the LGB employee group receive any internal company media
     coverage?   Y   N

5.   Does your company provide support for individuals with HIV/AIDS?
     (Please explain):

     _____

     _____

     _____

     _____

     _____

     _____

Comments: _____

_____

_____

_____

_____

_____

_____

_____

_____

_____

_____

_____

CRACKING THE CORPORATE CLOSET
Follow-up
Company Questionnaire

Company Name:—————————————————————

This form was completed by:

Name:—————————————————————————

Title:—————————————————————————

Tel/Fax:————————————————————————

Address:————————————————————————

Address:————————————————————————

City/State/Zip:———————————————————

Date Completed:—————————————————

IMPORTANT

Please include information about any particular initiatives, policies, or related data that you think might be relevant to our examination of your company in the context of gay and lesbian concerns. All supporting materials are welcome.

If you have any questions concerning *Cracking the Corporate Closet*

or this questionnaire, please feel free to contact either of the co-
authors. Thank you for taking the time and effort to cooperate with
this project.

EMPLOYMENT POLICIES

1. *If your company has a written policy barring discrimination based on
   sexual orientation in employment and promotion practices, have any
   claims ever been filed under this policy?*

   [ ]Yes   [ ] No

   If so, how many?

   *What actions were taken?*_____

   _____

2. *Has your company ever advertised employment opportuntiies in the gay/
   lesbian press?*

   [ ] Yes   [ ] No

   *If so, please provide a sample or list the publications.*_____

   _____

   *Would you do so if there were gay/lesbian community publications serving
   areas where you were hiring?*

   [ ] Yes   [ ] No

3. *Who is the highest-ranking employee in your company who would be willing
   to speak openly about being gay or lesbian for this project?*

   Name:_____

   Title:_____

   Tel/Fax:_____

   Address:_____

   Address:_____

   City/State/Zip:_____

4. *In what state(s) are the majority of your employees?*_____

_____

Do you have significant operations in any of the following states or cities, all of which have anti-discrimination laws based on sexual orientation that apply to private employers? (Please circle the ones that apply.)

Connecticut,   District of Columbia,   Hawaii,

Massachusetts,   New Jersey,   Vermont,   Wisconsin

Atlanta,   Austin,   Baltimore,   Chicago,   Cincinnati,

Columbus,   Detroit,   Iowa City,   Los Angeles,   Milwaukee,

Minneapolis,   New York City,   New Orleans,   Oakland,

Philadelphia,   Pittsburgh,   Sacramento,   St. Paul,

San Diego,   San Francisco,   Seattle,   Tucson

5. *How many of your company's top officers and directors have never married? (This question is designed to measure the advancement opportunities available at your company for persons who do not marry. It is not designed to measure how "gay" your company is. Many gay men and lesbians marry; most unmarried people are not gay or lesbian.)*

Officers:_____of_____

Directors:_____of_____

HEALTH ISSUES AND BENEFIT PROGRAMS

1. *Is your company self-insured?*
   [ ] Yes   [ ] No

2. *Does your company's pension policy extend to the unmarried domestic partners of employees?*
   [ ] Yes   [ ] Yes, but same sex only   [ ] No

3. *Are there any provisions in your group health insurance policy that restrict the amount of coverage for HIV- or AIDS-related illnesses?*
   [ ] Yes   [ ] No

4. *Does your company have any policies that restrict job-related activities of HIV-positive employees?*
   [ ] Yes   [ ] No
   If so, please detail.

5. *Does your company require blood tests of its employees?*
   [ ] Yes, new hires only
   [ ] Yes, all employees
   [ ] Yes, senior executives
   [ ] No
   [ ] Other. Please explain:_____

6. *Does your company carry out any AIDS awareness or education programs?*
   [ ] Yes   [ ] No

Advertising and Marketing

1. *Has your company ever advertised its products or services in gay or lesbian publications or other gay-oriented media?*
   [ ] Yes   [ ] No
   *If yes, what products?:*_____

2. *Has your marketing department ever researched your company's appeal to the gay market?*
   [ ] Yes   [ ] No

3. *Has your company ever produced advertising for any media that shows same-sex couples or that was designed to appeal to a lesbian/gay audience?*
   [ ] Yes   [ ] No
   If yes, please provide copies of advertising.

4. *Has your company ever served as the official sponsor of a gay or lesbian event or one in which gays and lesbians made up a large part of the audience?*
   [ ] Yes   [ ] No
   *If yes, please indicate which events:*_____

5. *Do you have an estimate of what percentage of your customers are gay?*
   [ ] Yes   [ ] No
   *If yes, please indicate how you arrived at your estimate:*_____

6. *Has your company declined to advertise on television shows or in other media in response to boycott calls from such organizations as Accuracy in Media or Donald Wildmon's American Family Association or any similar religious, fundamentalist, or conservative organization?*
   [ ] Yes   [ ] No
   *If yes, please provide details:*_____

CHARITABLE ACTIVITIES

1. *Does your company have a charitable foundation?*
   [ ] Yes   [ ] No

2. *Please detail any company donations in the last two or three years to AIDS organizations or to any charitable groups specifically serving the gay community.*

   _____

   _____

3. *Has your company contributed to other civil rights organizations, such as NAACP, NOW, the Urban League, the United Negro College Fund, etc.?*
   [ ] Yes   [ ] No
   *If yes, please indicate which ones:*_____

4. *Does your company match the charitable giving of your employees?*
   [ ] Yes   [ ] No
   *If yes, at what ratio?*_____

5. *Can any charity recognized by the IRS, including gay and lesbian organizations, qualify for matching funds?*
   [ ] Yes   [ ] No
   If no, please include description of criteria for matching.

6. *Has your company contributed to any of the following in 1991, 1992, or 1993?*
   [ ] Citizens for Excellence in Education
   [ ] Colorado for Family Values
   [ ] Concerned Women for America
   [ ] Council for National Policy
   [ ] Eagle Forum
   [ ] Family Research Council
   [ ] Focus on the Family
   [ ] Free Congress Foundation
   [ ] Heritage Foundation
   [ ] National Legal Foundation
   [ ] Oregon Citizens Alliance
   [ ] Traditional Values Coalition

INDEX

DATE DUE

Northwest-Shoals Community College		
Larry W. McCoy Learning Resources Center		
Shoals Campus		
Muscle Shoals, AL 35662		